Edward B. Segel

The Mirage of Power

FOREIGN POLICIES OF THE GREAT POWERS
Edited by C. J. Lowe

The Mirage of Power

volume three: the documents

British Foreign Policy 1902-22

C. J. Lowe
and M. L. Dockrill

Routledge & Kegan Paul
London and Boston

First published 1972
by Routledge and Kegan Paul Ltd
Broadway House, 68–74 Carter Lane
London, EC4V 5EL
and 9 Park Street,
Boston, Mass. 02108, U.S.A.
Printed in Great Britain by
Western Printing Services Ltd,
Bristol
© *C. J. Lowe and M. L. Dockrill 1972*
ISBN 0 7100 7094 2

Contents

Contents

Contents

(There are no documents referring to chapter 4)

5. BRITAIN AND EUROPE, 1912–14

Contents

The Anglo-Russian naval conversations

Documents to volume II

1. STRATEGY AND FOREIGN POLICY

Sonnino proposes an interim agreement

Contents

2. THE MIDDLE EAST, 1914–18

Contents

3. WAR AIMS AND PEACE TERMS

Contents

Negotiations with Austria-Hungary for a separate peace

Imperial objectives, August 1918

4. THE FAR EAST

Essential to renew the Japanese Alliance

British interests in China—the twenty-one demands

Expulsion of Germans in China

Recognition of Japanese claims

Incompatibility of Japan and the U.S.A.

Japanese intervention in Siberia

Renewal of the Anglo-Japanese Alliance

Washington Conference

Contents

5. BRITAIN AND THE RUSSIAN REVOLUTION

Contents

6. THE PEACE SETTLEMENT, 1919–22

The object of the Peace

The index appears at the end of volumes I and II.

Preface

As was pointed out in volume II of *The Reluctant Imperialists* (Routledge & Kegan Paul, 1967), the purpose of these documents is less to define what policy was than to give students some idea of the dialogue that lay behind it. The same criterion has been applied to these documents on the period from 1902 to 1922. Official despatches have been largely omitted in favour of the private correspondence of ministers and officials, memoranda prepared for the Cabinet, the prime minister's brief reports to the King on proceedings of the Cabinet and, after 9 December 1916, minutes of Cabinet meetings.

In contrast to the previous volume, however, every effort has been made in this collection to utilize material that has not hitherto been published. The reason is that an important published source already exists for the years 1898–1914 in the *British Documents on the Origins of the War* edited by G. P. Gooch and H. Temperley (11 volumes), which has recently been reprinted and is available in paperback. Another important source also published recently is the companion volume (in three parts) to *Winston S. Churchill, The Young Statesman, 1901–1914* (Heinemann, 1969) and consisting of letters to and from Churchill during these years. The student is commended to the study of these volumes in order to obtain a comprehensive picture of British foreign policy down to 1914. The short selection printed here is intended to supplement the above collections and to illuminate the analysis of foreign policy to be found in volume I; most are novel—it is hoped that all are significant.

There are no large printed collections of British documents for the period 1914–18, and very little of the material collected in this volume has been published before. For 1919 and beyond, the *Documents on British Foreign Policy 1919–1939*, 1st series, edited by E. L. Woodward and Rohan Butler, are especially valuable.

Our gratitude is due to the Controller of H.M.Stationery Office for permission to reproduce Crown Copyright Material at the Public Record Office, to the Trustees of the British Museum for permission to quote from the papers of J. A. Spender, to Mr Laurence Scott for permission to quote from the papers of C. P. Scott, to C. & T. Publications Ltd for permission to quote material by Winston Churchill, to the Cambridge University Library to quote extracts from the Hardinge papers, to Mr A. J. P. Taylor and the Trustees of the Beaverbrook Library for authority to quote from the Lloyd George papers, to Mr Mark Bonham-Carter for permission to quote from the Asquith papers, to the Keeper of the House of Lords Records Office for permission to quote from the Samuel papers, to Lord Harcourt for kindly allowing us permission to quote from the Harcourt papers and to the Trustees of the Smuts Archives, University of Cape Town, for permission to quote an extract by Field-Marshal Smuts.

C. J. LOWE
M. L. DOCKRILL

Authors' Note

The abbreviations used in this volume, e.g. B.D., are the same as those used in volumes I and II. A list of these abbreviations and an identification of the Cabinet and private papers at the Public Record Office (F.O. 800 series and Cab. series) can be found in volume II on pp. ix and 411.

C.J.L.
M.L.D.

Chapter 1

The Anglo-French Entente

LANSDOWNE'S VIEWS ON FRANCE AND MOROCCO

1. (*Lansdowne to Sir Edmund Monson (Paris), 26 December 1904, F.O. 800/126*)

The turn which affairs have taken in Morocco is very unlucky. We may in our secret hearts congratulate ourselves on having left to another Power the responsibility of dealing with so helpless and hopeless a country, but we need not proclaim our feelings.

The French never, I believe, intended to force the pace in Morocco, but events may be too strong for them. I have begged that we may be given ample notice of any vigorous measures which they may find themselves obliged to take, for it is evident that Europeans may have a very dangerous time ahead of them.

The New Year will be full of anxiety for us all. I incline myself to the belief that the closeness of our relations with France, and of her relations with Russia, may prove useful to all concerned when the time comes for bringing the [Russo-Japanese] war to a close.

ANGLO-JAPANESE RELATIONS

2. (*Lansdowne to Sir Francis Bertie (Paris), 21 March 1905, F.O. 800/126*)

Extract

I do not see how, as matters stand, we could take upon ourselves to say anything to the French Government as to the terms of peace which Japan will accept...

MacDonald [Tokyo] telegraphed to us on the 17th instant, in reply to a question of mine, to the effect that the Japanese Government were determined to prosecute the war to the end, that the entire press of the country urged the continuance of it until Russia sued for peace, and that serious trouble would arise were the Japanese Government suspected of promoting overtures for peace. If this is their attitude we ought I think to be extremely careful how we take upon ourselves to suggest to them or for them that certain terms should be acceptable.

I do not take very kindly to your idea of encouraging the German Emperor to mediate. We may, I think, safely trust His Majesty to take the initiative if he sees an opportunity of doing so for his own advantage, but I should mistrust his intervention.

3. (*Balfour to the King, 9 June 1905, F.O. 800/134*)

Mr. Balfour with his humble duty to Your Majesty begs respectfully to say that the discussions on the proposed Japanese Treaty which have extended over several Cabinets have now resulted in the preparation of a draft treaty for the consideration of the Japanese Government.

The main difficulties which had to be dealt with in framing the draft were (1) that the guarantees of assistance by Japan to Britain and by Britain to Japan, had to cover not merely the case in which the territories of the two Powers were attacked, but also the case in which adjacent territories were attacked—Japan (for example) must be able to call upon us to aid her if Corea were invaded; while we, in like manner, should claim her assistance if the same danger threatened Afghanistan (2) the assistance given by Britain could hardly be in the shape of a *military* force. The public would be alarmed, if we were under an obligation to land soldiers in Corea, perhaps at the same moment that they might be urgently required in India. (3) The naval force which in time of peace the two Powers are to keep in Eastern waters demands careful consideration—and (4) the number of troops which Japan should send for the defence of India raises points which cannot be determined by military considerations alone, but involves questions of home politics as well. There is, for example, a real danger that if a Radical Government came into power, they would reduce our Army below the limits of safety, and this danger will be greatly augmented if they think they can rely on an unlimited supply of men from Japan.

In the opinion of Your Majesty's present advisers it is not consistent with the Security or the dignity of the Empire that the defence of any part of it should depend upon a Foreign Power, however friendly and however peaceful. We have therefore endeavoured to frame the treaty . . . in such a manner as to make

Japanese assistance in the defence of India bear a fixed relation to the efforts *we* make to send adequate forces to the front . . .

Mr. Balfour is sanguine that a satisfactory agreement may be come to.

The Moroccan Crisis of 1905

4. (*Lansdowne to Sir Frank Lascelles (Berlin), 9 April 1905, F.O. 800/190*)

Extract

I entirely agree with you in looking upon the Emperor's Tangier escapade as an extraordinary clumsy bit of diplomacy . . .

I am afraid however that we can hardly regard this ebullition as an isolated incident. There can be no doubt that the Emperor was much annoyed by the Anglo-French Agreement, and probably even more so by our refusal to vamp up some Agreement of the same kind with Germany over the Egyptian question . . . We shall, I have little doubt, find that the Emperor avails himself of every opportunity which he can make in order to put spokes in our wheels and convince those who are watching the progress of the game that he means to take an important part in it . . .

I must have the documents carefully looked up, but my impression is that the German Government have really no cause for complaint of us or the French in regard to the Morocco part of the Agreement. We made no secret of its existence. It dealt exclusively with French and British interests in Morocco, and so far as other Powers were concerned, it provided adequate security for their interests by maintaining the policy of the 'open door' and equality of treatment, and the integrity of Morocco itself. What else does the Emperor want—unless perhaps it be to place orders for German guns?—but if he crams these down the Sultan's throat he will certainly not add to the reputation and popularity of his country.

As to the attempts of the German Government to ingratiate themselves, with the United States and Japan, I am under the impression that these two Powers, while certainly desiring to be well with Germany, know exactly how much value to place on such overtures, and are not likely to be drawn by them off their true course. All my information leads me to think that we have never stood better with the President, or with the Japanese Government than we do at this moment.

The Anglo-French Entente

5. (*Lansdowne to Bertie, 12 June 1905, F.O. 800/127*)

Extract

Delcassé's resignation has, as you may well suppose, produced a very painful impression here. What people say is that if one of our Ministers had had a dead set made at him by a foreign Power the country and the Government would not only have stood by him but probably have supported him more vigorously than ever, whereas France has apparently thrown Delcassé overboard in a mere fit of panic. Of course the result is that the 'entente' is quoted at a much lower price than it was a fortnight ago.

I gather from what Cambon told me Rouvier will not attend a Conference. I hope he will not, although if the French are really on the run, we might perhaps extract a not unsatisfactory settlement out of such a Conference. You will observe that Metternich . . . represents Germany as upholding what he calls the legal status of Morocco, an attitude which would scarcely be reconcilable with a proposal to steal territory from the Sultan.

6. (*Lansdowne to Sir Reginald Lister, 10 July 1905, F.O. 800/127*)

Extract

Whatever may be the feeling of the public upon the point the fact remains that we have received no hint from the French Government that they would like us to tell them how far we should be prepared to go in supporting them against Germany. We have been giving a great deal of thought to the question, but until it is asked I doubt whether we should be wise to volunteer a statement. The moment would not, in my opinion, be a very opportune one for suggesting either to the Cabinet or to the country an extension of the understanding already arrived at. Recent events have, I am afraid, undoubtedly shaken peoples' confidence in the steadfastness of the French nation . . . I am in hope that now that the Conference is to take place it may be more or less of a parade movement.

GREY ON RELATIONS WITH FRANCE AND GERMANY

7. (*Grey to Lascelles, 1 January 1906, F.O. 800/61*)

The atmosphere does not get less electric as the date of the Morocco Conference approaches, and I think, when you speak at Berlin, our intention to keep in letter and spirit our engagements to other countries, must be emphasised. It may be in the plural so as to include the Japanese Alliance as well as the French Entente and so avoid the appearance of being specially addressed to the Morocco question.

The subject might be introduced as an instance of how very open and frank British diplomacy is. Our Alliance and Entente, the terms as well as the facts, are published to the world. This would not be so if they were directed against any other country, and as a matter of fact we have no intention or desire, nor have our partners, to use them to the detriment of third parties. We entered into these engagements without *arrière pensée*, and if other countries will only believe that, they surely need not see a hostile intent in our keeping these engagements as we intend to do.

The danger of speaking civil words in Berlin is that they may be used or interpreted in France as implying that we shall be luke-warm in our support of the Entente at the Conference. I think it is essential to guard against this danger, even at the risk of sending a little shudder through a German audience.

The rest will be plain sailing: commercial rivalry is not resented here; we don't in the least feel that German methods are directed against British trade. German success in trade may stimulate us to fresh efforts, but will not cause political estrangement, and we want to see the commerce between the two countries grow. It is the same with the growth of the German Navy: we build ships when other Powers do, but we don't regard their building as a hostile act against ourselves: the natural motive is the general desire to protect an Empire. In fact, if we were only quite sure that Germany did not regard our public engagements as incompatible with German interests, and if she would only believe that we do not mean badly to her, recent friction would disappear.

There are reports that the Emperor is in a softer mood: if things go smoothly at the Morocco Conference and it is attributed to him, there will be a quick and favourable recognition over here of the part he has played.

But fine words butter no parsnips, and if the parsnips are to be buttered it must be done at the Conference. If that ends in conclusions not adverse to the Anglo-French Entente there will be a real clearing of the sky and an assurance of peace. If not, everything said now will go for nothing, and Europe will be very uncomfortable . . .

The Anglo-French Entente

January 8th

The lapse of a week since this letter was written has made me feel that it is more than ever important to prevent misunderstandings in France, Germany or England: to avoid these it must be made quite clear that your speech is in response to friendly and unofficial overtures from the German people; that you reply to these in friendly terms because to do otherwise would be not only uncivil but would give an impression that our policy was inspired by animosity or had a hostile intention against Germany. This is not the least true either of the Government or people in Great Britain. But they must remember in Germany that all depends upon reciprocity: that they must make it clear to us that our engagements to other Powers are not regarded as inimical to Germany: and nothing said must be taken either as an indication that our policy and intention to keep these engagements are in any way weakened.

The date of your speeches, just on the eve of the Morocco Conference, and the apprehension and uncertainty felt about the outcome of the Conference, make it essential that there should be no mistake about our attitude.

Chapter 2

Britain, France and Germany, 1908–12

ANGLO-GERMAN-FRENCH RELATIONS: BRITISH VIEWS

8. (*Grey to Lascelles, 27 March 1907, F.O. 800/61*)

Extract

When the Russian Government pressed for an answer about the Hague Conference [on disarmament], I sent for Metternich on purpose to tell him of the reply that had been sent.

I had previously explained to him that we had a lot of naval expenditure in suspense: that public opinion here was so strong that we were bound to do our best to discuss the question of expenditure at the Hague Conference; and I now made it clear to him that, in agreeing to a reference of the subject when raised at the Conference . . . I was adopting that course because I had understood . . . it was the one most likely to smooth over difficulties.

In short, I told Metternich that, though we were bound to attempt to raise the question, we did not wish to do so in a way which would provoke friction with Germany.

But all this met with no response.

If the Germans will not meet us halfway, and if they insist upon a blank, absolute refusal to have a discussion, we shall just settle down to building more ships than theirs.

And what the Germans do not realise is the extent to which this naval expenditure will grow if they insist on forcing the pace.

9. (*Grey to Haldane, 4 September 1907, Haldane MSS.*)

Extract

I am satisfied about the Russian Agreement, but I am not very comfortable about other things . . . I hear of a tendency in the press to whittle away our obligations to France about Morocco; to say that it is our business to let Germany put pressure on France in the interest of the open door. . . This will be a very mischievous line. Also I am not altogether without apprehension about the German Emperor's visit . . . the Emperor has a habit of turning his visits into demonstrations which is tiresome. All the other Sovereigns are so much quieter.

10. (*Minute by Eyre Crowe, 18 August 1908,*[1] *F.O. 371/461/28285*)

Extract

. . . It is somewhat alarming to see cabinet ministers with obviously imperfect understanding of foreign affairs plunge into public discussion abroad of an 'entente' with Germany.

An 'entente' means absolutely nothing more than a frame of mind, a disposition to view the action and thoughts of another party with friendly sympathy. Ententes are not 'negotiated'. They result from agreements concluded or from the logic of events.

Mr. Lloyd George himself admits that there are no points of quarrel which require settling with Germany. His view of an 'entente' is an agreement for mutual limitation of armaments. After what the Emperor said at Cronberg; what has appeared in the semi-official German press; and after what we remember took place in the 6 months preceding the Hague Conference, the public renewal of this proposal of the British Chancellor of the Exchequer is bound to create an unpleasant impression. If the desire is to arrive at a state of good relations with Germany, it must be doubted whether this is not the way to defeat the object . . .

I read in the papers that Mr. Lloyd George is going to Berlin to discuss the question further with Admiral von Tirpitz. Presumably Sir E. Grey will lay down for Mr. Lloyd George's guidance what he should say on such an occasion, and what he should not say. How much better it would be if he said nothing at all!

The more we talk of the necessity of economising on our armaments, the more firmly will Germans believe that we are tiring of the struggle, and that they will win by going on.

11. (*Minute by Eyre Crowe, 13 April 1909, F.O. 371/673/13621*)

Everything points to the fact that Germany's efforts are at present directed to the dissolution of the understanding between England,

---

[1] On Lloyd George's interview with the *Neue Freie Presse* on 12 August 1908 advocating an Anglo-German naval limitation agreement.

France, and Russia. Germany has realised that her bullying attitude towards France failed to detach that Power from England.
She now seeks the same object by making up to France and holding out prospects of commercial and financial advantage, to accrue
from co-operation between France and Germany. This is an
insidious weapon and may well prove effective at Paris. Towards
Russia the same policy of first bullying, and then cajoling, is
applied. Meanwhile England is to be kept quiet by throwing [out]
the bait of disarmament. We may be caught in a genuine difficulty
if Germany proposes to come to an agreement on the existing
basis of her naval programme and our present position. Whatever
agreement we could make with Germany would become a danger
as soon as third Powers take up the naval development where
Germany left off. We have already the menace of Austrian dreadnoughts.

I have already had occasion to point out that an agreement with
one Power alone is not compatible with the maintenance of the
two-Power standard.

12. (*Hardinge to Goschen, 26 April 1910, Hardinge MSS., vol. III,
1910*)

Extract

I have discussed with Sir Edward Grey the report of your interview with the Chancellor, and the conclusion to which we have
jointly arrived is that we must wait for the present at any rate and
as for the future (1) we cannot enter into a political understanding
with Germany which would separate us from Russia and France
and leave us isolated, while the rest of Europe would be obliged
to look to Germany: (2) no understanding with Germany would
be appreciated here unless it meant an arrest of the increase of
naval expenditure; and (3) we do not wish to deprive Germany of
the Baghdad Railway concession which, as the Chancellor says, is
in her pocket already, all we desire is that Germany should not
have the only door for trade in Mesopotamia: this could be
secured by getting the Turks to give us another door, and we
therefore cannot pay a high price for participation in the Baghdad
Railway. . .

13. (*Nicolson to Goschen, 28 February 1911, F.O. 800/347*)

Extract

The advanced Radical section here are girding at McKenna in regard to increased naval estimates, and in these quarters I am afraid there undoubtedly is a growing desire to make terms with Germany at any cost. There is certainly no great liking for our understanding with Russia, not only in Radical circles but in other quarters also, and I fear that there is an increasing feeling that France is a very weak reed to rely upon. So many people regard the maintenance of the equilibrium in Europe as merely an abstract principle, for the support of which it is not worth firing a shot, and they do not understand that, were the Triple Entente to be broken up, we should be isolated, and compelled to do the bidding of the Power which assumed the hegemony in Europe. Moreover in present circumstances we are certainly not strong enough to stand alone.

14. (*Bertie to Nicolson, 15 March 1911, F.O. 800/186*)

Extract

The Germans of course wish to sow discord between us and the French and the Russians. I cannot believe that by a paper agreement the fundamentally opposing interests of the British and German peoples can be reconciled . . .

Any political or armament agreement made by Germany would be observed by us in the spirit as well as the letter, but in neither probably by the Germans. The consequent dissatisfaction in England would cause more ill-will than there is already in the present condition of things between the two countries. The interests of the two peoples are so opposed that they cannot be settled by a diplomatic agreement. We ought to be thankful that Germany annexed Alsace and Lorraine as that act has made a combination between Germany and France against us impossible. There have been several attempts by Germany when our relations with France were bad but they failed. Our reconciliation and Entente with France have saved us from the danger of a French attack if we have a war with Germany and there is now no possibility of an Anglo-French war to give Germany her opportunity to attack us.

THE AGADIR CRISIS

15. (*Bertie to Nicolson, 14 May 1911, F.O. 800/180*)

Extract

You will see that Cruppi[1] is in a despondent state. What he, Jules Cambon and I suppose Paul Cambon and many others hanker after is something more visible to Germany and useful to France than the existing Entente between England and France. The French Government . . . do not feel sure how far they could rely on it if Germany became threatening or bluffed. This feeling is useful to us as a security against France committing imprudence in her discussions with Germany, but it is also a danger as France might if hard-pressed give us away in a question important to British and not to French interests, as Sazonov gave away at the Potsdam interviews both France and England. I quite understand and appreciate the difficulty for His Majesty's Government to anticipate events by a formal and binding agreement in furtherance of the entente with France, but everything military and naval ought to be arranged to meet the contingency of British and French forces *having* to act together. Otherwise in these days of quick locomotion we might arrive a day too late for the fray and find our essential interests already compromised. Perhaps these arrangements *have* been made.

16. (*Asquith to the King, 19 July 1911, Cab/41/33/22*)

Extract

The remainder of the sitting was occupied with the situation in Morocco. It was agreed that the proposals put forward by Germany to France for the practical absorption of the French Congo were such as France could not be expected, and probably was not intended to accept. It was also agreed that we should advise the French Government to submit without delay to Germany their counter-proposals for 'compensation' in that region.

Sir E. Grey was of the opinion that we should at once propose to the German Government the assembly of a Conference to deal with the new situation, with an intimation that, in the event of their refusal, we should take steps to assert and protect British interests. This suggestion was strenuously resisted by the Lord Chancellor [Loreburn] on the ground that our direct interest in

[1] French Foreign Minister.

the matter was insignificant, and that, as a result of such a communication, we might soon find ourselves drifting into war. There ensued a long and animated discussion, and, in the end, it was agreed to defer any communication to Germany until the matter had been further considered at the next meeting of the Cabinet on Friday. In the meantime, the French Government are asked whether they are prepared to resist *à/outrance* [sic], the admission of Germany under *any* conditions, into Morocco; and to be informed that, under proper conditions, such admission would not be regarded by us as fatal to British interests, and could not be treated by us as a *casus belli*. They are also to be told that we shall suggest a Conference, in which it will be our aim to work in concert with French diplomacy.

17. (*William Tyrrell to Hardinge, 21 July 1911, Hardinge MSS., vol. 1, part 1, 1911*)

Extract

We are in the midst of an Anglo-German crisis: far more severe than the Algeçiras Conference one of 1906. I am not sure that 'the Powers that be' appreciate the real inwardness of the German move; it is to test the Anglo-French entente. It should be viewed from that point of view alone: everything else is a side issue on this occasion. Bertie has been sent for from Paris and I have great hopes he will carry the day. I can't tell how I wish you were here. I should feel ever so much happier. It is depressing to find that after six years' experience of Germany the inclination here is still to believe that she can be placated by small concessions . . . What she wants is the hegemony of Europe. The French game in Morocco has been stupid and dishonest, but it is a vital interest for us to support her on this occasion in the same way in which the Germans supported the Austrian policy of 1908 in Bosnia. It is going to be a narrow shave and we may pull it off again but that is about all that I feel about it at present.

18. (*Morley to Asquith, 27 July 1911, Asquith MSS., vol. 13*)

I read with a good deal of concern the blue print last night, reporting Grey's talk with Metternich on July 25. I have seen Grey, George, Winston this morning. I cannot say that last night's concern is much or at all abated. The speech[1] reminds me uncom-

---

[1] Lloyd George's Mansion House speech on 21 July 1911, see Vol. I, p. 42.

fortably of Gramont's on July 6, 1870; received with tremendous applause, followed by bottomless mischief. It is all very well to say that the speech had nothing but *bona verba*. You cannot detach a speech from all the consequences that may surround (?) it. In one sense, it is the least part of itself. For my own part I feel the justice of every word of the language that Metternich was instructed to use about the speech, including the effect it may by and by prove to have had in 'embroiling' the negotiations between France and Germany. I utterly dislike and distrust the German methods. They are what they have always been. But that is no reason why we should give them the excuse of this provocation.

19. (*Note by Sir Edward Grey, 2 August 1911, Cabinet papers, Cab. 37/107/89*)

Extract

It was asked whether France had put herself in the wrong by violating her agreement with Germany of 1909.

I have called for a Memorandum of what is known in the Foreign Office and I circulate it to the Cabinet . . .

France was technically justified in going to Fez by the request of the Sultan and by the necessities of the case. There was real danger to her subjects at Fez, and there was none to German subjects at Agadir.

But I have not myself pressed this point because whatever justification there may have been for French action, the indirect consequences of it must in fact be to make the Sultan more dependent on her than was the case at the time of the Algeçiras Act, and it is open to any signatory Power of that Act to argue, that the status of Morocco has, in fact if not in theory, been offended.

I do not wish to attach too much importance to these points because motives that are really operative and the issues that are involved in the dispute between Germany and France lie deeper. . .

E.G.

20. (*Nicolson to Hardinge, 17 August 1911, Hardinge MSS. vol. 1, Part 1, 1911*)

Extract

I do not consider that we are by any means out of the wood over

this Moroccan question, and I should not be in the least aston-
ished if Kiderlin gave us some surprises. Our attitude at the outset
upset German calculations, as it was quite unexpected, and they
had to recover themselves a little. I may tell you privately that
Lloyd George and Winston, the two Members of the Cabinet
whom we always regarded as dubious and uncertain factors, were
those who took up the strongest line, and who were the readiest
to go to the utmost extremities. In fact I believe they were a little
disappointed that war with Germany did not occur. Winston
came to see me every morning and Lloyd George came once and I
was struck by the determination of both of them not to permit
Germany to assume the role of bully and at their belief that the
present moment was an exceedingly favourable one to open hostilities. I also hear that the extreme Liberals below gangway
benches were also quite ready to back up the Government whatever action the latter might take. All this is very satisfactory—and
I hope that it is not merely a passing whim or phase of mind. It is
quite possible that occasion may again arise productive of similar
conditions and when we shall have to decide whether we are prepared to support France *vis et armis*. . . . We are all topsy turvy at
home with these strikes, etc. and I should not be in the least
surprised if Germany took the opportunity to put the screw
suddenly on France in the expectation that our internal difficulties
would prevent us from moving. I am not quite at ease in my mind.

21. (*Loreburn to Grey, 26 August 1911, F.O. 800/99*)

Extract

It is quite unnecessary for me to tell you what I feel as to the
prospect of our being engaged in a war with Germany. You know
that and also you can contemplate for yourself the ruinous consequences on our future history which such a disaster must involve.
I wish only to say that, strongly as I feel the necessity of good
relations with Germany, I am no blind admirer and quite realise
the roughness of German methods, and so far as I can see the
sending of a ship to Agadir was very ill-advised. . . Now are you
quite sure you know all that has been mentioned to Germany in
the course of recent [Franco-German] negotiations? . . . It does
not seem likely that the sudden action of Germany was unpre-
ceded by anything in the nature of remonstrances or replies. Why
are we expected to make up our minds upon our action in this

controversy, which if taken in one sense would lead to war, without full knowledge upon these points? In fact our deliberations at the beginning of this crisis proceeded upon the hypothesis that the despatch of the Panther to Agadir was a bolt from the sky. Is it certain that it was so?

It looks to me as if there was either a misunderstanding between France and Germany as to the price France was in May willing to pay, or else that we have been unfairly treated by France in being left without this most important piece of knowledge. I believe the latter. . .

The time may be very near at hand when our Government will have to decide upon a choice of the most eventful character. Is it too late to try, before the choice has been made, whether a frank statement to Germany would do good, saying that we are in no way opposed to her expansion. . .

I fear France has not been quite frank with us. Are we in danger of incurring from France the reproach that we have not been quite frank with them? . . . Is it fair for us to let them imagine that Great Britain would join them in that war? Have you made up your mind as to the circumstances . . . in which you would take up arms? It is not an answer to say that you could not lay down that we would in no circumstances go to war over this quarrel. The real point is—what is our policy, what are the circumstances in which you actually contemplate such a step? I greatly fear that France expects our military and naval support. I believe you could not give it, if you wished, in this, which is a purely French quarrel . . . I cannot think of such a thing without distress, and I cannot think without the most profound sorrow and dismay of such a thing as war with Germany . . . It would postpone indefinitely the hope, which you yourself have done so much to encourage, of a gradual dying down of the use of force in national disputes . . . If there is war, and we stand neutral, as you will, I think, find this country means to do, then we shall be reproached beforehand . . . I fear that we have been drifting in this business, and that in a very natural desire to avoid making up our minds prematurely, and to avoid telling disagreeable things to our French neighbours, we have got into a position in which it will be more difficult than it would have been at an earlier stage. But I suggest to you that it is only fair to the French to tell them plainly that even if you and the Government desired to join them in any war against Germany, it is at least doubtful whether it would be possible to obtain the support of the country in such a course.

22. (*Grey to Loreburn, 30 August 1911, F.O. 800/99*)

Extract

I understand you feeling strongly for the question of war even if it be only possible is most serious and disagreeable.

But what can be said to Germany about expansion more than I have said to her about the Portuguese Colonies Agreement and the line we should take if Belgium ever sold her Congo Colony.

We can't offer her a free hand about the Bagdad Railway and Persian Gulf or about Morocco. Public opinion here would not sanction either and the second is barred by our 1904 agreement with France.

In my opinion an assurance that in the case of war between Germany and France we should remain neutral would not conduce to peace. Even if I thought such a statement should be made either to Germany or France it could not be made except as the result of a Cabinet decision.

The same is true of any statement that would commit us to war . . .

23. (*Grey to Nicolson, 13 September 1911, F.O. 800/350*)

If there is war between France and Germany everything here will depend upon its being clear that Germany has forced the war. A repetition of 1870, when France was manoeuvred into making war on Germany, would be a fatal mistake as regards public opinion here, on which everything as regards our attitude depends.

I do not like the indication . . . that the French Army are so ready that they might prefer war now . . . nevertheless I am glad that they are ready.

24. (*Grey to Bertie, 14 October 1911, F.O. 800/165*)

Extract

There is a difficult corner to turn in the French Congo. If the Germans ask more than the French have offered people will say Kiderlen repents of the Morocco part of the bargain and wants to upset it. If on the other hand the French Government were now to draw back from a reasonable offer, it would be thought very bad on their part. I don't suppose the French Government can think of doing that if the Germans hold them to it, but there seems to be some danger that the French Chamber may refuse to ratify the bargain. It would be very unfortunate if that happened, for it would upset public opinion here altogether . . . and alienate it from France. The French Chamber would have played straight into the hands of Germany by detaching England from France and no one here could help it. We are all for backing up France against the attempt of Germany to bully her, but if when France had made what seemed a good bargain she chucked it away, our people would say they couldn't fight for such folly.

25. (*Notes by C. P. Scott of conversation with Lord Loreburn, 1 December 1911, Scott MSS. 50901*)

As to *Germany* he said the recent statements would tell me a great deal, but not half or a tithe of what had really happened—he meant of course in the way of folly and provocation on our part. As to what should now be done he was rather in despair. Grey was helpless and impervious to any argument. It was impossible to control him in detail, yet everything depends in diplomacy on the handling of detail. Thus at a critical moment in the Moroccan dispute, Grey had informed the German Ambassador that we should decline to recognise any agreement to which our assent had not been obtained and this had been done on the authority of the Cabinet but he omitted to make it plain that this claim was asserted by us only in *respect to our rights as signatories of the Treaty of Algeciras*—and this made all the difference. Then as to securities, for the future he agreed with me that the root of the recent mischief was the perversion of the friendly understanding with France in to an alliance but that was a subtle thing and how could you prevent it except by changing the Minister? You could not take a vote in the Cabinet on an abstract proposition. Grey no doubt ought to go but who was to take his place? Either Churchill or Haldane would be worse, the one irresponsible the other with his cloudy mind and passion for intrigue. Morley was now really senile and Crewe was not at all the same man since his illness. Birrell, honest and able fellow, would be the best—but in any case the resignation of Grey would mean the break-up of the Cabinet as probably George, Churchill and Haldane would go with him. He saw nothing for it but a change of Government. Bonar Law and Lansdowne would be far better. They would not be deeply committed, like Grey, to an extravagant championship of France, and would have no difficulty in going straight to Germany and establishing a parallel understanding with her . . .

His own judgement counted for nothing with Grey so had gone to Asquith . . . and begged him to wrestle with Grey. He had pointed out that Grey's whole position rested on one or other of two really absurd propositions—either that our forming a close friendship with Germany would cause France to attack Germany or that our remaining close friends with France would cause Germany to attack France. Asquith was friendly enough and said he largely agreed with [sic] but whether he would really exert himself was another matter. The fatal thing was that the P.M. who alone was in constant communication with Grey and alone could really influence him never attempted to influence him at all. . .

BRITISH MILITARY PLANS AND PREPARATIONS

26. (*A Note upon British Military Needs, by Winston Churchill, 27 June 1908, Cabinet Papers, Cab/37/94/89*)

Extract

1. No proportion exists between British land forces and great contingencies. The troops maintained in time of peace in the United Kingdom are not, have never been, and probably will never be, equal to dealing with any peril of first class magnitude. They bear no relation to the needs which would arise in the course of a struggle with Russia upon the Indian frontier or with Germany upon the Continent. Arguments are therefore, in my opinion, irrelevant which are based upon the assumption that there exists at present between the British army and these tremendous possibilities some nice adjustments which a dozen battalions of infantry or a million or two in money would fatally derange . . .

2. Upon proposals being made to reduce the numbers or the expense of the army, we are at once invited to contemplate appalling possibilities. We are to counter Russia in Afghanistan, to stamp out the flames of 'a religious war' in India (and I gather simultaneously in Egypt too) and at the same time to be prepared with sufficient forces either to resist the German invader at home, or (perhaps even *and*) to co-operate effectually with some other

great Power upon the Continent. It is further assumed that these exertions should be maintained without departing from the regular organization of our forces and without the adoption of extraordinary measures. These nightmares should leave the advocates of economy undismayed. It is submitted that skilful diplomacy and wise administration should be able to prevent in the future, as in the past, such a formidable and sinister conjunction of disasters. But if diplomacy and administration should unhappily fail, it is then obvious that our existing army, whether doubled or halved, will be equally incompetent to cope with them.

3. The preparations of the British Empire cannot be adapted to meet *immediately* with military force all the needs and dangers which may arise, still less those which may be imagined. They should be adapted *ultimately* to meet reasonable and probable contingencies, and from this point of view our safety lies only in the possession of undisputed naval supremacy, which by itself will enable us *ultimately* to realize and apply the whole energies of our own people and of other peoples under our control. It is this, and this alone, which gives us our rank as a first-class Power, and the excessive expenditure upon purely secondary weapons adapted only to minor emergencies may easily lead us to impair the vital sources of our naval and financial strength. . .

27. (*Report of the Sub-Committee of the Committee of Imperial Defence, on the Military Needs of the Empire, 24 July 1909, Cab/38/15/15*)

Extract

1. The possible requirements of India are held to be one of the ruling factors that determine the size of the Regular Army that is to be maintained in peace time in the United Kingdom. Further investigation into possible theatres of war for the army was, however, desirable in order to give the War Office such indication of the general policy of His Majesty's Government with regard to the employment of a British military force on the Continent of Europe as would enable the General Staff to concentrate their attention only on such plans as they might be called upon to put into operation.

2. The countries selected by the Foreign Office as being those to which, either owing to British Foreign Policy or on account of Treaty obligations, it might be necessary to send a military force were France, Belgium, Holland and Denmark.

3. The fundamental reason for the selection of these countries was in each case the same viz possible aggression by Germany. Other countries were mentioned as possible theatres of war for the British Army. The most important of these were Canada, where Great Britain might be called to fight against the United States, and Southern Persia, where military action might have to be taken against Turkey in the event of British interests being endangered. War in these countries not being, however, considered as reasonably possible in the near future was not discussed by the Committee.

4. The nature of the assistance to France was freely discussed by the Committee. We were informed by the Foreign Office that 'in the event of Germany provoking hostilities with France, the question of armed intervention is one which would have to be decided by the Cabinet; but the decision would be more easily arrived at if German aggression had entailed a violation of the neutrality of Belgium, which Great Britain has guaranteed to maintain.

5. The decision of the question of whether Great Britain should intervene on behalf of France cannot, in our opinion, be left to turn on the mere point of violation of Belgian neutrality. We are strengthened in this conclusion by the opinion expressed by the General Staff as follows:

'It is considered extremely unlikely that Belgium will form part of the theatre of war during the first operations, as the prospective military advantages to be gained by advancing through that country do not seem to afford sufficient justification for such a serious step as the violation of the neutrality of Belgium, with its almost inevitable consequent political complications. It undoubtedly appears quite possible, however, that the tide of battle might bring about such a state of affairs as to make it inoperative (more especially Germany) to disregard Belgian neutrality.'

6. We also take into consideration the length of time that must elapse before a British force would be able to take the field in France or Belgium. This is considered by the General Staff to be twenty days in the case of four divisions and a cavalry division, and such a delay would prevent us from taking part in any operations which had for their object the support of the Belgians against the violation of their neutrality.

7. We have considered three methods by which armed assistance could be given by Great Britain to France . . .

(a) *The Assistance that can be given to France by Naval means alone* . . .

8. In support of (a) we have evidence regarding the extent of the economic and financial injury that Great Britain could inflict on Germany by the stoppage of imports through German ports and by the destruction of her sea-borne trade . . .

13. From the evidence that we have had, we are of the opinion that a serious situation would be created in Germany owing to the blockade of her ports, and that the longer the duration of the war the more serious the situation would become. We do not, however, consider that such pressure as could be exerted by means of naval force alone would be felt sufficiently soon to save France in the event of that country being attacked in overwhelming force. We therefore recognise the possibility that Great Britain's success at sea might only cause greater pressure to be brought to bear on France by land, and that the latter country might have to make terms with Germany which would be no less stringent owing to the losses suffered by the opponent at sea.

(b) *The Assistance that might be given to France by means of the Navy and a mounted Force of 12,000 men*

14. The suggestion that Great Britain might give military assistance to France by means of six mounted brigades was made by Lord Esher, who brought it forward as an alternative proposal to that of the General Staff, which involved the dispatch of a force of four divisions and a cavalry division. Lord Esher considered that, however anxious the British Government might be to send an army to assist the French, circumstances might render its dispatch impossible. He further pointed out that even if this were the case, Great Britain would still be acting up to the spirit of our Entente with France by giving that country the support of her fleet which might well be considered as a fair proportion of armed force to bring into the partnership of the two nations. The dispatch of the mounted contingent would, moreover, in Lord Esher's opinion, afford as much moral support as a larger force, and might prove to be of the highest military value.

15. Neither Sir John French nor the General Staff were in agreement with Lord Esher's suggestion. Their objections to sending a mounted force such as he had proposed were chiefly of a technical nature, since they did not consider such a force as homogeneous or capable of useful military action. The General Staff are of opinion that command of the sea would not necessarily

influence the immediate issue of a great land struggle, and might not be of use to the French at the time that it was required. They further considered that a military *entente* between Great Britain and France can only be of value so long as it rests upon an understanding that, in the event of a war in which both are involved alike on land and at sea, the whole of the available naval and military strength of the two countries will be brought to bear at the decisive point.

(c) *The Assistance that can be given to France by means of the Navy and the British Army*

16. The third manner in which Great Britain could give assistance to France is that which is presented by the General Staff on the assumption that we are in agreement with the opinions that they express in the last paragraph. Their proposal would involve the dispatch to France of an army of four divisions and a cavalry division, amounting in all to about 110,000 . . .

17. It would be possible to reinforce this army by the two remaining divisions in the course of a few months, and these would bring the strength of the British force up to 160,000 . . .

18. We have heard from the Foreign Office that the French are anxious that Great Britain should be able to afford them substantial military assistance, and that such assistance, if granted at the immediate outbreak of war, would be of immense *moral* value to them. In view of this and of the fact that Great Britain's value as a continental ally must to a large extent be judged by her military strength, we are of the opinion that attention should be given to plans which have for their object the utilizing for Imperial purposes of such portions of the scattered forces of the Empire as can be spared from the duty of purely local defence.

19. Various schemes for the employment of the British force were considered by the Committee. It was pointed out that no relief could be given to the armies of France by any threat by the British army to make a descent on the coast of Germany, since the latter Power has ample troops both for watching its own coasts and for an attack on France, and those detailed on the former service would not in any case be used for active operations. It was further pointed out that the Belgian army is weak, and would be unable effectively to resist the violation of the neutrality of Belgium by Germany; and since the British force could not be concentrated and ready to take the field until twenty days after the

order to mobilize had been given, that force could be more effectively used as a reinforcement to the French left than in co-operation with what would probably be a broken or dispirited Belgian army.

20. The plan to which preference is given by the General Staff is therefore one in which the British force shall be concentrated in rear of the left of the French army, primarily as a reserve. The possibility of its being called upon to cover Antwerp has not however been lost sight of, and plans will also be worked out for landing in Belgium with a view to this operation.

Conclusion:

(*a*) The Committee, in the first place, desire to observe that, in the event of an attack on France by Germany, the expediency of sending a military force abroad, or of relying on naval means only, is a matter of policy which can only be determined when the occasion arises by the Government of the day.

(*b*) In view, however, of the possibility of a decision by the Cabinet to use military force, the Committee have examined the plans of the General Staff, and are of opinion that, in the initial stages of a war between France and Germany, in which the Government decided to assist France, the plan to which preference is given by the General Staff is a valuable one, and the General Staff should accordingly work out all the necessary details.

28. (*Memorandum by the General Staff: The Military Aspects of the Continental Problem, 13 August 1911, Cab/38/19/47*)

Extract

In this paper it has been assumed that the policy of England is to prevent any one or more of the Continental Powers from attaining a position of superiority which would enable it or them to dominate the other Continental Powers. Such domination or control would place at the disposal of the Power or Powers concerned a preponderance of naval and military force which would menace the independence of the United Kingdom and the integrity of the British Empire.

This policy, if correctly defined, may possibly be held to apply to Germany at the present time, just as it applied to France in our struggle with Napoleon. It is proposed to examine what course of action England should adopt if, in pursuance of a policy of continental domination, Germany, with the support of Austria, were to attack France. England can either remain neutral or become the active ally of France. And here it must be pointed out that, though England possesses a powerful navy, the military force that she has immediately available for continental intervention is comparatively small; and as sea power exercises only an indirect influence on land operations on a large scale, England can only assist France to a very limited extent in promptly resisting a German invasion. Thus, for example, Trafalgar gave us unquestioned command of the sea, but that victory did not prevent Napoleon from pursuing his course of conquest in Central Europe, though it rendered England safe from invasion.

(a) What is likely to be the result if England remains neutral?

In the case of our remaining neutral, Germany will fight France single-handed. The armies of Germany and the fleets of Germany are much stronger than those of France, and the results of such a war can scarcely be doubted . . .

It is true that France might have the active assistance of Russia. In point of fact, however, in the early stages of the war this assistance would not be likely to relieve the hostile pressure along the line of collision to any material extent. It has no value on the sea, and on land it could be met by German and Austrian troops, with no appreciable diminution of the German troops on the French frontier.

It follows that in a single-handed war France would in all probability be defeated, Holland and Belgium might be annexed by Germany, and a huge indemnity would be placed on France, who would also lose some of her colonies.

In short, the result of such a war would be that Germany would attain to that dominant position which has already been stated to be inimical to the interests of this country. It would appear, therefore, to be imprudent for England to remain neutral in a war of this description, provided she possesses the means of affording such assistance to France by land and sea as might give that Power a reasonable chance of resisting German aggression.

(b) What would be the result if England becomes the active ally of France?

In this case also we can ignore the action of Russia.

In the first place the English and French fleets will command the seas, with the result that the chief fiscal dislocation and commercial loss will fall on Germany. The longer the war lasts the more this strain will be felt by that country.

In the second place the actual disparity in numbers becomes less, and owing to causes which it would take too long to enumerate here, the numbers of the opposing forces at the decisive point would be so nearly equal during the opening and early actions of the war that it is possible for the allies to win some initial successes which might prove invaluable.

In the third place, and perhaps this is the most important consideration of all, it is believed that the moral of the French troops and nation would be greatly strengthened by British co-operation; and there might be a corresponding decrease, or at least some decrease, in the moral of the Germans.

It seems, therefore, that in a war between Germany and France in which England takes active part with the French the result in the opening moves might be doubtful, but the longer the war lasted the greater the strain would be on Germany. This course may therefore be the best for England to pursue, as it is the only course which offers a hope of preventing Germany from attaining the dominant position on the continent of Europe which would be likely in the long run, to prove fatal to this country.

Our navy is powerful, while our expeditionary force is very small if measured in terms of European armies, but these two in alliance with France might prove a formidable obstacle to German victory; whereas if we once allow Germany to defeat France, our expeditionary force would be valueless and the duration of our naval predominance could be measured by years.

Two things, however, are essential. We ought to be able to mobilize as soon as the French and Germans, and to put our whole available strength of six divisions, 1 cavalry division, and army troops into the field so as to be present at the opening actions to which reference has already been made. If we fail to do so, the value of our assistance would be seriously diminished . . .

As regards the naval aspect of the problem, what we ask from a military point of view is that it shall be possible safely to transport troops and supplies across the Channel and in the other directions indicated in this paper, and that the Navy will protect the United Kingdom from organised invasion from the sea. If that cannot be done the scheme falls to the ground. I should not anticipate decisive naval conflicts in the early part of a war between Germany and England. The weaker naval Power generally adopts a defensive attitude, and would endeavour to impose a severe strain on its opponent by means of destroyers, submarines, possibly floating mines, and other methods of naval warfare.

Finally, I must say that, from the information at my disposal I estimate the French commanders and staff to be in no way inferior to those of the German Army, the cavalry to be equal in efficiency to the German, unit for unit, the French artillery to be superior to the German, and the French infantry to be equal to the German if not disheartened by repeated defeats. Perhaps the German infantry being less emotional, may possess greater staying power, but it is difficult to judge, as in the Franco-Prussian War the Prussians gained great initial successes, and we do not know what would have happened had the reverse been the case. . .

29. (*Asquith to the King, 2 November 1911, Cab/41/33/28*)

Extract

Mr. Asquith, with his humble duty to Your Majesty, has the honour to report that a meeting of the Cabinet was held yesterday.

Lord Morley raised the expediency of communications being held or allowed between the General Staff of the War Office and the General Staff of Foreign States, such as France, in regard to possible military co-operation, without the previous knowledge and directions of the Cabinet. Lord Haldane explained what had actually been done, the communications in question having been initiated as far back as 1906, with Sir H. Campbell Bannerman's sanction, and resumed in more detail during the spring and summer of the present year. The Prime Minister pointed out that all questions of policy have been and must be reserved for the decision of the Cabinet, and that it is quite outside the functions of the military and naval officers to prejudge such questions. He added that he believed (and Sir E. Grey concurred), that this was fully recognised by the French Government. Considerable discussions ensued, and no conclusion was come to, the matter being adjourned for further deliberation later on.

30. (*Extracts from 116th Meeting of the Committee of Imperial Defence, 25 April 1912, Cab/38/20/9*)

7. ATTITUDE OF GREAT BRITAIN TOWARDS BELGIUM IN THE EVENT OF A VIOLATION OF BELGIAN NEUTRALITY IN TIME OF WAR

LORD HALDANE said . . . the only case presenting real difficulty was one in which Belgium adopted an attitude of neutrality, but refrained from attempting to enforce respect for her attitude . . .

SIR ARTHUR NICOLSON said that the neutrality of Belgium was guaranteed just as much in the interests of other guarantors as in that of Belgium, and we should be perfectly within our lawful rights in taking steps to enforce her neutrality, even were she unwilling that we should do so. The other guarantors might, of course, raise objections. They were France, Prussia, Austria and Russia.

MR. CHURCHILL said that it would be a great pity if we had to rescue Belgium against her will, for in that case the resentment of the Belgians might counterbalance any strategical advantage which our forces might otherwise gain. Friendship with Belgium was therefore very valuable to us.

If she were a co-belligerent with us we should be able to close Antwerp to German trade. It was probable also that in this case the German forces would be compelled to violate the neutrality of Holland as well. This from the strategical point of view was important as it would give us an excuse to blockade Dutch ports also, and so add to the efficiency of the sea pressure upon Germany. Similar action might perhaps be taken if the Dutch obstructed the transport of troops or supplies to Antwerp.

It was therefore most desirable to secure Belgium as a co-belligerent with us against Germany.

LORD HALDANE said that in order to close Antwerp from the sea it would be necessary to blockade the mouth of the Scheldt, but as the entrance was situated in Dutch territory that would involve a breach of Dutch neutrality.

THE PRIME MINISTER said that everyone would agree with the First Lord that the active co-operation of the Belgians was most to be desired, but we did not know what their views were.

SIR JOHN FRENCH said that the impression that he had gained in Paris and Brussels was that the Belgians were disposed to favour us and that proposals would not be unwelcome. It would certainly make an immense difference to a British army employed on the Continent which attitude the Belgians were to adopt.

LORD HALDANE said that the Belgians had just dismissed a War Minister who was supposed to entertain views which were not favourable to us.

THE HALDANE MISSION

31. (*Lord Sanderson to Hardinge, 26 January 1912, Hardinge MSS. 1912*)

Extract

There is a considerable amount of discontent against Grey in the Liberal Party. A good deal of it is the inevitable result of that enthusiastic philanthropy which insists on messing about in other peoples' affairs which it does not understand. But part also arises from want of information. There has been no call for bluebooks and the F.O. have really given none for the last three years except a collection of Persia papers. I do not think this is wise and I have just made a suggestion to that effect. Of course Bluebooks are troublesome things to prepare but it is quite a mistake to suppose that the public can be satisfied by an occasional speech or by scattered answers to Parliamentary questions which are merely *ex parte* statements and not easy of access for reference. The consequence is that false impressions remain uncorrected and eventually come to be regarded as facts.

32. (*Asquith to the King, 3 February 1912 (held 2 February), Cab/41/33/34*)

Extract

. . . Ministers confined themselves to a review of the foreign situation, and in particular, to the best means of improving the relations between Germany and England . . .

The Cabinet, while most anxious to take the fullest advantage of this or any other opportunity for a fresh start towards more cordial relations between the two countries, were unanimous that it would be premature, at this stage, for the Foreign Secretary to go to Berlin. But, after much consideration, they adopted Sir E. Grey's proposal that Lord Haldane, who has occasion to go to Berlin . . . might be commissioned at the same time to see the Emperor and the Chancellor . . . to feel the way in the direction of a more definite understanding. He would point out to the German Government the bad effects which would be produced on public opinion in both countries by a fresh development of naval rivalry, and would, at the same time—if the question of naval competition can be got out of the way—indicate our readiness to deal in a cordial and generous spirit with German aspirations and interests.

33. (*Nicolson to Bertie, 8 February 1912, F.O. 800/171*)

Extract

This is a private line for your eyes only—as it expresses my personal views which are not quite in accordance with those of the Cabinet. . . I do not myself see why we should abandon the excellent position in which we have been placed, and step down to be involved in endeavours to entangle us in some so-called 'understandings' which would undoubtedly, if not actually impair our relations with France and Russia, in any case render the latter countries somewhat suspicious of us. Moreover, is it likely that we shall be able to obtain from Germany an undertaking of a really formal and binding character that she will not increase her naval programme—and will always be content to leave us in undisputed and indisputable supremacy? . . . The idea is preposterous —so that there is practically no hope that any acceptable arrangements can be come to in respect to naval expenditure.

In these circumstances *if* we adhere to our repeated deduction [sic, declaration?] that we will not discuss formulas for political understandings until a naval agreement has been reached, the failure of Haldane's mission seems certain. Then the relations instead of being impressed [sic, improved?] will be worse. . . I cannot feel quite reassured that we shall not be let in for some kind of engagement of a political kind, and be content with some vague assurances as to naval construction to be carried out at some future date.

I have discharged my soul to you, as I should not like you to think that I have been instrumental in this journey, which I hope will not be one to Canossa.

34. (*Memorandum by Bertie of conversation with Grey in London, 16 February 1912, F.O. 800/171*)

Extract

I warned Grey that the Press and public in France are very nervous and suspicious as to the result of the Haldane mission . . . and that if we signed a formula binding ourselves not to join any combination to attack Germany, we might tie our hands very inconveniently as regards France. He said, Do you mean that it is possible that France will attack Germany? I replied that the first attacker is not necessarily the real aggressor. . . In France it is feared that Germany is making preparation for an attack on France as soon as England has been hoodwinked by Germany. . .

The Government are in a hesitating state. The Lord Chancellor Harcourt and some others are for coming to arrangements with Germany. Grey is wavering Churchill is against tying our hands. I don't know as to Lloyd George and Asquith.

35. (*Memorandum by Bertie on conversation with Lloyd George at the House of Commons, 19 February 1912, F.O. 800/171*)

Extract

Mr. Lloyd George asked me whether I was opposed to any agreement with Germany for there was a growing feeling in England in favour of one. I said, No, for though I believed that it was chiefly the noisy section of the radicals who urged it I thought that a formula of some kind had become necessary but it should be of a very general and anodyne character. As he mentioned a feeling in the City in favour of an Agreement, I observed that financiers have no 'patrie' . . .

Mr. Lloyd George expressed the opinion that the French Government had thrown away the finest opportunity they had ever had or were ever likely to have again, to try conclusions with Germany. They had the certainty of our armed support. The aid of 150,000 English troops would have had a great moral effect. Our Navy would have cut off Germany commercially from the West, Russia would have put pressure on the Eastern frontier of Germany, there would have been shortness of food and famine prices in Germany, commercial stagnation and financial disaster. He did not think France would have crushed Germany as Germany had France in 1870, but it would have brought home to the

Germans that they could not ride rough shod over Europe as they appeared to think. I asked Mr. Lloyd George whether it would not have been a very expensive and not uncertain demonstrations [sic] to the German people. He said that the armed state might in the end be more costly.

Mr. Lloyd George thought that it might be difficult to bring England again to fighting point unless there happened to be a conspicuous aggressive action against France by Germany. I put it to him that if A spat in B's face and the latter knocked down the former the real aggressor would be A. If Germany made great preparations for the evident purpose of attacking France and moved troops to her frontier, France could not be regarded as the aggressor if her troops were the first to cross the frontier between France and Germany. Mr. Lloyd George thought that to bring the British people to fighting point it would be requisite that Germany should have passed into Belgium for the purpose of attacking France or should have crossed the French frontier.

36. (*Nicolson to Bertie, 6 April 1912, F.O. 800/171*)

Extract

I had sent Grey, who is in the country, the substance of a private letter which Cambon had written to de Flurian [sic] reporting the impression and uneasiness which existed in the minds both of the President and M. Poincaré in regard to our discussions with Germany, with especial reference to formulas of any description. I sent your letter on to Grey yesterday. I am glad these communications have arrived, as they give one additional texts on which to discourse on the points which I have been labouring for many a day. I have told Grey that it is clear that if we proceed with any formula we shall affect our relations with France, and indirectly with Russia, and that the ultimate consequences of such a contingency are not pleasant to contemplate. We have, I have pointed out, an easy exit from the position in to which we are drifting, as the Germans have practically rejected our original formula, and have demanded something which we cannot possibly grant. We can, therefore, now abandon all formula of any description with good reason, but there is no reason why we should not maintain our friendly relation with Germany and discuss in an amicable manner any question which may arise between us, but that we should retain perfect liberty of action, and not tie ourselves up in any way. If we do one of the chief guarantees of peace is removed. I feel confident that Grey would not sign any formula acceptable to the Germans, but there are some of his colleagues who, in their ignorance and shortsightedness would go very far towards pleasing Germany, and they exercise considerable pressure on our Chief . . .

As to territorial cessions on exchange in Africa, I do not know exactly what is proceeding. I believe, but I am not sure, that Harcourt is conversing with Kühlmann, and I have urged that we should ascertain whether Kühlmann has been authorised either by his Government or his Chief to discuss these matters. If he is not, we are showing all our cards to an unauthorised agent, who can be disavowed if convenient. The whole proceeding is most irregular, and these matters should not be allowed to be taken out of the hands of the Foreign Secretary. It is rather absurd our dealing with the property of other people, especially of people whose integrity we have more or less undertaken to defend. The '98 Treaty was not a happy transaction, but apparently Harcourt is willing to confirm and extend it. He is you know, a most ardent Germanophil. I doubt if anything will result from these irregular conversations, as even Harcourt would not dare to make any serious surrenders. The whole history of these recent German negotiations is an extraordinary episode, and I have never seen any discussions conducted in such a strange manner. I am doing my best to get us out of the quagmire into which we are plunged, and into which we have been led by our unscrupulous adversaries and our singularly naive and feeble negotiators.

BRITISH NAVAL POLICY

37. (*Memorandum by Winston Churchill, 15 March 1911, Cabinet Papers, Cab/37/105/27*)

Extract

The Mediterranean Fleet

I am anxious that the Mediterranean position should be examined *de novo*.

1. It is suggested that the maintenance there of a strong and costly subsidiary establishment is inconsistent with accepted modern naval theory. The sea is all one, and the fleet which has established its superiority over the main battle fleet of the enemy is supreme . . . all over the world. . .

2. From this point of view it is suggested that what matters to Great Britain is not to be able to hold the Mediterranean permanently but to be sure of being able to enter it in preponderant strength at any moment when circumstances require. Gibraltar, which is unable to close the Straits, is of immense importance in assuring that they will be kept open. On the basic assumptions that we secure supremacy in the decisive waters and that Gibraltar prevents the entrance to the Mediterranean being closed to us, there seems to be no adequate reason why we should remain in the Mediterranean until the moment is reached for specific action there.

3. It should be further remembered that we are no longer the strongest Power in the Mediterranean, and that to have an inferior fleet in those waters would lead, on the declaration of war, to great risks. . . This is in effect an admission of the faulty strategic position involved in the separation from the waters of decisive superiority of so important a division of the fleet as the Mediterranean command . . .

4. It should further be remembered that it is no longer possible to force the Dardenelles, that nobody would expose a modern fleet to that, therefore the one decisive method of putting pressure upon the Turks which depended upon speed has become inoperative and that other naval demonstrations would be quite as effective if they took the form of the departure of a fleet from British waters for a particular purpose.

5. It is inconceivable that a descent would be made on Egypt by sea in face of the interruption of communications which would follow the entry of the British Navy in force into the Mediterranean. The invasion of Egypt by land would be necessarily a lengthy business . . . and if it were part of a general European struggle . . . the victor in that struggle would, whatever might have happened to Egypt in the meanwhile, decide the future destinies of that State.

6. It seems, therefore, a matter for consideration whether the Mediterranean establishments should not be reduced to that of a cruiser squadron. . .

38. (*Memorandum by Reginald McKenna on the naval situation, 24 June 1912, Cabinet Papers Cab/37/111/79*)

Extract

It must be assumed that Mr. Churchill's policy is to withdraw into the home waters on the outbreak of war the squadron of battle-ships which he proposes to base upon Gibraltar. If he does not it is obvious that they would be an even cheaper spoil than when reinforced by the fleet at Malta . . . the allied [enemy] fleets would have the whole Mediterranean open to them and there would be nothing to prevent them passing through the Straits into the Atlantic. On Mr. Churchill's hypothesis we should be unable to spare a fleet of sufficient strength to drive the Allies back into the Mediterranean, and they could establish themselves off the coast of Portugal in complete control of a trade route which is of vital importance to us. Their cruisers would capture our merchant ships coming from South America, Africa, Australia and the East. . . Mr. Churchill conceives that we could obtain relief from these disasters as soon as we have disposed of the German fleet in the decisive theatre of war. I imagine, however that the Germans are as much alive to the function of a navy as we are. The purpose of a fleet is to keep the sea open for ourselves and closed to our enemy. So long as Germany is able, by the mere postponement of a battle, in which she is sure of defeat, to secure the destruction of our trade and the consequent starvation of our people, what inducement has she to do more than remain in her fortified harbours until we are either exhausted from lack of supplies or have weakened ourselves to Mr. Churchill's point of danger by dispatching a fleet to drive off the allies.

I do not think I am misinterpreting Mr. Churchill's strategy when I say that an alliance with France is its essential feature. Without such an alliance I cannot think that his naval advisers would recommend the distribution of the fleet which he now proposes.

It is, of course, for the Cabinet to decide whether we should be allowed to be forced into this alliance, but, for my part, I should view with the gravest concern any action being taken which must necessarily lead to such a conclusion. I would far rather—if it were necessary, which I hesitate to believe—give my vote for an addition to our fleet in ships and men, than be driven into dependence on an alliance with any European power.

39. (*Asquith to the King, 16 July 1912, Cab/41/33/58*)

Extract

Mr. Asquith, with his humble duty to Your Majesty, has the honour to report that the naval situation in the Mediterranean was further considered at meetings of the Cabinet yesterday and today.

The subject was exhaustively discussed in all its respects, particularly in view of the criticisms offered, especially by Mr. McKenna, to the proposals of the Admiralty . . .

Mr. Churchill dealt today in detail with these objections and satisfied his colleagues (i) that there would be no need to withdraw the four battle cruisers from the Mediterranean, in the event of a war with Germany, unless to meet some unlikely and unforeseen contingency and, (ii) that in the opinion of his best expert advisers, the proposed Cruiser squadron would, during the next two years, be more than a match in the Mediterranean for any force that Austria would oppose to it.

After a full discussion, the Cabinet unanimously approved the proposals of the Admiralty . . .

It was agreed that, in continuing the communications which had taken place in the past between French naval and military experts and our own, it should be plainly indicated to the French Government that such communications were not to be taken as prejudging the freedom of decision of either Government as to whether they should or should not co-operate in the event of war.

40. (*Memorandum by Bertie on conversations with Grey on 17 and 23 July 1912, F.O. 800/165*)

Extract

I told Sir E. Grey that if we withdraw our ships from the Mediterranean and left the care of our interests to the French they would before long ask for a quid pro quo, and I suggested that it might be in the form of an exchange of notes defining the major interests of England and France and stating that in the event of any of those interests being in the opinion of either endangered the Governments of the two Countries would confer together as to what steps, if any, should be taken to defend those interests.

Sir E. Grey said he would submit to the Cabinet my formula for the communication to the French Government but he thought

that they would prefer the one they had already sanctioned. . .
I saw Sir Edward Grey again on the 23rd.

He told me that the Cabinet adhered to their formula. He told
me that *he* would not remain in the Cabinet if there was any question of abandoning the policy of the Entente with France. To my
observation that the Cabinet could not afford to lose him and that
if the Prime Minister was with him it would be the Dissenting
Ministers who would have to drop out and they would not be a
loss, Sir E. Grey said that he did not wish to break up the Cabinet
and that it would be he that would go and I might put this to
M. Poincaré in defending the Cabinet formula. I gathered that
Harcourt is the Anti-French leader and that Asquith to a great
degree, Churchill strongly and Haldane moderately are with Grey.

41. (*Memorandum on the General Naval Situation prepared for the
information of the Right Hon. R. L. Borden, K.C., M.P. (Prime
Minister of Canada) August, 1912, F.O. 800/87*)

Extract

. . . The purpose which governs the creation of a weapon may be
unconnected with any intention to employ it. It would not be fair
to draw from the character of the German Fleet the conclusion
that the German Government, or still less, the German people,
have formed any conscious intention of attacking the British
Empire; and so long as we maintain a good and sufficient superiority in naval power it is unlikely that they will ever do so.

It is permissible to believe that Germany wishes to be powerful
at sea, simply for the sake of being powerful and of obtaining the
influence which comes from power without any specific danger
to guard against or settled purpose to employ the power. Still the
German Empire has been built up by a series of sudden and
successful wars.

Within the lifetime of many of us she has carved a maritime
province out of Denmark, and the Rhine provinces of France. She
has absorbed half the ancient Kingdom of Poland; she dominates
Austria, Italy, and Sweden. Her policy has been such as to place
her in a position to absorb Holland with scarcely an effort. Her
military strength renders her alone, among the nations of Europe,
free from the fear of invasion. But there is not a State on her
borders, nor a small State in Europe, but has either suffered at
her hands or lies under the impression of her power. From these

anxieties Great Britain, and the British Empire, sheltered by the Navy of Great Britain, have hitherto been free.

In this connection the disparity of the naval risks of the British and German Empires must not be overlooked.

Great Britain can never violate German territory even after a defeat of that Power at sea, her Army not being organised or strong enough for such an undertaking. Germany with her large Army could, however, if she chose, invade and conquer Great Britain after a successful naval campaign in the North Sea. Germany has no overseas territory desired by Great Britain. Great Britain has overseas territories, the cession of which might be demanded by Germany after a successful war. A decisive battle lost at sea by Germany would still leave her the greatest Power in Europe. A decisive battle lost at sea by Great Britain would for ever ruin the United Kingdom, would shatter the British Empire to its foundations, and change profoundly the destiny of its component parts. The advantages which Great Britain could gain from defeating Germany are nil. There are practically no limits to the ambitions which might be indulged by Germany, or to the brilliant prospects open to her in every quarter of the globe, if the British Navy were out of the way. The combination of the strongest Navy with that of the strongest Army would afford wider possibilities of influence and action than have yet been possessed by any Empire in Modern times.

Chapter 3

Anglo-Russian Relations and the Middle East

BRITISH POLICY TOWARDS RUSSIA

42. (*Grey to Nicolson (St Petersburg), 1 April 1907, F.O. 800/71*)

Extract

It would be much better not to bring the Dardanelles and Bosphorus into this Asiatic Agreement. . . The fact is that if Asiatic things are settled favourably, the Russians will not have trouble with us about the entrance to the Black Sea, but France at any rate must be taken into our confidence before we take engagements, and we should expect Russia's support about some Egyptian and other kindred things in the Near East, which matter to us and are important to us.

The real rock ahead is the prospect in Russia itself. If the Duma is dissolved and there is a regime of pogrom and courts martial, feeling here will be very adverse. We could carry a settlement of Asiatic frontier questions in any case, but I don't think we could do more if things were very bad in Russia, for there would be resentment at our choosing this moment to make a concession about the Straits. But this would not be the worst consequence of reaction in Russia: the worst is that things would be said in Parliament and in our Press, which would mightily offend the Czar and the Russian Government, and might make it impossible for you to make progress at St. Petersburg.

43. (*Nicolson to Grey, 19 July 1908, F.O. 800/73*)

Extract

If we wish, and I presume we do wish, in the interest of peace, to avert the possibility of any Power assuming a position from which she could dictate to others, a close understanding [with Russia] is, I submit, an object for the attainment of which every effort should be made. We have secured an understanding with France. That with Russia is in its very early infancy, and will require, for reasons which I need not explain, careful nurture and treatment. Any serious check to this infant growth may kill it before it has advanced in years and its disappearance would doubtless eventually react on our relations with France.

GREY IS GLOOMY ABOUT THE PROSPECTS OF TURKISH REFORM

44. (*Memorandum by Sir E. Grey on Turkey, January 1908, Cab/37/91/5*)

There are three questions connected with Turkey to which I wish to draw the attention of the Cabinet.

1. The Turks have in the most flagrant manner violated the Persian frontier, and have practically annexed a slice of North-Western Persia.

The Persians have been pressing Russia and ourselves to protect them.

The matter concerns Russia more than us, as it is in a part of Persia which is close to her own frontier, and it is remote from the sea. I have therefore taken the line that we will support the representations which Russia makes, but that we are not ourselves prepared to resort to coercive measures. Russia herself is reluctant to undertake such measures, but is much perplexed by the loss of prestige which attaches in some degree to both of us if the integrity of Persia is violated, but in a special degree to Russia, by allowing the Turks to remain where they are, as the region affected is near her frontier.

Should Russia propose to take coercive measures, the question would arise as to what support we should give her. Till that arises, or till the Turks do something which involves British subjects or property, it is not necessary to take a decision. In the meantime, a Turco-Persian Commission has met on the frontier, and, in the event of their failing to agree, we and Russia have a claim by Treaty to act as mediators.

2. The state of Armenia is lamentable.

The misgovernment is so bad, that in at least one place, the Mussulmans have combined with the Christians and practically expelled the Governor. The worst sufferings are those of the Christian population; but the whole population suffers, and the country is in a state of starvation and misery.

I see nothing that we can do, except to urge the Turks diplomatically to give assistance, which, however, I fear that they have no money to afford; and to allow the population the right to emigrate, which it is in their power to do.

On the occasion of the massacres in Armenia in 1895 and 1896 Lord Salisbury used the strongest language in his speeches; but we were unable to take any action in a part of the world which was out of the reach of our fleet, and the massacres went on quite unchecked. The present evil can only be cured by a complete reform of the government of Armenia, and this it is out of our power to impose or enforce.

3. In Macedonia the state of things gets worse.

Armed bands of Greeks, Bulgarians and Servians are all killing each other and the unarmed population. There are a certain number of outrages by Mussulmans upon Christians, and vice versa; but the greatest evil in the country is the outrages of Greeks, Bulgarians and Servians upon each other.

A year ago it was the Greek bands which were doing nearly all the mischief. The Turk probably could have stopped them, and thus pacified the country; but either his troops are incompetent or else he is unwilling to use them; it has even been said that they were in collusion with the Greek bands. I am reluctant to urge too strongly that the Turk should use his troops, for fear that if he did use them energetically they would commit excesses.

The Powers have agreed to put forward a proposal for introducing judicial reforms. But this will not pacify the country.

I have therefore proposed to the Powers that we should urge the Turkish Government to use the gendarmerie under European officers, giving the European officers executive control over this force. I believe that a mobile column of gendarmerie, if the European officers were given executive control, might put down the bands and establish something like order.

I have little hope that the Powers will agree to press this proposal upon the Turks. Lord Lansdowne with great difficulty induced the Powers (except Germany) to combine in a naval demonstration in 1905 to secure the Financial Commission. The Powers were no sooner committed to this than they wished to get out of it, and I doubt whether they will agree to join in one again. Moreover, there have been so many naval demonstrations during the last few years that they are beginning to lose their effect as a means of coercion. I am not prepared to ask the Powers to resort to coercive measures for any proposal such as that for judicial reforms alone, which would not pacify the country; if there is to be coercion it should be for something which will really be effective.

But I must bring matters to a head with regard to Macedonia by a statement in Parliament if I am pressed there. I cannot go on holding out hope when there is no hope. I propose, therefore, to press the Powers to agree to put forward and to resort to any measures necessary to make the Turk accept some large proposal of reform, such as the appointment of a Turkish Governor irremovable except with the consent of the Powers, which would be really effective in Macedonia; and, in the event of the Powers refusing, I see nothing for it but to explain in Parliament what we have done, and that, without the consent of the other Powers, we can do no more.

If we separate from the concert of the Powers and try to act alone, we shall not solve the Macedonian question; we shall raise the Turkish question. It will certainly mean war between us and Turkey, and that will raise other grave questions, under pressure of which the question of reforms in Macedonia will be lost to sight.

For two years we have, as Lord Lansdowne did, taken the initiative; either openly, as in regard to the customs dues, or virtually, as in regard to judicial reforms, which we urged Russia and Austria to put forward. The other Powers leave the brunt of everything to us, and we incur increasing odium at Constantinople, by which others benefit and our commerce suffers, while Macedonia is gaining no advantage.

It is not reasonable to go on with this policy, nor do I think it expedient or honest to do so when no good results are to be expected from it.

If therefore, I am pressed in Parliament upon the question of Macedonia, I propose to take some such line as I have sketched out; and I have thought it well to give the Cabinet an opportunity of reviewing the matter beforehand, if they desire to do so. Shortly put, what I propose to do is to write a despatch to the Powers and present it to them on the first suitable occasion (1) pointing out faithfully what the present state of Macedonia is: (2) stating what would be an effective remedy; and not pretending that anything short of this effective, and (3) asking whether they are prepared to press this remedy upon the Turks, and pressing our co-operation and support in doing so if they agree.

HARDINGE'S VIEWS ON THE YOUNG TURK REVOLUTION

45. (*Hardinge to Barclay (Constantinople), 30 June 1908, F.O. 800/193A*)

Extract

I hope you approve the attitude we have assumed towards recent developments in Macedonia, which are intensely interesting and towards which everybody in this country has the greatest possible sympathy. We are quite convinced that a good administration in Turkey will be of the greatest advantage to British interests, although perhaps it will not be to the advantage of other more interested Powers. I am always afraid that the Russians may be tempted to revert to the intrigues which took place in 1876 to upset the Constitution, which were in reality the precursors to war between Russia and Turkey. I can only hope that the Young Turk movement has a permanent basis, and that it may perhaps be a bulwark to the new Constitution. Unless this is so, I cannot help feeling that the Sultan will not accept the present situation, but will endeavour to upset it on the first possible occasion. In this course he would no doubt be encouraged by Germany, since that Power cannot feel at all pleased at the blow her influence will receive in Constantinople. It is a splendid opportunity for Gerard Lowther to arrive at Constantinople after such a crisis, and we cannot help thinking that it may be possible in the near future to entirely reverse our attitude and policy towards Turkey of the last few years.

In view of the change in the situation in Macedonia, we have suggested to the Russian Government to drop our scheme of a mobile force for the time being, such a force being no longer necessary since the disappearance of the bands. It also seems to me that the prosecution of our reform scheme will be superfluous until we see whether the Turkish Government will really undertake the internal regeneration of Turkey...

BRITAIN AND THE BOSNIAN CRISIS

46. (*Hardinge to Lowther, 1 December 1908, F.O. 800/193A*)

Extract

As regards Austria taking over part of the Turkish debt, I have repeatedly urged it upon Mensdorff as the only possible means of compensation to Turkey which she would be in a position to accept, without exposing the new regime to having sold the two Provinces to Austria. Aehrenthal has categorically refused to accept any such proposal—consequently, we can do no more. I cannot conceive what form of compensation Austria can find to offer to Turkey, which the latter would be ready to accept.

The Conference seems to be receding daily. It is a very strong order for Austria to demand that Turkey and the five Great Powers should go gagged to a Conference, and not say a word about Bosnia and Herzogovina. . . . I do not very well see how Russia can possibly give way, and Aehrenthal seems to have burnt his boats.

In the meantime the *impasse* at which Austria has arrived in her negotiations with Russia and Turkey seems to make it all the more desirable that Turkey should make a strenuous effort to come to terms with Bulgaria. The same might equally be said of Bulgaria. Were these two countries to come to terms, the question of Bulgarian independence might be settled by the Ambassadors at Constantinople or elsewhere, without any Conference at all. Bulgaria would then be encouraged to be on friendly terms with Turkey, and if Bulgaria at the same time made friendly ententes with Servia and Montenegro, the position of the Balkan States, supported by a friendly Turkey, would be a very strong one, and would practically spell checkmate to Aehrenthal's policy of obtaining Austria's supremacy in the Balkans. This is the line of policy which would suit all the Powers, except perhaps Germany and Austria, and I think we shall do all we can to achieve this result. This is not merely my own opinion, but also that of Sir Edward Grey.

47. (*Hardinge to Nicolson, 12 April 1909, F.O. 800/342*)

Extract

I quite realise the strength of German traditions at St Petersburg and the power enjoyed by German sympathisers at Court, but with a full knowledge of the extreme sensitiveness of the Emperor it seems to me almost impossible that he will ever get over the brutality of German methods and the humiliation that has been inflicted upon him. The fact that he himself had to bow before the German demarché is what he will never get over and what will in the end save Isvolsky, although the latter is much to blame for not having foreseen it and for not having modified his policy accordingly.

Isvolsky's excuses and recriminations in connection with the Montenegrin question have not impressed us favourably. It is evident that he fancied that it might be possible to retrieve his hopeless position by pressing to obtain for Montenegro what we and all clear sighted people could see that there was no possible hope of obtaining. I think that we have come out of it well, especially as we refused to agree to Aehrenthal's last exigencies and he gave way in the end. Isvolsky should realise the great advantage of war in the Balkans having been postponed to a later date when Russia may be in a better state of preparation, and I only hope that Russian statesmen will take the lesson to heart. . .

The future must necessarily be a source of anxiety and there can be no doubt that big events are in store for us. I agree that it is very desirable that we should draw nearer to Russia, but there is no prospect of this while the present Govt. is in office in this country. I am almost absolutely certain that certain members of the Cabinet assiduously spread the report that, in the event of a general conflagration, England would stand on one side. This was naturally reported to Metternich and the Germans were thereby emboldened. Please regard this as private but I know it as a fact. I mention this to show you how impossible it is to hope for any step forward by this Govt. towards a closer 'entente' or even an alliance with Russia. When Balfour comes into office it may be different, but we must hope that it may not be too late. This is not said in any party spirit as I have none and I would sooner have Grey as my Chief than anybody.

I cannot help thinking that these new Austrian Dreadnoughts are intended as a thank offering to Germany for her recent support and to force us to place Dreadnoughts in the Mediterranean and so relieve the strain in the North Sea. I am very glad of the announcement as it will knock out entirely the little Navy people in the Cabinet of whom there are less than six:—Winston Churchill, Lloyd-George, Harcourt, Burns, Morley and Loreburn. If it were generally know [sic] these would lost [sic] caste entirely in the country.

GREY AND HARDINGE GAZE INTO THE CRYSTAL BALL

48. (*Grey to Bertie, 30 April 1909, F.O. 800/180*)

Extract

I observed [to Cambon] that I thought one of the most important factors, perhaps the most important factor, in European politics during the next generation would be the struggle between Slav and Teuton for the upper hand in the south-eastern corner of Europe. This struggle used to be considered as one between Russia and the Western States, more especially Britain, but this idea has now disappeared, and the struggle would be one simply between Slav and Teuton. The Bulgarians counted for very much amongst the Slavs. Russia, it was true, was as yet unprepared for war, but this was partly compensated for by the increased strength of Bulgaria, who was already prepared for war. If the German Emperor were to do what he said and attempted to repress Bulgaria [if she marched on Salonika] the struggle between Slav and Teuton would be precipitated. Russia could not keep out of the struggle; she would be dragged into it by Bulgaria, and then the German object of detaching Russia from others and attaching her to Germany would be completely defeated.

49. (*Hardinge to Lowther (Constantinople), 18 May 1909, F.O. 800/193A*)

Extract

It is quite true that the Turks will probably turn to what they consider to be the strongest combination, which at the present moment is that of the Central Powers. Yet, if peace and quiet continue in the Balkans for the next two years, and if in the meantime the Turks lean on Austria and Germany, they will, in my opinion, find that they have put their money on the wrong horse, and that it would have been much better for them to have made friends with the Bulgarians and to have leaned on the Powers of the Triple Entente. Provided that Russia and France do not yield in the near future to German pretensions to obtain a position of domination in Europe, there is, in my opinion, little doubt that their combination, together with Bulgaria, will be the strongest one before long. It is all very well to talk of detaching Italy from Germany and Austria. That is not at all our policy, since it is preferable to us that the Triple Alliance should be maintained and even renewed, because Italy is, and must always be dependent on the goodwill of France and England in the event of a continental war. Her coast line is too long for her to be able to protect it from the attacks of the two Powers, and to contribute military assistance at the same time to the other members of the Triple Alliance. Moreover Italy is lukewarm in her sentiments towards Germany and Austria, her sympathies in reality being with us and France.

THE BAGHDAD RAILWAY

50. (*Hardinge to Sir Charles Marling* (*Constantinople*), *16 November 1909, F.O. 800/193A*)

Extract

We are quite determined not to give way as regards the four per cent [Turkish customs increase] until we get all we want, and that is the full control and construction of the Baghdad end of the Baghdad Railway, and possibly a promise of a concession for a railway from Baghdad to the Mediterranean . . .

Nobody would be more pleased than I if we could only come to terms with the Germans about the Baghdad Railway. It is what I have been trying for ever since I came to this Office; but the last two years have been quite hopeless owing to the hostility of the Emperor and some of his *entourage*. Things look a little more hopeful now.

51. (*Grey to Hardinge, 16 May 1911, Hardinge MSS., vol. 1, 1910–13*)

Extract

We have two objectives about the Baghdad Railway negotiations (1) to secure an agreement as to the limits of Turkish territory in the region of the Persian Gulf, which is consistent with our strategic interests and prestige. I think it is not inconsistent with that, if we recognise Turkish suzerainty over Koweit, provided his [the sheikh's] autonomy is guaranteed and our treaties with him are recognised as part of the *status quo*. His position then will really be more secure than now. (2) to get such a footing on the prolongation of the Baghdad Railway beyond Baghdad, as shall give us a say in through routes and enable us to see that our trade gets in fairly at the gate and has fair treatment along the road.

Till we get these two points we cannot give way about the Turkish customs. The weak point is that, even without increase of Turkish customs, the Turks and Germans can at a pinch complete the railway to Basrah, and as we cannot prevent that, it will be a mistake for us to push them so hard that negotiations fail and that it is completed without our having any say.

POTSDAM AND TURKEY

52. (*Nicolson to Lowther, 23 January 1911, F.O. 800/193A*)

Extract

We are still puzzled as to what actually took place at Potsdam as the communications which Sazonow makes to Buchanan are not entirely of a satisfactory nature, and he seems to be in an attitude of mind which disposes him to yield to whatever demands are made to him from Berlin. I am quite at a loss to understand his policy, as he seems to me to be giving everything away and receiving nothing in return. . . At the same time, now that the Germans have got him on the run, I doubt if they will allow him to stop until he has yielded to all that they desire, and, were we to endeavour to check his downward career, and possibly thereby lead to a rupture of negotiations, we should incur the odium and responsibility of having prevented the establishment of a good understanding between Russia and Germany. In short, Sazonow is getting both us and France into a tangle . . .

Personally I am not particularly keen on seeing the present Turkish regime too well provided with funds. This would only assist towards the creation of a power which, I think, in the not far distant future—should it become thoroughly consolidated and established—would be a very serious menace to us and also to Russia. It would be curious if, in this twentieth century, we witnessed a revival of the Ottoman Empire of the seventeenth century, and there is the additional danger that it would be able to utilise the enormous Mussulman populations under the rule of Christian countries. I think that this Pan-Islamic . . . movement is one of our greatest dangers in the future, and is, indeed, far more of a menace than the 'Yellow Peril' which apparently produces such misgivings in the mind of the German Emperor... A union between her [Germany] and Turkey would be one of the gravest dangers to the equilibrium of Europe and Asia.

THE TRIPOLI WAR AND ANGLO-TURKISH RELATIONS

53. (*Asquith to the King, 2 November 1911, Cabinet Papers, Cab/41/33/28*) (*held 1 November 1911*)
Extract

Sir E. Grey reported a rather *naif* communication from the Ottoman Government, proposing an alliance between Turkey and this country or (in the alternative) the admission of Turkey as a party to the Triple Entente. It was agreed to reply that the obligations of neutrality forbid us to entertain any such proposals while a state of war exists between Turkey and Italy, but that we appreciate their spirit and object, and when peace is restored we shall be prepared to do all in our power to reciprocate the Turkish wish for a solid and friendly understanding...

ANGLO-RUSSIAN RELATIONS, PERSIA AND CENTRAL ASIA

54. (*Nicolson to Barclay (Tehran), 24 October 1911, F.O. 800/315*)
Extract

We can have no possible confidence in the Persian Government being able to take effective measures for some time to come—in any case in safeguarding the trade routes and re-establishing order . . . I, personally, have always been of the opinion that we should utilise the troops which are coming from India for patrol work on the trade roads, but the India Office are much opposed to such a project, being influenced, I understand, by the fear that possibly an Escort of say 50 men, might be overwhelmed by disorderly tribes, and in that event it would become necessary for India to send a regular military expedition to avenge such a disaster. Of course one cannot guarantee that such misfortunes would not arise, but I doubt very much if it is likely that any tribes would venture to attack a body of well armed Indian Cavalry, or, should they do so, that the latter would not be able to give them a lesson . . . The reinforcements . . . are to be there ostensibly and primarily for the protection of the Consulates and all British lives and property. In the meantime we will wait to see what effective measures the Persian Government are able to take for re-establishing order and maintaining security on the trade roads. Should they be unable to effect any thing of a serious character, we shall then have to decide whether our people should patrol the roads themselves or whether they should be employed for escorting down to the coast our Consuls and other British subjects. The latter will, of course, amount to abandoning South Persia to complete chaos and anarchy, and personally I think it would only be the prelude to our having to take eventually very serious and extensive measures ourselves. However, we shall have to proceed for the moment on the limited lines which have been settled in consultation with the India Office and the Government of India. We have now before us the threat of the Russian Government to proceed to what seems to be tantamount to an occupation of the whole of the Northern Provinces of Persia. We are in conversation with St Petersburg on the subject . . .

Among the many disturbing factors which have of late given us all so much trouble, the attitude of Shuster is by no means one of the least. . . The early attitude of Shuster towards the two Legations indicated pretty clearly that he intended to take a perfectly free hand and to ignore completely the positions which we and Russia hold in Persia and listen to no advice or take into consideration the Anglo-Russian Convention. Of late, with the assistance of his extreme friends in the Medjliss and I daresay also under the inspiration of Major Stokes, he seems to be desirous of acquiring powers which go far beyond those which properly appertain to a Treasurer-General. He seems also to have put himself at cross-purposes with the Regent and the Persian Government, and he seems to have alienated the sympathy of Russia and ourselves. It would be a good thing if matters should so work out as to lead to his resignation. We must maintain our understanding with Russia as were it to break down in Persia, the relations between the two countries would be most materially affected, and in the present condition of affairs, not only in Europe, but elsewhere, it is of the highest importance that we should remain on the most friendly terms with Russia. It would be disastrous to our foreign policy were the understandings with Russia, France and ourselves to be weakened in any way whatsoever . . .

In reply to numerous memoranda which we have received from the Persian Minister here, we have given him a memorandum enumerating the various deplorable incidents that have occurred in Southern Persia and which it was quite impossible for any Government to tolerate indefinitely, and which exposed their subjects and commercial interests to dangers which the Persian Government are unable to control. . .

55. (*Hardinge to Lord Crewe, 17 September 1912, Hardinge MSS., vol. II, 1912*)

Extract

I have been considering very carefully and with much anxiety developments in Persia and Kashgar. . . I regard the general advance of Russia in Asia, undertaken under the guise of friendship, and in agreement with us, as really a very serious situation. Although the scheme that I have suggested for Persia maintains Persia as an entity on the map of Asia, it is impossible to close one's eyes to the fact that it is another big step towards partition. That partition is absolutely bound to come one day, but it is our duty to do our very utmost to postpone it. The day will inevitably come when we shall have to hold the Gulf Ports and Shiraz as an outpost. I do not like the prospect of that contingency at all. In any case what strikes me as very essential is the maintenance of friendly relations with Russia. Otherwise, I fear, we shall be left in the lurch; and whatever settlement is made by Russia, must be made in agreement with us and not in opposition.

56. (*Crewe to Hardinge, 26 September 1912, Hardinge MSS., vol. II, 1912*)

Extract

I have not yet had any intimation from Balmoral about Persian colloquies there with the Russians, but on Saturday next Sazonoff and Benckendorff, also Arthur Nicolson, . . . are coming here [Crewe Hall] for Sunday, so we shall go into the whole thing. Last week in London Asquith, Grey and I, John Morley also being there, laid down the general lines as it seems likely they may be drawn. I have been anxious that Persia should be taken as a separate subject, and not treated as one pawn in a game where Tibet and Kashgar are others: and I think my colleagues see the merit of this. In my belief, and here again there is much agreement, whatever the intrinsic advantages of restoring the ex-Shah, and there may be some, the public effect would be so bad, the

Convention would appear to be so futile, and we should consequently look such utter fools,—that the step should be avoided at almost any cost, and it seems that the Russians don't want to press him if anybody else at all can be found. They have also said that they do not desire to push on the Trans-Persian Railway, as public opinion here now stands, and this looks as if our debates on the subject had not been unfruitful. . .

57. (*Grey to J. A. Spender, 24 September 1912, F.O. 800/111*)

I am bombarded by letters here from people who want me to break with Russia over Persia; how on earth can we help Persia if we do? And it is these same people who denounce partition because it would increase our responsibilities! I agree with the dislike of partition, but it would be less formidable than a policy of destroying Russian influence in the North of Persia, which is pressed upon me. Partition however is not yet in question and I trust may never be.

58. (*Grey to Harcourt, 26 September 1912, Harcourt MSS. Box 29*)

Extract

Almost the first thing Sazonow said to me was to deprecate any partition of Persia and I don't suppose our conversations will result in any new agreement being proposed. Whether we can make things in Persia much better is very doubtful. We are discussing details such as a change of Regent, Gendarmerie, finance, etc. There is no question of the return of the ex-Shah. Of course I shall submit the record to the Cabinet. . .

59. (*Nicolson to Hardinge, 11 June 1914, F.O. 800/374*).

Extract

The consequence is that in the Russian sphere [of Persia] the Russians have succeeded in keeping order and security and pushing their trade with great vigour and in practically bringing the administration more or less indirectly under their control. While in the South we have no very definite aims or policy and the result has been a chaotic state of affairs. It is no use our sitting down and criticising the methods of Russia or in reading them lectures on the subject. We are about to open up discussions as to the situation in Persia. Though I do not for one moment imagine that they will lead to Russia withdrawing her troops or seriously modifying her attitude, I trust they may result in our being able to have a free hand not only in our sphere but also throughout the South of Persia. In fact to put it bluntly I think the time will eventually come when we shall have to face the question of a partition of Persia. The present state of things really cannot last for any length of time, and does really lead to serious friction between us and Russia. When we see Russian influence pushed right down into the neutral zone we really must take some steps to consolidate our own influence, both political and commercial, in those regions. Of course we shall do nothing without full consultation with your Government but I do think you ought to keep in view the possibility that some such step will have to be adopted before very long. Also we must not leave out of account the possibility of German activity in the Gulf and on the Karun where it has already begun to make itself rather unpleasantly manifest. The great trouble in all these questions is that on the one hand we have an autocratic and if you like a somewhat unscrupulous Government, with unlimited resources at its disposal, while on the other hand we have a country under a parliamentary government with very limited means at its disposal and obliged to consider political and parliamentary exigencies at home. There is little doubt that under such conditions which country is likely to gain the upper hand eventually. . . We must not quarrel with Russia if it can possibly be avoided.

Chapter 4

Britain and Europe, 1912–14

THE BALKAN WARS

60. (*Minute by Winston Churchill to be read to the Cabinet on 3 April 1913, Lloyd George Papers, C/3/15/21A*)

Although I agree to the principle of an international demonstration provided it is unaccompanied by bloodshed, I earnestly hope that we shall not be drawn into any position distinct from that of France and Russia and still less of giving any support to Austria, whether active or tacit, in attacking Montenegro.

If a great war breaks out, we cannot take sides, in sympathy or action, in favour of Austria and against the Balkan States; nor ought we to be drawn at this juncture into an opposite system to that of France and Russia. Earnest efforts to preserve peace and maintain the Concert ought not to compromise the clearness of our position should they fail. The Montenegrins have made terrible sacrifices and they ought not to be deprived of the fruits of their victories except as the result of the united action of the Concert of Europe.

61. (*Grey to Hardinge, 13 May 1913, Hardinge MSS. vol. II, 1913–15*)

Extract

There are a lot of troubles ahead in the Balkans and more questions there are unsettled than settled but I think we are past, though only just past, the greatest danger—that of war between the Great European Powers being precipitated by the Balkan question. It was touch-and-go more than once, but the Emperors of Russia and of Austria and Sazonow and Berchtold (though neither of them strong men) have just managed to prevent being carried off their feet by the war parties in Russia or in Austria. The Ambassadors in London have all been fairly well disposed, and each individual, to the utmost limit that his personal position would allow, has worked for peace. . .

62. (*Nicolson to Sir Fairfax Cartwright (Vienna), 8 July 1913, F.O. 800/368*)

Extract

Our policy is to endeavour to maintain and consolidate Turkish dominion in Asia. I should not if I were called upon to do so defend such a policy upon any higher ground than simple expediency and an unwillingness to be parties to any measures that might alienate or disappoint our moslem population in India. In my heart of hearts I have the very gravest doubts, apart from any question of morals, whether it will be possible to maintain the Turkish dominion for any great length of time. The prestige of the Turk as a fighting machine and also as the soldier of Islam has entirely disappeared and there are many indications to show that the spirit has gone out of the Turks and that they are no longer capable of maintaining the position they have hitherto enjoyed. This fact will I doubt not soon become general throughout the Asiatic provinces and will I expect lead to movements tending to disintegration. We shall find the liquidation, should it of necessity come to pass, of the Turkish succession in Asia a far more delicate and difficult performance than that which has recently taken place in Europe. It will not be the small countries like the Balkan States which will be filled with the desire of acquiring rich provinces, but it will be the Great Powers who will be scrambling to obtain their share of the spoils. We shall certainly do our best to co-operate in any measures which may help in maintaining Turkish rule surrounded naturally by all limitations and safeguards for the welfare of subordinate races. I think that a very long time will elapse before we have done with these matters and they will afford us many months if not years of very anxious work and anxiety.

63. (*Grey to Bertie, 31 July 1913, F.O. 800/180*)

I entirely agree that for France, Russia and England to take coercive measures against Turkey without the other Powers would be the worst conceivable course. It would, in my opinion, be absolutely disastrous, and we could not join in it.

If anything is done separately, it will be preferable that it should be done by Russia alone. When the Turks entered Bulgaria, I thought that the hand of Russia might be forced; but now that the Turks have withdrawn from Bulgaria and it is only a question of

Thrace, I hope that Russia will not take separate action. Even if she confined her action to Thrace, there would always be the risk that some other Power, presumably Austria, would deem it necessary to assert itself by some separate action: and that no one could foresee what would be the end.

I am not very sanguine about getting the Turks out of Adrianople by bargaining and diplomatic pressure; but we must see what can be done.

I think that the Powers should review the settlement of Macedonia, Thrace and the Islands as a whole. If they could come to an agreement on all points, and announce that they were prepared to take coercive measures to impose their will on any State that disputed any of their decisions, it would be much less invidious than taking action piecemeal against one particular State while war is still going on.

THE NAVAL ESTIMATES CRISIS, 1913–14

64. (*Memorandum by David Lloyd George, December 1913, Cabinet Papers, Cab/37/117/97*)

Extract

If the programme of new construction be adopted by the Government in its entirety, not merely will the 60% superiority over Germany be more than attained, but it will be exceeded by a figure which is distinctly provocative. It would be construed as a direct challenge to Germany, and such a policy, at a time when our relations with that country are better than they have been for ten years is, to say the least of it, highly inopportune. To commit the country to an expenditure of millions, unless it is abundantly clear that it is necessary to maintain the security of our shores, would be a proceeding that would lay the Government open to a serious charge of extravagant folly, and to do so now, when trade is on the decline, when we are confronted by a political crisis of the gravest possible character, and when there is a widespread revolt not merely in this country, but throughout the whole of Europe, against the grievous burden imposed by increased armaments, would be not merely to invite but to deserve disaster for the party and the Government responsible for such a proceeding.

65. (*Memorandum by Winston Churchill, Naval Estimates, 1914–15, 10 January 1914, Asquith Papers, vol. 25*)

Extract

V

The General Situation

No survey of British naval expenditure and no controversy arising out of it can be confined to our naval strength. It must also have regard to our military readiness compared to all the other European States that are building Navies. Even the modest establishments which Parliament has regarded as necessary have not been and are not being maintained. In 1913, when the five Great Powers of Europe have added over 50 millions to their military expenditures, when every power in the world is increasing the numbers and efficiency of its soldiers, our regular army has dropped by 6,200 men. The Special Reserve is 20,000 short, and the Territorials are 65,000 short. Only the belief that the naval strength of this country is being effectively maintained prevents a wide-spread, and in important respects a well-justified, alarm. If at any time we lose the confidence which the country has given to our naval administration in the last 5 years, the public attention cannot fail to be turned into channels which, apart from raising awkward questions, will lead directly to largely increased expenditure.

Our naval standards and the programmes which give effect to them must also be examined in relation not only to Germany but to the rest of the world. We must begin by recognising how different the part played by our Navy is from that of the Navies of every other country, [sic] Alone among the great modern States we can neither defend the soil upon which we live nor subsist upon its produce. Our whole Regular Army is liable to be ordered abroad for the defence of India. The food of our people, the raw material of their industries, the commerce which constitutes our wealth, has to be protected as it traverses thousands of miles of sea and ocean from every quarter of the globe. Our necessary insistence upon the right of capture of private property at sea exposes British merchant ships to the danger of attack not only by enemy warships but by converted armed-merchantmen. The burden of responsibility laid upon the British Navy is heavy, and its weight increases year by year.

All the world is building ships of the greatest power, training officers and men, creating arsenals, and laying broad and deep the foundations of future permanent naval development and expansion. In every country powerful interests and huge industries are growing up which will render any check or cessation in the growth of Navies increasingly difficult as time passes. Besides the Great Powers, there are many small States who are buying or building great ships of war and whose vessels may by purchase, by some diplomatic combination, or by duress, be brought into the line against us. None of these Powers need, like us, Navies to defend their actual safety or independence. They build them so as to play a part in the world's affairs. It is sport to them. It is death to us.

These possibilities were described by Lord Crewe in the House of Lords last year. It is not suggested that the whole world will turn upon us, or that our preparations should contemplate such a monstrous contingency. By a sober and modest conduct; by a skilful diplomacy we can in part disarm and in part divide the elements of potential danger. But two things must be remembered. First; that our diplomacy depends in a great part for its effectiveness upon our naval position, and that our naval strength is the one great balancing force which we can contribute to our own safety and to the peace of the world. Secondly; we are not a young people with an innocent record and a scanty inheritance. We have engrossed to ourselves, in times when other powerful nations were paralysed by barbarism or internal war, an altogether disproportionate share of the wealth and traffic of the world. We have got all we want in territory, and our claim to be left in the unmolested enjoyment of vast and splendid possessions, mainly acquired by violence, largely maintained by force, often seems less reasonable to others than to us.

Further, we do not always play the role of passive unassertiveness. We have intervened regularly—as it was our duty to do, and as we could not help doing—in the affairs of Europe and of the world. We are now deeply involved in the European situation. We have responsibilities in many quarters. It is only 2 years ago that the Chancellor of the Exchequer went to the Mansion House and delivered a speech which to save Europe from war, brought us to the very verge of it. I have myself heard the Foreign Secretary say to my predecessor that he had received so stiff a communication from the German Ambassador, that the Fleet must be placed in a condition of readiness to be attacked at any moment. The impression which these events produced in my mind is ineffaceable. I saw that even a Liberal Government, whose first and most preferred resolve must always be to preserve peace, might be compelled to face the gravest and most hateful possibilities. All Governments in England will not be Liberal Governments; all Foreign Secretaries will not have the success of Sir Edward Grey. We have passed through a year of continuous anxiety and, although I believe the foundations of peace among the great Powers have been strengthened, the causes which might lead to a general war have not been removed and often remind us of their presence. There has not been the slightest abatement of naval and military preparation. On the contrary, we are witnessing this year increases of expenditure by the Continental Powers beyond all previous experience. The world is arming as it has never armed before. Every suggestion of arrest and limitation has been brushed aside. From time to time awkward things happen, and situations occur which make it necessary that the naval force at our immediate disposal, now in this quarter, now in that, should be rapidly counted up. On such occasions the responsibilities which rest on the Admiralty come home with brutal reality to the Minister at its head, and unless our naval strength is solidly, amply and unswervingly maintained, with due regard to the opinions of the professional advisors of the Government, I could not feel that I was doing my duty if I did not warn the country of its danger.

VI
Points for Decision

Bringing, then, these Papers to the point of action, it will be seen that there are five distinct questions on which the Cabinet must give a decision:

1. *Is the Battleship programme for 1914–5 to be 4 ships or 2?*
2. *Is the Supplementary Estimate to be limited to £1,400,000, although £3,150,000 will be actually due to the contractors?*
3. *The 7 months gained by the acceleration of the 3 1913–14 battleships having expired, and the Canadian ships not being begun, are we again to accelerate ends of 1914–15 programme to maintain the position meanwhile? If not, how are we to justify to Parliament the*

£450,000 *required in the Supplementary Estimate which must now* *be presented?*

4. *Is the Cabinet decision to maintain a one-Power standard in the* *Mediterranean to stand or to be revoked?*

5. *Are we to make any addition to our programmes in consequence of* *further Austrian or Italian building now imminent or are we to* *ignore it?*

HARCOURT, GREY AND THE TRIPLE ENTENTE

66. (*Harcourt to Grey, 8 January 1914, F.O. 800/91*)

You will remember that I have often protested to you against the use by our Ambassadors—mainly at St. Petersburg and Constantinople—of the phrase '*Triple Entente*'.

You have more than once promised that you would draw the Ambassador's attention to this inaccuracy.

You can therefore imagine my horror when I find the phrase—in all the glories of capitals and italics—in your telegram (no 440) of 31st December '13 to Sir E. Goschen.

This telegram will find its way in the sections to most of our Embassies and will seem to give *your* imprimatur to this mischievous and misleading phrase.

I object to 'Triple Entente' because no such thing has ever been considered or approved by the Cabinet.

In fact the thing does not exist.

We had an 'Entente' with France over Morocco with some obligations which are now happily resolved.

This 'Entente' left behind it greatly improved relations between the two countries, but no mutual obligations of any kind whatever.

At a later date we came to an 'understanding' with Russia over Persia—and *over nothing else*.

It is true that there is an Alliance between France and Russia (in which we are not concerned) and that when we are acting with one of these powers we are likely to find ourselves in agreement with the other.

But none of these facts entail any community of action between the three in European diplomacy: and in my opinion it is the frequent and unfortunate use of the phrase 'Triple Entente' which has led to the expectation by Russia of British support (as of right) against Germany in the matter of the Military Mission at Constantinople.

This sort of assumption that we are in fact members of a new Triple Alliance (under another name) opposed to the old is so mischievous and dangerous that I think some early opportunity should be taken of making it clear to both France and Russia that any such assumption is wholly opposed to our policy and intention.

If the present state of misapprehension is allowed to continue the time is not far distant when we shall be denounced with some truth as 'Perfide Albion'.

67. (*Harcourt to Grey, 9 January 1914, F.O. 800/91*)

Extract

Since writing to you I have read with still greater alarm Buchanan's telegram (no 4) of Jan 6th '14 from St. Petersburg in which the Russian Foreign Minister is reported to have said that 'if England failed to support Russia . . . [on the German Military Mission to Turkey] there would be an end to our understanding' and he added that 'separate action by Russia would inevitably cause war into which *we should be dragged in the end*' . . .

It seems more than ever necessary to make it clear that there is no 'Anglo-Russian understanding', as apart from Persia, and that we have little or no interest in the German Military Mission to Constantinople.

In fact so slight is our locus standing that before we can obtain one we must reduce the status of Admiral Limpus (who already has a Fleet Control which we are supposed to decline to the Germans for the army) before we can make a protest over a matter which does not concern us. This is I fear 'Triple Entente' run mad—a result which I always feared from the use of this terminological inexactitude.

68. (*Grey to Harcourt, 10 January 1914, F.O. 800/91*)

It is true that I have hitherto deprecated the use of the phrase Triple Entente. It is in its proper sense quite accurate, but it was a new phrase without a settled meaning. It has however become so exceedingly convenient and common that I can no more keep it out of use than I can exclude split infinitives.

I was not however aware that I had put it into one of my own telegrams and with nothing but the date of the telegram before me (for you don't send the text and I keep no print here) I have no recollection of what the telegram referred to or the connection in which I used the phrase.

I think it is quite a mistake to assume that there is any mis-apprehension on the part of Russia or of France as to our obliga-tions. It is precisely because Russia knows that an Entente is not an Alliance and that an Entente does not entail any obligation upon us, that she is so sensitive and anxious to know how she stands as regards our support of her respecting the German command at Constantinople—a point on which I have been very careful to avoid committing H.M. Government.

If there is to be, as you desire, any new declaration, it must now be one that recognises the use of the phrase Triple Entente and confirms it with a proper understanding of what it means. The phrase has ceased to give offence even at Berlin.

The best course I think is to let things go on as they are without any new declaration of policy. The alternatives are either a policy of complete isolation in Europe, or a policy of definite alliance with one or other group of European Powers.

My own desire has been to avoid bringing the choice between these two alternatives to an issue: and I think we have been fortu-nate in being able to go on for so long as we are.

But if you think the time has come when it is necessary to discuss and to choose I cannot object to discussion, though there may be difficulties in the course of it.

69. (*Grey to Harcourt, 11 January 1914, F.O. 800/91*)

I have now got your letter of the 9th. I do not consider that I have done anything that ought to cause alarm and I think you must be alarmed rather at what you think I am going to do. If so I can only assure you that I shall do nothing that commits the Cabinet before they have discussed and decided upon this question and I think the caution I have shown in dealing with the German command at Constantinople entitles me to a little more con-fidence.

I begin to think there is more divergence of view between us about Foreign policy than I had thought, but if any decision is necessary I will bring it before the Cabinet before taking any step that commits the Cabinet to action.

NICOLSON ON ANGLO-RUSSIAN RELATIONS AND BRITAIN'S
WEAKNESS

70. (*Nicolson to Hardinge, 29 October 1913, F.O. 800/370*)

Extract

I am afraid personally, supposing that a collision did occur between France and Germany, that we would waver as to what course we should pursue until it was too late, and moreover our home defences are so utterly inadequate and deficient that I doubt very much whether we should be able to send any substantial force abroad. No one for one moment believes that our territorials are of any real use, while our own regular army is far below normal strength and there is increasing difficulty in finding recruits. It is unfortunate that the Government will not lay the state of the case frankly and openly before the country and endeavour to stimulate the public to follow the example of every other country in the world and be ready to make certain sacrifices for their own defence. I think that Churchill's speech as to a naval holiday was most unfortunate and renders us somewhat ridiculous. The Germans specially asked us not to raise the question again but Churchill persuaded Grey that it was necessary that he should do so in order to conciliate the radical wing of the party and show them that every effort was being made to moderate naval armaments. Of course he will now say that the large increases in the navy budget which he will no doubt have to demand have been necessitated by the refusal of Germany to listen to the handsome offer which he made to them.

71. (*Nicolson to Sir M. de Bunsen (Vienna), 30 March 1914, F.O. 800/373*)

Extract

My own personal idea is that this recent Press campaign against Russia was not really seriously meant on the part of Germany, and that she will do her utmost to come to terms with Russia, or in any case create more friendly and intimate relations. Of course there is no doubt that for the moment there is a very strong anti-German feeling in Russia and a determination not to accept any longer German dictation, but I have known such phases of feeling to have arisen in Russia and to have passed away without leaving much trace behind. We must always remember that there has never been any conflict between Russia and Germany and that on more than one occasion and for some lengthy periods the two countries have worked and fought together in close co-operation. We must also not forget that among many high and influential circles in Russia there is a desire to keep on the friendliest terms with Germany as representing the great bulwarks of the monarchical system. I have no doubt that the people who are now in office in Russia are largely imbued with this feeling, which I am sorry to say has no doubt been greatly deepened and emphasised by the deplorable condition in which France and ourselves are at present placed. A country with the traditions and institutions of Russia can hardly view with much favour the events which are occurring both in France and here, and she may well consider whether it is to her interest to be linked to countries who seem to be on the high road towards revolution and ruin, and whether it would not be more to her interest to ally herself with that great central Power which in any case on the surface has the appearance of stability and where the monarchical system is firmly established. I do not mean that next week we shall hear that Russia has denounced her alliance with France or that she has broken off abruptly her understanding with us, but as events develop in this country and in France I do think that the tendency in Russia will become more and more marked towards a friendly understanding with Berlin. One of the chief obstacles to this friendly understanding in recent times has been the strong support which Germany has always accorded to the aims and objects of Austria, but if it is true that Germany is now beginning to doubt the value of her alliance with Austria and is disposed to treat it as of little account, indeed perhaps an encumbrance, I think it is extremely probable that before very long we shall witness fresh developments and new groupings in the European political situation. I am afraid I have treated you to rather an academical essay, but I do think we are approaching a period when we must be prepared to see a new course adopted among some of the great European Powers.

72. (*Nicolson to Buchanan, 7 April 1914, F.O. 800/373*)

Extract

What we have done with France goes very little further than an exchange of views between our military and naval staffs and those of France and indeed in respect to any military co-operation with France, matters are still in an undecided state. Moreover it has been carefully laid down and is thoroughly understood between the two Governments that these exchanges of views in no way binds either Government and it seems to me that they have little real practical value . . . I am afraid that should war break out on the continent the likelihood of our despatching any expeditionary force is extremely remote, and it was on such an expeditionary force being sent that France at one time was basing her military measures. I believe that of late she has gradually abandoned the hope of ever receiving prompt and efficient military aid from us . . .

Moreover in the present welter in which we find ourselves in respect of internal affairs, it is hopeless to expect that the Cabinet will seriously consider any new departure in our foreign policy. We must I am afraid therefore rub along for the present as best we can . . . I fear that there is no help for it as matters at present stand, though it is possible that before long we shall find that this hesitating policy will lead to unfortunate results and that we shall find that we are being given up as untrustworthy and undecided friends. This increases my fear that Russia in giving us up in despair will take steps towards bringing herself into closer relations with Germany and of course such a new course of policy on her part would seriously react upon our relations with her in the Mid and Far East.

THE ANGLO-RUSSIAN NAVAL CONVERSATIONS

73. (*Asquith to the King, 14 May 1914, Cab/14/35/13*)

Extract

Mr. Asquith, with his humble duty to Your Majesty, has the honour to report that the Cabinet met yesterday.

Sir E. Grey averted to his conversations in Paris with M. Doumergue . . . in regard to the desire of Russia for closer and more formal relations between the members of the Triple Entente. The Cabinet warmly approved the language used by Sir E. Grey to M. Doumergue and agreed that he should communicate to the Russian Government the terms of the note of 22 November 1912 —in which he explained to M. Cambon the exact extent of our obligations and intentions in the event of a war of provocation or aggression being directed against France.

As regards the interchange of views between the Staffs of Russia and Great Britain—on the same footing as that which prevails between the Staffs of Great Britain and France—it was agreed that there was no reason for any military consultation. On the naval side, the large contemplated increase in the Baltic fleet of Russia must necessarily ease our position *vis à vis* of Germany in home waters. Mr. Churchill was of the opinion that the naval staffs should keep in contact also in regard to the position in the Mediterranean, where the Black Sea fleet (now in course of construction) may become to a certain degree a counterpoise to those of Austria and Italy. The Prime Minister pointed out that this must depend on the way in which the question of the Straits developed: at present Russia and Germany are in acute rivalry for ascendancy in the Councils of the Porte. It is also a material fact that both Turkey and Greece are developing their navies— Great Britain in each case supplying both the ships and the training officers. . .

74. (*Nicolson to Grey, 7 July 1914,* F.O. *800/374*)

I hope that you will allow me to make an observation or two in regard to that portion of the conversation which Pce [Prince] Lichnowski had with you yesterday relating to a naval understanding with Russia.

He practically warned us that if we were to enter into any kind of naval arrangements with Russia, certain unpleasant consequences would ensue, and we may, therefore, infer that if we wish to avoid these consequences we must abandon any naval conversations with Russia. In short, we are to abstain from taking the most elementary precautions and from discussing any arrangements which might be necessary to our defence in certain contingencies. This request or suggestion is a pretty strong one for one Power to make to another—and it comes oddly from a Power who quite rightly makes secret arrangements with her allies— arrangements which for all we know may comprise certain measures against us in possible eventualities. We must not forget that only a year or two ago Germany pressed Russia to engage to remain neutral in the event of hostilities between Germany and England as she also strove to secure our neutrality in case of a Franco-German conflict. She therefore, very rightly, looks ahead and seeks to avert any possible danger or conflict against herself, whether near or remote. This liberty apparently she wishes to deny to us. I sincerely trust that we shall not walk into this trap but keep our hands perfectly free—and our friendships un-impaired.

(*Minute by Grey*)

Certainly what Lichnowski has said is not going to alter our conversations with Russia or France or our relations to them. The difficult question is whether I should say nothing to Lichnowski or whether I should admit that we have had and may continue to have such conversations both with France and Russia. I will talk this over with you.

GREY ON GERMANY'S STRATEGIC PREDICAMENT

75. (*Memorandum by Bertie of conversation with Grey in London on 16 July 1914, F.O. 800/161*)

Grey says that whereas hitherto Germany has feigned alarm at the encircling policy against Germany falsely attributed to H.M. Government under the inspiration of King Edward, and has made it an excuse for largely increasing her Navy, she is now really frightened at the growing strength of the Russian Army, and she may make another military effort additional to the recent large expenditure to meet which the special capital tax was instituted, or bring on a conflict with Russia at an early date before the increases in the Russian Army have their full effect and before the completion of the Russian strategic railways to be constructed with French money.

I told Grey that if Germany make [sic] a further military effort of any importance France will be bound to do something and a very dangerous situation will be created.

Grey talked of cricket, football and fishing. He deprecated the supplanting of cricket to a great extent by football which has become a medium of betting.

Grey had intended to go home this evening to see his roses, but there is a Cabinet tomorrow and he cannot get away. He has not been home since April.

BRITISH POLICY DURING THE SARAJEVO CRISIS

76. (*Asquith to the King, 28 July 1914 (held 27 July 1914)*
    Cab/41/35/21)

The main subject of consideration was the situation in the Near
East. Sir E. Grey reported conversations with Count Mensdorff,
who stated that Austria regarded the Servian reply as in effect a
non-acceptance of her conditions: and with Prince Lichnowski,
whom he urged to press upon the German Government the importance of persuading Austria to take a more favourable view of
the Servian note.

Austria has given assurances that she will not in any event
annex Servian territory, but this will not satisfy Russia.

Sir E. Grey further explained his proposal for a Conference *à
quatre* of the less interested powers in London. France would
agree, and possibly Italy, but Germany's adhesion is more than
doubtful.

As far as this country is concerned, the position may thus be
described. Germany says to us, 'if you will say at St. Petersburgh
that in no conditions will you come in and help, Russia will draw
back and there will be no war'. On the other hand, Russia says to
us 'if you won't say you are ready to side with us now, your
friendship is valueless, and we shall act on that assumption in the
future'.

It was agreed to consider at the next Cabinet our precise
obligations in regard to the neutrality of Belgium.

The action of the First Lord in postponing the dispersal of the
First and Second Fleets was approved.

77. (*Herbert Samuel to Mrs Samuel, 2 August 1914, Samuel MSS.*
    A/157/697)

Extract

The Cabinet sat today from 11 to 1–30 and from 6.30 to 8. This
morning's Cabinet almost resulted in a political crisis to be super-
imposed on the international and financial crisis. Grey expressed a
view which was unacceptable to most of us. He is outraged by the
way in which Germany and Austria have played with the most
vital interests of civilisation, have put aside all attempts at
accommodation made by himself and others, and while continuing to negotiate have marched steadily to war.

I expressed my own conviction that we should be justified in joining in the war either for the protection of the northern coasts of France, which we could not afford to see bombarded by the German fleet and occupied by the German army, or for the maintenance of the independence of Belgium, which we are bound by treaty to protect and which again we could not afford to see subordinated to Germany. But I held that we were not entitled to carry England into the war for the sake of our goodwill for France or for the sake of maintaining the strength of France and Russia against that of Germany and Austria. This opinion is shared by the majority of the Cabinet with various degrees of emphasis on the several parts of it. We sanctioned a statement being made by Grey to the French Ambassador this afternoon, followed by a statement in Parliament tomorrow, that we should take action if the German fleet came down the Channel to attack France (Almost the whole of the French fleet is in the Mediterranean) . . . Burns dissented, feeling that Germany may regard this declaration as an act of hostility and may declare war on us because of it. He is for neutrality in all circumstances. It is probable that he will resign tomorrow and Morley may go with him. Strong efforts are being made to persuade them not to go.

I lunched at Beauchamp's, and afterwards there was a talk between L.G., Harcourt, Beauchamp, Simon, McKinnon Wood, Pease, Morley and myself. They all agreed with my formula except Morley, who is now so old that the views he expresses are sadly inconsequent and inconsistent. I went from there to see McKenna, whom I found in bed, worn out. He concurred . . . At 6, several of us, including Crewe, met again at Lloyd George's. When the Cabinet resumed at 6.30 the situation was easier, the point of contention was not pressed, and with the exception of the two I have mentioned, we remained solid.

Had the matter come to an issue Asquith would have stood by Grey in any event, and three others would have remained. I think all the rest of us would have resigned. The consequence would have been either a Coalition Government or a Unionist Government, either of which would certainly have been a war ministry. Moreover, the division of or resignation of the Government in a moment of utmost peril would have been in every way lamentable.

I still have hopes that Germany will neither send her fleet down the Channel nor invade Belgium, and we shall be able to keep England at peace while rendering to France the greatest of all services—the protection of her northern coasts from the sea and the protection of her 150 miles of frontier with Belgium. If we can achieve this, without firing a shot, we shall have accomplished a brilliant stroke of policy. For this object I have been working incessantly all the week. If we do not accomplish it, it will be an action of Germany's, and not of ours which will cause the failure and my conscience will be easy in embarking on the war. . .

78. (*Notes by C. P. Scott of conversation with Lloyd George on 3 August 1914, Scott MSS., 50901*)

He [Lloyd George] confirmed all that Simon had said about the provocative attitude of *German diplomacy* and said the despatches when they were published would prove it up to the hilt. Up to last Sunday only two members of the Cabinet had been in favour of our intervention in the War, but the *violation of Belgian territory* had completely altered the situation. He had gone so far, however, as to urge that if Germany would consent to limit her occupation of Belgian territory to the extreme southerly part of Belgium . . . he would resign rather than make this a *casus belli* . . . At the same time he said we could not have tolerated attacks on the French coasts of the Channel and had the Government done so public opinion would have swept them out of power in a week. He had done his utmost for peace but events had been too strong for him.

79. (*Nicolson to Hardinge, 5 September 1914, F.O. 800/375*)

Extract

I may tell you quite privately that I passed an anxious 48 hrs at one moment. The Cabinet were not prepared to stand by France and the argument was used that the quarrel originally an Austro-Serb one, then developing into a Russo-German-Austro-Serb one, had only brought in France because she was bound by Treaty to come in, and that as we were free from any obligations to anybody and our British interests were not for the present involved, we shd stand out and hold ourselves free as circs. might demand. Cambon declined to communicate this message to his Government, and pointed out that we should inevitably be drawn in later, with much loss of prestige, and at a moment when our aid would be belated and of little use. I was appalled by the outlook—this was on Friday July 31—and I wrote to Grey in as strong language as possible in regard to our deserting our friends. The Cabinet were at sixes and sevens over the matter, but the majority were in favour of standing aside, and with the exception of Winston the minority was weak. Winston, I hear, in view of the differences in the Cabinet, which might lead to a disruption was away for a time in indirect negotiations with the leaders of the opposition for a coalition cabinet. On Saturday Cambon pointed out that at the request some time ago of our Admiralty the French had sent all their fleet to the Mediterranean on the understanding that we would protect their northern and western coasts. This was a happy inspiration on the part of Cambon and to this appeal there could be but one answer and on Sunday 2nd Aug Cambon was told that if the German fleet came out to attack French shipping or coasts we would defend them. Grey in his speech in the House of Commons on the 3rd stated this. So far matters had improved by the statement that we were to a great extent pledged to support France in any case at sea. On the 3rd in the morning we had positive information as to the violation of Belgium neutrality by Germany and then our course was plain and you know the rest.

The whole country is now united and the German behaviour in Belgium has raised a feeling against her the depth and fervour of which cannot be estimated.

Chapter 1

Strategy and Foreign Policy

SONNINO PROPOSES AN INTERIM AGREEMENT
80. (*Rodd to Grey, 7 November 1914, F.O. 800/65*)

Extract

Referring to the idea that a form of agreement with Italy could not be negotiated till she had definitely pledged herself to join the allies, he [Sonnino] said something about not altogether appreciating the idea of her support being put up to auction—which I believe is the significance of the phrase he used '*al incanto*'. I said that there must be some misapprehension if he had been allowed to suppose that this was in your mind. You had never made any secret of the general lines to which you would be prepared to agree if Italy should range herself on our side. But you had not considered it opportune to enter into a long and elaborate discussion of points of detail constituting a state document, which would involve elaborate negotiations, until there was some definite indication of Italy's real intentions. The general lines which had been indicated should suffice, and matters of detail could not be dealt with at this stage.

He said that so far as he had at present been able to gauge the situation, Italy was hardly yet ready for action. Her preparation was still incomplete, and with the winter advancing there was little on her northern frontier that she could hope to achieve. A little more time would enable her to become a much more valuable asset. Of course if she were driven into action now, she would do the best she could, but he was not sure that the psychological moment had yet come for her. At the same time it was very possible that circumstances might precipitate matters. He even thought it possible that the action of Turkey might contribute to this. Personally he thought the war was destined to be a long one and that there might be a period during which events would drag. At the same time they often surprised us by new and unexpected phases, and it was quite conceivable that such a surprise might suddenly force the hand of Italy and that she might be compelled to take a decisive step with only a few days or hours notice. He would therefore have thought it would be well if we could have some concrete scheme ready, which though binding on neither party until the moment of decision, could be rapidly put into a binding form, either as it stood or with such modifications as the subsequent movement of events indicated as opportune, and which could be signed by the parties concerned with the briefest possible delay.

He did not see why some such draft scheme could not be very confidentially prepared between us. He would prefer that it should only be known to the fewest possible people.

THE CABINET AGREES TO ITALIAN TERMS

81. (*Asquith to the King, 24 March 1915, Cab/37/126/21*)

Considerable discussion took place upon the territorial demands formulated by Italy as the conditions of her taking an active part on the side of the Allies. The main difficulty arises in regard to the Italian claims for the whole of the Dalmatian coastline with the islands, except the strip from Ragusa to Cattaro which she is willing that Serbia should obtain, and from Cattaro to San Giovanni which she wishes to see 'neutralised'. She also asks for Valona in Albania.

It was agreed that these were very sweeping claims, depriving Serbia of Spalato and other convenient points of access to the Adriatic, and that it might be very difficult for the moment at any rate to obtain Russia's consent to them. On the other hand the Italians have a very strong strategic case, as under the conditions of modern maritime warfare their coast will never be safe if the Dalmatian islands can be used by a rival Power as a shelter and base for submarines and destroyers.

The importance of bringing in Italy without delay appears to be so great that it was agreed to give a general consent to what she asks and to press on Russia to do the same provided the Italians will agree to bring all their forces into the common stock against all our enemies (including Germany) and will bind themselves not to make a separate peace. They should also be urged to consent to Spalato becoming a free port.

GREY PROTESTS AGAINST EXTENT OF ITALIAN DEMANDS

82. (*Grey to Rodd, 1 April 1915, no. 222, Cab/37/127/4*)

My telegram No. 221, Private and Secret.

I fear that there may be some danger of the discussions about Dalmatia acquiring an importance quite out of proportion to the sum of material and territorial acquisitions which will accrue to Italy if she joins the Allies, and obscuring the extent and magnitude of those acquisitions.

Your Excellency should therefore make an earnest personal representation to the Minister for Foreign Affairs in the following sense:

The terms which the Allies are ready to accord to Italy include the Trentino and Cis-Alpine Tyrol, the countries of Gorizia and Gradisca, and the whole of Istria, including Trieste and Pola, and the Istrian Islands. She secures practically half of Dalmatia, the islands of Lissa and Lagosta, and she seals the entrance to the Adriatic by obtaining definite possession of Vallona.

Her material gains are no less extensive. At one stroke Italy gets rid of the Austrian naval and mercantile marine, and obtains the great port of Trieste and the immensely valuable naval arsenal of Pola. The economic wealth of her new territories is not a question of possibilities, but of known and proved existence, and there is no one to dispute the complete supremacy of Italy in the Adriatic.

I cannot believe that when these really vast gains are calmly considered the Italian Government will seriously maintain that they are valueless unless she is placed in possession of the remaining Dalmatian islands and the peninsula of Sabbioncello, neutralised as they will be, and therefore incapable of ever becoming a menace to the Italian position.

The Allies have, in order to meet Italy, allowed serious inroads upon the principle of nationalities, for which they hope this war will secure general recognition, and they feel that to yield more would not only involve a sacrifice of that principle, but would permanently disturb the relations between Italy and her new neighbours.

It is in this spirit that the Allies ask that the portion of Dalmatia assigned to Italy should share the neutralisation of the rest of the province. It forms a detached portion of the Italian kingdom, and to keep it as an armed warder over the unarmed surrounding territory will provoke the very spirit of unrest and suspicion which it is in the general interest to allay.

ITALIAN INFLUENCE UPON BALKAN STATES

83. (*Rodd to Grey, 2 April 1915, no. 181, Cab/37/127/11*)

Your telegram No. 222.

Prime Minister is absent from Rome for a day or two, and point referred to in my immediately preceding telegram as requiring explanation gives a little time for examination of following considerations, which I most earnestly recommend as representing views of Minister for Foreign Affairs. His Excellency must consult the Prime Minister, but his own view is emphatically that rejection of proposal would deprive Italy of sufficient inducement to assume grave responsibility. If she were already involved in war she might welcome solution proposed in *aide-mémoire* in order to terminate it. It is another matter to provoke war with many elements in the country opposed to it and a prospect of obtaining some concessions in certain eventualities as compensation for neutrality.

Her object in taking hazard of war would be to make Adriatic her naval base. She has no safe or satisfactory one at present.

Russia, if she obtains control at Constantinople, may become in the future the leading naval Power in the Mediterranean. Cursola islands, south of Cape Planca, are regarded by the naval experts here as political key to Adriatic, where a naval or submarine base established by strong enemy could neutralise the value of Pola and expose the whole Adriatic coast of Italy to danger. Neutralisation would not suffice to eliminate danger as experience had proved. Only possession offers adequate guarantee. Vallona does not really seal the Adriatic, as it could only be converted into a naval base or defensive station by works of such magnitude that they cannot be contemplated. It is only to prevent others from going there that Italy wishes to retain Vallona.

Neutralisation of that part of the coast and islands which it is suggested should accrue to Italy would not be acceptable. Croatian coast is not to be neutralised, and its future destiny is not yet clear. Southern road out from Fiume passes Zara. Neutralisation of the Dalmatian coast and islands would limit Italian naval defences to the extreme north of the Adriatic, and majority of Italian coast would have no additional guarantee of security than at present except that of neutralisation of Serbian coast. Small islands enumerated in section 3 of *aide-mémoire* have little or no value even if not neutralised. If, therefore, proposals there made are final, he would have to advise that negotiations should close, and Italy should remain neutral and take her chance. He feared that it was tending to this. Meanwhile we remained good friends.

I cannot anticipate that Prime Minister's view is likely to be essentially different. Minister for Foreign Affairs is, I think, the dominant personality. I had yesterday pointed out that there were other inducements beside the great ones in the Adriatic. He said that as regards Asia Minor these were now limited to admission of Italy to eventual discussions. Other Powers had already considerable claims actually earmarked, and equilibrium of Eastern Mediterranean was a vital interest to an exclusively Mediterranean Power. One definite inducement an Italian statesman could therefore effectively put forward for leading country into war was prospect of acquiring absolute security now and for the future in the Adriatic.

From my knowledge of Minister for Foreign Affairs I think we must accept this as his final view. He is very frank with me and does not conceal his thoughts.

We are therefore up to a critical issue. We can have immediate co-operation of Italy, ensuring, I believe, the co-operation of Roumania and affecting that of all the other Balkan States, with great results ensuing if we do not insist on applying to her acquisitions the very unreliable condition of neutralisation, and if we agree to her occupation of Cursola islands with Sabbioncello, which could be neutralised together with Serbian coast. Alternative is, I think I can guarantee, neutrality. But it might readily become a less benevolent neutrality as regards passage of contraband if she retains the hope of concessions from Austria as its price. She could even enhance that price by indiscretions as to the offers which the Allies were prepared to make to her. In certain eventualities, which I trust will not arise, even her neutrality might not be permanently assured.

Price of Italian co-operation involves sacrifice of Dalmatia. But unity of that province is already sacrificed by rent [*sic*] which Allies agreed to. Can we afford to renounce their co-operation on account of Cursola islands?

SUMMARY OF NEGOTIATIONS WITH THE BALKAN STATES

84. (*Drummond to Asquith, 26 October 1915, F.O. 800/100*)

The attitude adopted by Great Britain at the beginning of the war was that it was better for the neutral Balkan States, if they remained separate, to remain neutral. The best course would be a confederation which should include Roumania, but it was recognised that for this purpose Greece and Serbia would have to propose something which would be attractive to Roumania. Russia wanted, however, the immediate co-operation of Roumania but failed to obtain it and an offer made by Greece on the 18th of August, to give full assistance, was refused on the ground that it would render the policy of the Balkan bloc impossible and might involve this country in purely Balkan conflicts.

Early in September it appeared that Bulgaria was likely to join the Central Powers and negotiations were entered into with Serbia asking her to make concessions to Bulgaria, if the latter were prepared to help Serbia in case of an attack on Turkey or Roumania. Serbia expressed her willingness to make some concessions but nothing further came of the negotiations. In October war broke out with Turkey. Bulgaria was approached again and territories in Thrace and advantages in Macedonia offered to her if she would attack Turkey. She however decided to remain neutral. From this time till March when M. Venizelos fell various attempts were made to secure Greek assistance for the Allies but all these endeavours failed owing to the Greek objection that before moving she must be definitely certain of Bulgaria's attitude. Greece insisted that assurances on the part of Bulgaria were of no avail and the only method of acquiring such certainty was either that Bulgaria should herself co-operate with the Allies or that Roumania should undertake that if Bulgaria moved she would take forcible measures against her. Roumania always declined to give any such undertakings to Greece and the negotiations accordingly had no result. In April the Greek Prime Minister said that he was prepared to co-operate against Turkey if he could receive a guarantee for Greek territory during and after the war and also large concessions in Asia Minor. It looked as if the Greeks would, if an agreement were come to, make an immediate attack on Bulgaria, and in view of her attitude and her large demands it was thought wiser not to proceed further with the Greek offer.

Negotiations were now begun with Bulgaria and suggestions were made for the acquisition by Bulgaria of the Enos Midia line and the uncontested zone in Macedonia; Cavalla was also mentioned. The Bulgarian Prime Minister asked for considerably larger territories including the contested zone in Macedonia, the reason being clearly that the military situation was becoming less favourable to the Allies. No definite offer was therefore made. Meanwhile, on May 5th, the Greek Prime Minister, as a personal suggestion, offered the Allies the use of the Greek fleet, ports and territory, though no use was to be made of the army which was to be kept for use against Bulgaria if necessary. Unfortunately this proposal was never made officially and the illness of the King of Greece prevented all further action. At the end of May the Entente Powers made a definite offer to Bulgaria and simultaneously a declaration to the Serbian Government, telling the latter that it was necessary to make sacrifices to the common cause. The offer to Bulgaria included the uncontested zone, the Enos Midia line and the assurance that the Powers would endeavour to obtain Cavalla and would arrange a concession of the Dobruja. The Serbian Government refused authority to the Powers to cede Serbian territory and the Greek Government protested against the mention of Cavalla. The Bulgarian Government replied to this offer asking for more definite information. This took place on June 15th and on August 4th the Allied Governments replied that no extension of territory would be given to either Greece or Serbia till they had made the concessions promised to Bulgaria by the Entente Powers in their note of May. Meanwhile, further pressure was brought to bear on Serbia to cede definitely the uncontested zone to Bulgaria and after considerable negotiations and a further protest by the Greek Government, who were told of the note to Bulgaria, the Serbian Government consented to promise the greater part of the uncontested zone. This promise was, however, so hedged round by conditions that it was of little value in persuading the Bulgarian Government to accept the offers of the Entente Powers. Meanwhile the situation in Bulgaria was becoming more and more serious and on September 14th a formal guarantee was given to Bulgaria that the Powers would see that Serbia ceded the uncontested zone immediately at the end of the war provided Bulgaria attacked Turkey. The reply to this note was not sent till October 20th after diplomatic relations with

Bulgaria had been broken off. It asked for further information and especially as regards Cavalla and the Dobruja and stated that formal and positive assurances that her national aspirations could be fulfilled would be necessary before she would depart from her neutrality.

DARDANELLES OPERATIONS HINDERED BY RUSSIAN ATTITUDE

85. (*Grey to Buchanan, 4 March 1915, F.O. 800/57*)

His Majesty's Government are risking British ships, sailors and soldiers with the object of rendering Turkey valueless as an ally to Germany, to destroy Turkey's power of attacking Russia and Great Britain, and to influence all the Balkan States to join the allies. The operations in the Dardanelles have been undertaken in the common cause and in the most ungrudging spirit in regard to the recognition of the Russian interests in that region and with the full knowledge that the direct fruits of them will be a gain for Russia and not for Great Britain. In these circumstances, the Anglo-French forces ought not to be deprived of any available assistance in their sphere of operations though it was agreed that such assistance should not be given on any condition or establish any claim except such as may be agreed to by France, Great Britain and Russia together. In the circumstances, it is unreasonable and impossible to hamper the operations in the Dardanelles by refusing the aid of Greece if it were offered, especially military assistance, which may be important and which might prove essential on the Gallipoli peninsula to ensure complete success. The Russian Government must bear in mind the disastrous consequences which would ensue if the operations in the Dardanelles do not succeed. His Majesty's Government readily agree that Greece must not have a footing on the Straits which would conflict with Russian interests. They have never contemplated the annexation of any part of the Straits to Greece. Smyrna would be the compensation for that Power. H.M. Govt agreed with the Russian and French Governments as to that matter, and were ready to forego any British claim there—although the Smyrna–Aidin railway is the only British vested interest in Asia Minor at present—in order that Greece should join the allies. Russian ships, assistance, and the presence of Russian ships and troops in connection with the operations against the Straits have been invited and welcomed from the beginning.

RUSSIA AND CONSTANTINOPLE

86. (*War Council, 10 March 1915, Cab/42/2/5*)

THE PRIME MINISTER said that the principal business for which this meeting had been called, and for which Lord Lansdowne and Mr. Bonar Law (whom he cordially welcomed) had been invited, was to consider the political, as well as the strategic, questions likely to arise after the fall of Constantinople.

SIR EDWARD GREY said that some months ago it had become clear that Russia wanted to know how she stood with Great Britain and France in regard to the questions of Constantinople and the Straits. The economic pressure on Russia had become great owing to the closing of the Straits on the intervention of Turkey in the war, as the Baltic entrances were closed by the German fleet; and Archangel and Vladivostok, both of them liable to be ice-bound, were the only available ports. We then gave a general assurance that a settlement of the question of the Straits in the Russian interest was necessary. The question had recently been raised again, and M. Sazonoff had furnished an *aide-mémoire*[1] setting forth the Russian demands. In dealing with this question it had to be remembered that Germany was very desirous of concluding a separate peace with Russia and France; he had been informed by a neutral that Herr Jagow had admitted this, and had said that Germany quite expected to settle with France and Russia on the basis of concessions, and would give an indemnity to Belgium, but that there would be no peace with England except on terms of a German victory. As regards France, he had no apprehensions. They were as anxious as we ourselves to see the business through to a final conclusion, and was as determined as we ourselves. When the question had first been discussed M. Sazonoff had expressed his personal opinion that Russia would be content with the possession of the Bosphorus and the neutralization of Constantinople. Now, however, they put forward a claim for Constantinople, the Straits, and Turkey in Europe up to the Enos–Midia line. In making this claim their principal idea was to obtain an outlet to the sea. Russia had already so much territory that the acquisition of German Poland or Galicia would not confer any great advantage, but one of her principal hopes from this war was to obtain an outlet to the sea. It had to be remembered that at

[1] See Appendix.

one time Russia had absolutely vetoed Greek co-operation, though she had now somewhat modified this attitude, but she still was apprehensive of the effect of other Powers, such as Italy, Roumania, and Bulgaria, joining the Allies. She feared that Bulgaria, Greece, and Roumania might prejudice her claims for Constantinople, and, remembering our historical attitude towards this question, was suspicious that we might again check her aspirations. The urgency of the question was to remove Russian suspicions as to our attitude and to get rid of the Russian objections to the participation of other nations. It was therefore essential to the progress of the war that Russia should know where she stands, more especially as the occupation of Constantinople might be imminent.

THE PRIME MINISTER said that the Russian *aide-mémoire* referred to a *final* settlement, and not to an interim arrangement.

MR. BALFOUR said that he personally had no objection to an assurance being given to Russia for the realization of her aspirations as regards Constantinople and the Dardanelles, provided that the other Allies received similar assurances as regards their own wishes. The sentiments of the Russians, he said, were probably a good deal more moved by Constantinople than by Poland. If they obtained what they wanted now, they might slacken their efforts in the main theatre of war. We ought to consider what we wanted, for example, in the Persian Gulf and elsewhere.

MR. LLOYD GEORGE said that the Russians were so keen to obtain Constantinople that they would be generous in regard to concessions elsewhere. It was vital for us, if we made concessions, to say what we wanted in return.

LORD LANSDOWNE suggested that the matter depended to some extent on what each of the Allies had accomplished in the war. Supposing, for example, that the Allies in the West were very successful and crushed Germany, while the Russians in the East were to fail, ought we still to give an undertaking as regards Constantinople?

MR. BALFOUR replied that each of the Allies would have to do its share of the war, and that it would be invidious to differentiate between their efforts.

SIR EDWARD GREY said that, in any case, Russia might claim that the sacrifices she had made in East Prussia in the early days of the war had saved the Allies from defeat.

THE PRIME MINISTER said that, when Russian proposals were first put forward, the naval and military advisers were asked to consider them on their merits. They were asked if there was any objection on naval and military grounds to granting Russian claims? Their reply was that there were no objections. The naval authorities appeared to think that the establishment of Russia at Constantinople, and the granting of all she asks, would make it desirable for us to have an additional naval base in these waters, viz., Alexandretta, the probable terminus on the Mediterranean of the Baghdad Railway.

LORD KITCHENER agreed in the naval view. Alexandretta, he said, had a military as well as a naval importance.

MR. BALFOUR thought it injurious to our interests to allow Russia to occupy a position on the flank of our route to India, but considered that this would have to be accepted.

SIR EDWARD GREY said that M. Sazonoff could now rely on French support to his proposals, as the French Government had agreed to them in principle, and wished to have a conference on the subject. He thought it probable that the Russians had communicated to the French their suspicion of the British attitude, and he (Sir E. Grey) had sent a reassuring telegram to our Ambassador in Petrograd, for communication to M. Sazonoff, to the effect that we had asked for the French views without making any comment. M. Sazonoff had expressed great satisfaction with this.

MR. BONAR LAW suggested that we ought not to give Russia exactly what she wants immediately. He was in favour of taking up an attitude similar to that adopted by the French, that is to say, to tell Russia that she can count on the entire goodwill of the Government for a satisfactory settlement in regard to Constantinople on the conclusion of peace.

LORD LANSDOWNE agreed with Mr. Bonar Law. He suggested that, if Russia was granted all she wished for now, the result might be to choke off Italy and the Balkan States. This would be very unfortunate.

SIR EDWARD GREY pointed out that it would be still more disastrous if we conveyed the impression to Russia that we intended to join with the Balkan States and Italy in preventing her from obtaining Constantinople. He was inclined to suggest to Russia that they should offer Bessarabia to Roumania in the event of Russia herself obtaining Constantinople, as an inducement to join the Allies.

LORD KITCHENER did not think there was any chance that Bulgaria would fight Russia for Constantinople. Religious sentiment was too strong.

MR. BONAR LAW said that perhaps the best plan would be to say we would not oppose Russia, provided that we and France obtained what we wanted.

SIR EDWARD GREY agreed. Our acquiescence should be conditional on a successful termination to the war.

THE PRIME MINISTER read out the last sentence of the Russian *aide-mémoire*, as follows:

'Imperial Government likes to hope that above consideration will meet with sympathy of the two Allied Governments. Said Governments are assured of meeting with, at the hands of Imperial Government, the same sympathy for realization of desiderata which they may form in other regions of Ottoman Empire and elsewhere.'

LORD LANSDOWNE asked if we were to formulate these desiderata now.

MR. LLOYD GEORGE hoped we should do so.

SIR EDWARD GREY said that France would of course ask for Alsace and Lorraine, and perhaps for Syria. He proposed that we should agree to the Russian claims on some such terms as the following: 'Subject to the war being prosecuted to a victorious conclusion, so as to enable Great Britain and France to realize the desiderata referred to in the last sentence of the Russian *aide-mémoire.*'

MR. MCKENNA expressed a preference for the French reply referred to above by Mr. Bonar Law.

MR. BONAR LAW and MR. BALFOUR both expressed a preference for Sir Edward Grey's form of words.

MR. LLOYD GEORGE pressed that our desiderata should be formulated at once.

MR. CHURCHILL agreed. After the war there might be mutual jealousies and heartburnings. He suggested it was very desirable to block in the general lines of the terms we required. As regards Alexandretta, we had already been hampered by French susceptibilities.

[*Proposed Conference*]

THE PRIME MINISTER read a telegram sent by the French Minister for Foreign Affairs to Russia, proposing a Conference at Paris on the question of the ultimate terms of peace.

MR. LLOYD GEORGE said that any interchange of views ought to be between the Foreign Ministers themselves, and not through the medium of Ambassadors. He suggested that they should meet either at Salonica or Lemnos or on board a British man-of-war in those waters, which could easily be reached from either country. He suggested also that a hint should be given to Italy, and perhaps to Greece and Bulgaria, that the fate of Asia Minor would probably be settled at the Conference. By this step we might perhaps bring in all the hesitating neutral States.

SIR EDWARD GREY said he did not want to prejudge this proposal or to negative it, but he would put some of the objections. It nearly always happened that allies quarrelled over the spoils, and this might happen in our case. It would be very difficult, and perhaps very risky, to discuss such delicate questions now as were involved. For example, we might have serious friction with France if we put in a claim for Alexandretta. It would also be very difficult to all the Foreign Ministers to absent themselves from their own countries for two or three weeks.

[*Alexandretta*]

MR. LLOYD GEORGE said that the reason for friction in the division of the spoils was usually that the nations concerned did not discuss the matter beforehand. He felt considerable misgivings about the expediency of occupying Alexandretta. He suggested Palestine as an alternative owing to the prestige it would give us.

LORD KITCHENER said that Palestine would be of no value to us whatsoever. He saw no reason why the French should oppose our occupation of Alexandretta, provided it was put to them in the right way. Alexandretta was beyond the French sphere of influence in Syria.

MR. BALFOUR asked what was the military case in favour of an occupation of Alexandretta.

LORD KITCHENER said it was a question of communications. Troops could be sent rapidly by rail from Alexandretta to India and Mesopotamia.

MR. CHURCHILL said that the German Admiral Suchow, when on a visit to Alexandretta, had made a statement to the effect that Germany would have gone to war in order to secure Alexandretta alone, as it was the only good harbour between Smyrna and the Suez Canal.

LORD FISHER said that Alexandretta had a special importance as an outlet for the oil supplies of Mesopotamia and Persia.

MR. MCKENNA said that the question hinged largely on that of the balance of naval power in the Mediterranean after the war. A naval base would be of no value without command of the sea. We ought, therefore, to consider what we are committing ourselves to. In 1912 the whole question of our naval policy in the Mediterranean had been reviewed, and we had deliberately come to the conclusion that we could not simultaneously retain command of the Mediterranean as well as of the North Sea. He suggested, therefore, that in return for concessions made to Russia at Constantinople and the Straits we should ask for compensation outside the Mediterranean.

LORD KITCHENER said it was essential we should retain command of the sea in the Mediterranean.

MR. CHURCHILL said that in 1912 we had been justified in reducing our peace strength in the Mediterranean owing to our concentration of naval force in the North Sea and our close friendship with France. After the war he hoped that our naval position would be very strong. If we succeeded in shattering German naval power we ought to be able to build a Mediterranean fleet against France and Russia.

MR. LLOYD GEORGE questioned whether it was worth while to press the question of Alexandretta up to the point of a quarrel with France.

LORD KITCHENER laid great stress on the importance of Alexandretta. With Russia in Constantinople, France in Syria, and Italy in Rhodes, our position in Egypt would be untenable if any other Power held Alexandretta.

MR. BALFOUR said he was somewhat loth to oppose on a point on which the Admiralty and War Office appeared to be in complete agreement. He wished, however, to point out that, from a military point of view, the natural line of communication with the Persian Gulf was maritime. If we come to defend on a line of railway communication from Alexandretta to Mesopotamia we should be in an embarrassing position in the event of its inter-ruption in war.

SIR EDWARD GREY said that if we acquired any territory on land we should have to be prepared to defend it against someone. We ought to determine first whether we require a harbour, and, second, whether we want any more territory.

LORD KITCHENER said that we could not count on holding Egypt if Alexandretta were in the hands of some other Power.

MR. CHURCHILL asked if we were to give Constantinople to Russia, and Syria to France, and to receive nothing in return? He reminded the War Council that at the end of the war our naval and military strength ought to be very great indeed.

[German Colonies]

SIR EDWARD GREY asked what would be the fate of the German colonies?

LORD KITCHENER said it would be a mistake to acquire more of these than we could avoid, as it would more than anything else interfere with the future establishment of goodwill between Germany and ourselves after the war.

SIR EDWARD GREY agreed. He was strongly opposed to the acquisition of German colonies, but feared that South Africa and Australasia would never allow us to cede German South-West Africa and the Pacific colonies.

[German East Africa]

MR. HARCOURT agreed. He suggested that German East Africa might be acquired in order to settle the question of Indian emigration.

[Egypt not part of the bargain]

MR. CHURCHILL was strongly opposed to the acquisition of German East Africa. He also said that Egypt ought not to form part of the bargain. The question of Egypt had been decided long ago when it was bartered for Morocco. We ought not, as it were, to have to buy it over again.

MR. BALFOUR said that Lord Lansdowne and he had practically arranged the question of Egypt as part of the general settlement leading up to the *Entente cordiale* with France.

LORD LANSDOWNE agreed. He thought it possible that France had welcomed the Russian claim to Constantinople as a set-off against our occupation of Egypt.

[*The German fleet and the Kiel Canal*]

MR. CHURCHILL asked what was to happen about the German fleet and the Kiel Canal? The destruction of the fleet and the removal of the Canal from German control were great objects of British policy. It was essential that we should not come out of this war leaving Germany the power to attack us again in a few years' time. He also pointed out the enormous strategic value of the Kiel Canal, which enabled Germany to transfer her fleet within a few hours from the Baltic to the North Sea and *vice versa*. Ought we not, he asked, to demand the surrender or destruction of the German fleet?

MR. BONAR LAW said that, in his opinion, the first condition of peace was the elimination of the German fleet.

MR. BALFOUR drew a distinction between the destruction of the German fleet and the neutralization of the Kiel Canal, as the fleet could be rebuilt in a few years.

LORD LANSDOWNE pointed out that both these desiderata were as important to Russia as to ourselves.

LORD FISHER said that if, after the war, Germany started to build a new fleet, we ought to go and smash it at once.

LORD KITCHENER said that the question of armaments was entirely one of finance. The way to stop Germany from building a new fleet was to inflict an indemnity to be paid over a long term of years.

LORD HALDANE said he hoped that the possibility of some agreement for the restriction of armaments would not be abandoned.

[*The reply to Russia*]

THE PRIME MINISTER said that this discussion made him somewhat apprehensive. Russia had made a definite proposition with primary reference to the Ottoman Empire, which was the main subject of the present meeting. The discussion of this proposition had raised every subject which would arise at the end of the war. The conditions at the end of the war, however, could not be foreseen, and the present discussion ought to be limited to the Ottoman Empire. The question which really had to be decided immediately was the reply to be given to Russia. Personally, he advocated the adoption of Sir Edward's Grey formula. If the desiderata were to be formulated, they should be confined for the present to the Ottoman Empire.

[*Alexandretta*]

SIR EDWARD GREY said that this practically confined the issue to the question of Alexandretta.

MR. HARCOURT said that he was not agreed at present as to the desirability of acquiring Alexandretta. He asked whether it was required as a harbour, or as the terminus of a railway from Mesopotamia. He suggested that Marmaris was a better harbour.

MR. BONAR LAW suggested that we should put off Russia with a statement that we should at the end of the war give them what they asked for, provided that we obtained what we wanted, without any attempt at present to define our desiderata.

LORD CREWE said that then Russia would be completely dealt with. Early in the war the Russians had said what they wanted with regard to Germany and Austria, and now they had stated their requirements from Turkey. If we did not block out what we want we might get left in the lurch. He added that he thought we ought to consider the expediency of leaving some territory to the Sultan of Turkey as the head of the Khalifate. The Mohammedans of India, for example, had in no way diminished their reverence for the Sultan by reason of the war.

LORD KITCHENER said that the location of the Khalifate was solely a question for the Mohammedan world.

SIR EDWARD GREY said he proposed to suggest to Russia to keep secret for the present the arrangement proposed as regard the future of Constantinople, otherwise the Balkan States might be alienated. There were three other stipulations which he considered necessary:

1. Free passage of the Straits to the commerce of all nations.
2. Constantinople to be a free port for goods in transit.
3. Arabia and the holy places to remain in Mussulman hands.

THE PRIME MINISTER suggested also that a hint should be given to Russia that we are abandoning a traditional attitude and that a large section of public opinion in this country would be opposed to it. Also that Russia should be asked to interpose no obstacle to the intervention in the war on the side of the Allies of other nations.

Conclusions

1. *A reply to be sent to Russia in the sense that we should agree to the proposals put forward in the Russian* aide-mémoire, *subject to the war*

being prosecuted to a victorious conclusion, and to Great Britain realizing the desiderata referred to in the last sentence of the Russian aide-mémoire. *These desiderata will be put forward by the British and French Governments as soon as there has been time to consider them. (A telegram in this sense was sent in March* 1915.)

2. *The War Office to prepare a memorandum setting forth the strategical advantages of Alexandretta.*

APPENDIX

Sir G. Buchanan to Sir Edward Grey.—(Received March 5.)

(Telegraphic.)   *Petrograd, March* 4, 1915.

(No. 249. Secret.)

I READ to Minister for Foreign Affairs this afternoon your telegram No. 298 of 2nd March, and his Excellency begged me to assure you that he had never doubted your sympathy, and that he was much touched with terms in which you had referred to Russian aspirations.

He thought, however, that the time had come for preparing public opinion in Great Britain and France for their approaching realisation. French Government were, equally with His Majesty's Government, fully acquainted with the views of Russian Government on Constantinople and the Straits, and the French Minister for Foreign Affairs expressed himself in entire sympathy with them except on one point which, as a matter of fact, Russian Government never raised. French Minister for Foreign Affairs had been under the impression that Russia intended to claim both shores of the Dardanelles. This was a mistake, as she had never intended to ask for the Asiatic shore, provided it was left in the possession of Turkey, and on the understanding that no fortifications were to be erected on it.

On my way to Ministry for Foreign Affairs with French Ambassador, latter had told me that in the audience in which he had presented General Pau yesterday to the Emperor His Majesty had in conversation himself said that there was one question—that of Constantinople—on which he must speak with precision. Passions of his subjects with regard to its possession were deeply stirred, and he had no right to impose on them the tremendous sacrifices entailed by the war without securing for them in return the realisation of a secular ambition. His decision was taken, and he must insist on a radical solution of the question of Constantinople and the Straits. He asked French Ambassador to call on Minister for Foreign Affairs the same afternoon and to repeat to him what he had said. Minister for Foreign Affairs had in the meanwhile received a [group omitted: ? message] from the Emperor informing him of above conversation and desiring him to come to Tsarskoe Selo to see His Majesty this morning.

This afternoon Minister for Foreign Affairs handed to me and French Ambassador *aide-mémoire*, of which translation follows, embodying result of his Excellency's conversation with Emperor and definitely recording Russian claims. His Excellency does not ask us publicly to announce our approval of these claims, but I gather that he would be grateful for an assurance that we would not raise any objections to them. [? Subsequently] public opinion might be gradually prepared for desired solution.

Aide-mémoire begins:

'Course of latest events leads His Majesty the Emperor Nicholas to think that the question of Constantinople and the Straits must be definitely solved in accordance with traditional aspirations of Russia.

'Any solution would be unsatisfactory and precarious if it did not incorporate henceforward in Russian Empire the city of Constantinople, western shore of the Bosphorus, of the Sea of Marmora, and of the Dardanelles, as well as Southern Thrace up to the Enos–Midia line.

'*Ipso facto* and by strategic necessity, part of Asiatic shore included between the Bosphorus, River Sakharia, and a point to be fixed on the Gulf of Ismid, islands of the Sea of Marmora, islands of Imbros and Tenedos, ought to be incorporated in the empire.'

Special interests of France and of Great Britain in the region above described will be scrupulously respected.

Imperial Government likes to hope that above considerations will meet with sympathy of the two allied Governments. Said Governments are assured of meeting with, at the hands of Imperial Government, the same sympathy for realisation of desiderata which they may form in other regions of Ottoman Empire and elsewhere.

CONDITIONS UNDER WHICH RUSSIA TO HAVE CONSTANTINOPLE

87. (*Aide-mémoire of 12 March 1915, F.O. 371/2988/46142*)

Subject to the war being carried on and brought to a successful conclusion, and to the desiderata of Great Britain and France in the Ottoman Empire and elsewhere being realised, as indicated in the Russian communication herein referred to, His Majesty's Government will agree to the Russian Government's *aide-mémoire* relative to Constantinople and the Straits, the text of which was communicated to His Britannic Majesty's Ambassador by his Excellency M. Sazonof on the 4th March 1915.

Petrograd, March 12, 1915.

Memorandum

His Majesty's Ambassador has been instructed to make the following observations with reference to the *aide-mémoire* which this Embassy had the honour of addressing to the Imperial Government on the 12th March, 1915.

The claim made by the Imperial Government in their *aide-mémoire* of the 4th March, 1915, considerably exceeds the desiderata which were foreshadowed by M. Sazonof as probable a few weeks ago. Before His Majesty's Government have had time to take into consideration what their own desiderata elsewhere would be in the final terms of peace, Russia is asking for a definite promise that her wishes shall be satisfied with regard to what is in fact the richest prize of the entire war. Sir Edward Grey accordingly hopes that M. Sazonof will realise that it is not in the power of His Majesty's Government to give a greater proof of friendship than that which is afforded by the terms of the above-mentioned *aide-mémoire*. That document involves a complete reversal of the traditional policy of His Majesty's Government, and is in direct opposition to the opinions and sentiments at one time universally held in England and which have still by no means died out. Sir Edward Grey therefore trusts that the Imperial Government will recognise that the recent general assurances given to M. Sazonof have been most loyally and amply fulfilled. In presenting the *aide-mémoire* now, His Majesty's Government believe and hope that a lasting friendship between Russia and Great Britain will be assured as soon as the proposed settlement is realised.

From the British *aide-mémoire* it follows that the desiderata of His Majesty's Government, however important they may be to

British interests in other parts of the world, will contain no condition which could impair Russia's control over the territories described in the Russian *aide-mémoire* of the 4th March, 1915.

In view of the fact that Constantinople will always remain a trade *entrepôt* for South-Eastern Europe and Asia Minor, His Majesty's Government will ask that Russia shall, when she comes into possession of it, arrange for a free port for goods in transit to and from non-Russian territory. His Majesty's Government will also ask that there shall be commercial freedom for merchant-ships passing through the Straits, as M. Sazonof has already promised.

Except in so far as the naval and military operations on which His Majesty's Government are now engaged in the Dardanelles may contribute to the common cause of the Allies, it is now clear that these operations, however successful, cannot be of any advantage to His Majesty's Government in the final terms of peace. Russia also will, if the war is successful, gather the direct fruits of these operations. Russia should therefore, in the opinion of His Majesty's Government, not now put difficulties in the way of any Power which may, on reasonable terms, offer to co-operate with the Allies. The only Power likely to participate in the operations in the Straits is Greece. Admiral Carden has asked the Admiralty to send him more destroyers, but they have none to spare. The assistance of a Greek flotilla, if it could have been secured, would thus have been of inestimable value to His Majesty's Government.

To induce the neutral Balkan States to join the Allies was one of the main objects which His Majesty's Government had in view when they undertook the operations in the Dardanelles. His Majesty's Government hope that Russia will spare no pains to calm the apprehensions of Bulgaria and Roumania as to Russia's possession of the Straits and Constantinople being to their disadvantage. His Majesty's Government also hope that Russia will do everything in her power to render the co-operation of these two States an attractive prospect to them.

Sir E. Grey points out that it will obviously be necessary to take into consideration the whole question of the future interests of France and Great Britain in what is now Asiatic Turkey; and in formulating the desiderata of His Majesty's Government with regard to the Ottoman Empire, he must consult the French as well as the Russian Government. As soon, however, as it becomes known that Russia is to have Constantinople at the conclusion of the war, Sir E. Grey will wish to state that throughout the negotiations, His Majesty's Government have stipulated that the Mussulman Holy Places and Arabia shall under all circumstances remain under independent Mussulman dominion.

Sir E. Grey is as yet unable to make any definite proposal on any point of the British desiderata; but one of the points of the latter will be the revision of the Persian portion of the Anglo-Russian Agreement of 1907 so as to recognise the present neutral sphere as a British sphere.

Until the Allies are in a position to give to the Balkan States, and especially to Bulgaria and Roumania, some satisfactory assurance as to their prospects and general position with regard to the territories contiguous to their frontiers to the possession of which they are known to aspire; and until a more advanced stage of the agreement as to the French and British desiderata in the final peace terms is reached, Sir E. Grey points out that it is most desirable that the understanding now arrived at between the Russian, French, and British Governments should remain secret.

Petrograd, March 12, 1915.

GREY'S VIEW OF BULGARIAN CLAIMS

88. (*Grey to Crewe, 15 June 1915, F.O. 800/95*)

I don't believe a special mission to the Balkans will do any good, unless the Russians can turn the tables on the Austro-German forces or we can force the Dardanelles. What prospect there is of either of these things happening, you probably know better than I do. It looks to me as if the Russians would lose both Lemberg and Warsaw and have an internal revolution as well.

Under these circumstances a special mission to the Balkans headed by a man of high rank would be a ghastly fiasco, but I see no objection to Tyrrell and Chirol going there. They will avoid pitfalls and if there is any chance of doing good those two men are not likely to miss it. I think it would be a good thing if they got in close touch with Fitzmaurice who is at Sofia and made use of him while they were in the Balkans.

The Bulgarian minister first asked me to promise the uncontested zone in Macedonia, subsequently Noel Buxton succeeded in whetting his appetite, and after meeting Lloyd George under Noel Buxton's auspices he added Cavalla. Personally, I think Bulgaria ought to have the uncontested zone in Macedonia, the Dobrudja, the Enos–Midia line and Cavalla, but it is not our business to whet the Bulgarian appetite. I think, now matters have gone as far, we might perfectly well say to the Bulgarians that Greek and Serbian claims to large tracts of new territory will receive no support from us unless Greece and Serbia agree to give the uncontested zone and Cavalla to Bulgaria. But I believe our last offer at Sofia was quite definite enough to move the Bulgarians if they were disposed to move.

I told the Bulgarian minister some time ago that if Bulgaria joined us, I was sure there would be no difficulty in assuring Bulgaria against any aggression on the part of Greece or Roumania. Presumably France, Russia and Italy would join in saying this at Sofia.

THE STATE OF NEGOTIATIONS WITH BULGARIA

89. (*G. H. Fitzmaurice to Eric Drummond, 4 July 1915, F.O. 800/43*)

I found considerable difficulty in executing your instructions, owing to my having no representative character, and owing to the extreme seclusion which the King of the Bulgarians has imposed upon himself. I yesterday conveyed to His Majesty, through a trusted agent, your message concerning hostility to his person or position, and also as to the gift, the amount of which I thought better not to mention at present stage (? and which might not have wished result) but feel that no gift can replace guarantee for recovery of Macedonia.

When our proposals were presented (May 29), Central Powers, whose orgy of lies and bribery was redoubled after the entry of Italy, developed intense activity and backed by their sweeping victories in Galicia they menaced Bulgaria with the advance of a huge Army through Serbia to Bulgarian frontier, if Bulgaria dared to accept our proposals. Bulgarian reply of June 14, though it was favourable in tone and avoided re-affirmation of neutrality, was not their real reply.

Governing idea here is to have some thing palpable with a view to dissipating distrust arising from past broken Treaties, and thus securing a rapid and enthusiastic mobilisation, and the Macedonian leaders, when informed privately that immediate occupation of even a part of the uncontested zone was practically impossible, fell back on the demand for partial or entire occupation of that zone after Bulgaria had brought about the fall of Constantinople, on the grounds that 'end of the war' may be very far off, and the Army, 60% of whose Officers are Macedonians, would be impatient to realise the national ideal after fresh sacrifices in Thrace. There is also a tendency to request that, after Bulgaria has done her duty as our Ally, perhaps on two Fronts, the four Powers should agree to decide the future of the contested zone on the basis of nationality, either by an impartial plebiscite or by joint arbitration to replace Russian arbitration, provided for by the Treaty of 1912. I believe that the real Bulgarian 'desiderata' would be on foregoing line, and that in view of the vital necessity of keeping up appearances 'vis-à-vis' of the Central Powers and Turkey, final decision may be reached by other than ordinary diplomatic channels. Bulgaria's action may come suddenly, over the Turco-Bulgarian railway negotiations, now reported to be proceeding unsatisfactorily at Constantinople.

As regards draft reply, wording suggested for hinterland of Kavalla will fall far short of Bulgarian expectations, based on our Note of May 29, and as real Bulgarian interests would seem to require the strengthening of M. Venizelos (? platform) it might be best to say 'In presence of such pertinent facts as departure of Greece from neutrality and extent of her effort in Asia Minor, Bulgarian Government will doubtless realise that it is impossible for the four Powers to determine accurately at the present stage the extent of Hellenic compensations in Asia Minor, and consequently the extent of the hinterland of Kavalla, both matters being inter-dependent.'

As regards after-compensation word 'minimum' will be harmful here, and might be elided. The fact that our guarantee of the uncontested zone was made conditional on Serbian acquisitions in Bosnia, etc., was severely criticised here, and was cleverly exploited by German agents and their subsidised Press here. It might perhaps be omitted.

My personal analysis is that the King of the Bulgarians hates the German Emperor, has a moral respect for the Emperor of Austria, has Hungarian sympathies, has a now diminishing fear of Russia and a greater fear of the nearer Macedonians, and that he must go with the Powers that can give a real guarantee as regards

Macedonia. Over 90% of the people would never fight against Russia or her Allies, and would only occupy Serbian Macedonia in the event of the disappearance of the Serbian State. It is again Russian action in Serbia which can convert this negative Bulgarian force into a positive one on our side.

Serbia has perhaps played the Austrian game in re-occupying Northern Albania, but if the four Powers do not disturb her present possession and allow her to have access to the Adriatic at Durazzo, the Serbian original pretext for the revision of the 1912 Treaty will have disappeared, and she might be induced to revert to the 'status quo' of that Treaty. The four Powers might also give her guarantee that she will get Bosnia, etc., and receive material aid when Bulgarian action liberates a portion of the Dardanelles Expeditionary (? Force), in the way of artillery, etc., for the capture of Cattaro, Sarajevo, etc., on the lines of Serbian aid to Bulgaria for the capture of Adrianople in 1913.

Russian Minister yesterday telegraphed to the Russian Government in the sense of the above paragraph, and also suggested that, if we cease 'pourparlers' with Bukarest regarding the Banat, Serbian Government may realise that by making sacrifices to Bulgaria in Macedonia she will eventually get larger slice of the Banat, through indirect Bulgarian assistance. He has also reminded the Russian Government of Serbian Crown Prince's telegram to the Emperor of Russia at the beginning of the war, practically placing Serbia in the hands of His Majesty, and further suggested that Russia or the four Powers should invite Serbia, in return for the undisturbed occupation of Northern Albania and material help for the acquisition of Bosnia, etc., to agree to either immediate occupation, or occupation after the fall of Constantinople by Bulgaria or by international regiments (see my telegram of May 16) of part of, e.g.: Ishtip, Kochana region, or even of the whole of the uncontested zone. Landing of the Allied Forces at Dedeagatch with the secret consent of the Bulgarian Government would mean automatic rupture with Turkey.

As regards Rodosto, I glean that Russian objections on the point have weakened, and if Serbia cannot be induced to consent to the immediate occupation of at least part of the uncontested zone it would probably have the required effect. It ought not, however, to be included in our official proposals, but reserved for the King of the Bulgarians, whose hobby it is.

As regards 'chances of securing immediate Bulgarian action on our side', I would venture to state that our proposals of May 29 were three months too late, and their effect was therefore diminished by Russian defeats in Galicia and failure, as interpreted here, of the Dardanelles operations. The harvest is now in full swing, and there is a natural reluctance to mobilise unless the principle of immediate occupation of at least part of Macedonia is admitted. Heavy part of the harvest will, however, be over in a fortnight.

There is a strong underlying fear here of an Austrian advance here some weeks hence through Serbia, and of Bulgaria having to choose between becoming a Belgium or a Luxemburg as regards the passage of troops, etc., to Turkey. There may thus be no time to lose.

I may add that, though the Minister of Finance and a couple of his Colleagues are devoted German adherents, partly owing to our past mistakes, the general sense of the King and the country is that Bulgaria must throw in her lot with the Entente Powers, and that His Majesty is far from hostile to us, though unfortunately he is hostile to the British Minister here. Decision to give the latter leave of absence is generally interpreted as a tardy proof of the earnestness of H.M. Government to secure redress of 'injustices of the Treaty of Bukarest', and the realisation of Bulgarian aspirations on the basis of nationality.

Exarch of Bulgarian Church, who for forty years has been the architect of the Macedonian edifice, has just died, and a message of condolence from H.M. Government on the great loss thus suffered by the Bulgarian nation would be much appreciated.

ROUMANIAN POLICY

90. (*A. P. Bennett to T. Russell, 6 November 1915, F.O. 800/71*)

Events in this corner of Europe are marching so rapidly that in all probability by the time this letter reaches you the situation which it depicts may have radically changed but that you would of course understand.

The defection of Bulgaria, and the big enemy push south of the Danube have produced a profound impression in this country. The fall of Venizelos and the doubtful attitude of Greece is another and a very serious adverse factor in the situation. All this, as you may readily imagine, makes our work here more than doubly difficult. Influential people, both in politics and society, who up to a few weeks ago regarded the ultimate victory of the Allies as an absolute certainty, are now beginning to waver in their views, and this change of opinion is very visibly reflected even in the pro-Ally press. As to the sentiments of the country, however, there can, I think, be no reasonable doubt that it is overwhelmingly on our side. But even our staunchest supporters reluctantly admit that if the situation continues to develop to the advantage of the Central Empires, Roumania might find herself in such a position as to necessitate her co-operation with our enemies. Our friends here, however, look to the Allies, and above all to England, to prevent such a situation from arising.

Both the Cabinet and the General Staff appear at present to be entirely dominated by the personality of Bratiano. The King is regarded as a nonentity, and probably is, and although pro-German in sentiment and obstinate in character, it is generally believed that he would not be likely to oppose Bratiano's advice, if and when the latter considers the moment ripe for action. This is also the opinion of the Queen, as personally expressed to me in the course of a recent private conversation.

The enigma of the situation is Bratiano himself. His caution is so excessive as to render him suspect in many quarters. Whether this suspicion is justified it is impossible to say, but his general attitude of 'funk' and his constant wriggling when circumstances seem to call for a prompt decision, certainly seem to give some justification to those who say that he is preparing to come 'au secours des Vainqueurs'. It is fairly certain, however, that Bratiano believes in our ultimate success, and as long as he maintains that opinion the position would seem to be negatively safe. But I much fear that he will continue to temporise and to find excuses for non-intervention until some big alteration in the general situation renders the Allies' success in the Balkans a certainty even without Roumania's help. It is the general opinion here that should Bratiano resign, the military situation, being as it is, a position dangerous to the Allies might well ensue. The King would probably send for Marghiloman or Maiorescu. In the former case a declaration of martial law to be followed by co-operation with the Central Empires might be expected to result, in which case all would depend upon the loyalty of the Army. In the latter—at best—it would mean a Roumania pledged to neutrality benevolent to our enemies. Neither Take Jonescu nor

Filipescu have sufficient weight in the country to make their advent to power at all probable, although they are very useful to us in opposition.

Under the circumstances there appears nothing for it but to make the best of Bratiano. With him at least we are on a rock, although an uncomfortable one. In the alternative we might find ourselves on dangerous quicksands.

There are perhaps four different developments, any of which might influence the present position sufficiently to make Bratiano afraid *not* to come in with us:

1. A really successful Russian offensive. At present nobody here believes in its possibility.

2. The forcing of the Dardanelles.

3. The cutting of communications between Germany and Constantinople, e.g. the landing of a big force in Thrace which would enable us to command the railway at Demotiko.

4. The intervention of Greece on the side of the Quadruple Entente.

Great importance is of course laid in any event on the establishment of a definite line of communication which would ensure a constant supply of ammunition to the Roumanian Army.

This is briefly the position as it appears to me for the moment, and I will continue to keep you in touch with fresh developments.

LACK OF CO-ORDINATION IN BALKAN POLICY

91. (*Memo. by Eustace Percy, Comments by Eric Drummond, 11 October 1915, F.O. 800/95*)

Balkan White Paper

It has been suggested that a preface to such a White Paper should be written at the Foreign Office. As it has also been suggested that I might take part in writing it, I venture to raise certain points which must inevitably either be dealt with or concealed in such a preface. These points are far outside my competence, and perhaps outside departmental competence altogether, but I must ask leave to raise them, with all due apologies.

Up to the end of 1914, our Balkan negotiations are pretty plain sailing. They revolve round a perfectly clear and obvious event— the Austrian attack on Serbia. There should be no difficulty in giving an adequate account of these negotiations.

From the beginning of 1915, however, there are various crucial points on which, so far as I know, the Foreign Office to this day has no information.

First. Throughout January and February we were urging Greece to enter the war in support of Serbia. Why? Events have shown that no attack on Serbia was intended at that moment. Our diplomacy was about six months too early; we rushed the situation too soon. The question will immediately be asked in public: why were we misled as to the German plans; did the Foreign Office never consult the General Staff?

[*To forestall any possibility of a possible Austro-German attack on Serbia by showing that they would have to deal with both the Greek and Serbian Armies.*]

Second. Greece offered at the end of January to enter the war in return for two Allied Army Corps at Salonika.

Our practical refusal, indicated by our offer of two *divisions* in the middle of February—combined of course with a serious error of judgement on the part of M. Venizelos—was really responsible for the Greek fiasco at the beginning of March. Why did we refuse to send two Army Corps if we contemplated sending far more than that number to the Dardenelles? Here again it will be asked: what co-ordination was there between diplomacy and military plans?

[*Plus a guarantee that Rumania would attack Bulgaria if the latter moved. Rumania showed no willingness to respond to suggestions put forward by Greece to this effect.*]

Third. The experience of all the previous months was that Bulgaria was the stumbling-block, and that she had to be either coerced or bribed. Why then did we initiate a military operation which prevented us from sparing any troops to coerce her and which, moreover, directly tended to raise Bulgaria's price by placing the Allies in a situation of obvious difficulty and danger? Once more, it will be asked by the public: where was the co-ordination?

[*Military opinion thought the operations would be successful and that if successful Rumania would join the allies and the other Balkan States would follow.*]

Fourth. We landed troops at the Dardanelles at the end of April. We did not make our first definite offer to Bulgaria till the end of May. Why, it will be asked, was diplomacy so behind-hand? Was the diplomatic situation which would be caused by prolonged operations at the Dardanelles, and the military situation which would arise if Bulgaria could not be brought in, never discussed? Was there no effort to bring Bulgaria in *concurrently* with those operations?

[*Again because it was not till some time had elapsed that it was clear that the military operations were going to be a very difficult job.*]

Fifth. If Bulgaria's co-operation was necessary to success in Gallipoli, why did diplomacy in Bulgaria hang fire from the middle of June to the beginning of August, and why was our second offer of August 4 made just before the Suvla Bay attack, too short a time before to bring Bulgaria in concurrently with that attack? Made at that moment, the offer would be unnecessary in the event of success and futile in the event of failure?

[*Objections to bringing pressure on Greece, military opinion thought Suvla Bay operation was going to be successful.*]

[*This is a difficult point to answer.*]

Sixth. Why did we make a third offer to Bulgaria only about a fortnight or less before her mobilisation? If it was a forlorn hope and if the possibility of mobilisation was in the mind of the F.O. (as it was), why did the event find us without military plans? And why did we go out of our way (as the public will say) to offend Greece when we knew we might shortly need her as an Ally or at least as a front door?

[*On the chance of neutrality.*]

All these circumstances will be difficult to explain and it is impossible to explain them at the F.O. The Department can confess to many mistakes of its own, but the crucial errors referred to above cannot be confessed or explained by it alone. There has rarely been an opportunity for departmental officials of the Foreign Office to exchange adequate information with officers at the War Office and Admiralty; there has never been any opportunity whatever for common deliberation or a steady working out of common plans over a protracted period between these Departments. If I may venture to say so, I do not see how a preface to a Balkan White Paper could be written without showing clearly that there has been no *General* Staff work in regard to the Balkans.

I hope it will be clear that this conveys no criticism of the military or naval staffs. They have no doubt been as much crippled by their ignorance of pending diplomatic plans as the Foreign

Office has been crippled by ignorance of pending military plans. The point seems to be that there has been no departmental link between the two, except a few desultory conversations.

As to the C.I.D., there is in the Foreign Office, so far as I know, no information as to the decisions of its Committees as they affect diplomacy, nor is there any record of Foreign Office assistance at their deliberations. I speak of course only of the C.I.D. as an inter *Departmental* organisation.

I only state these difficulties in order to make it clear why it seems that the Foreign Office is too much in the dark to be able to write an account of Balkan negotiations. Any account written departmentally would, I feel, only deflect the criticism now being levelled on all hands at the Foreign Office into a far more dangerous criticism of the whole work of Government and the whole machinery which the public has hitherto believed exists to secure co-ordination in the conduct of the war.

A preface written departmentally could not fail to breathe a general atmosphere of helplessness.

Chapter 2

The Middle East, 1914–18

THE PARTITION OF TURKEY IN ASIA

92. (*War Committee, 19 March 1915, Cab/42/2/14*)

THE PRIME MINISTER said that the French Ambassador in Petrograd had laid claim to a very large part of Turkey in Asia as French desiderata in return for permitting a Russian occupation of Constantinople and the Straits. These desiderata included Cilicia, Syria, and Palestine. The Russians objected most strongly to the Christian Holy Places being in French hands.

SIR EDWARD GREY said that we had to make up our mind first on two great questions of principle:

1. If we acquire fresh territory shall we make ourselves weaker or stronger?
2. Ought we not to take into account the very strong feeling in the Moslem world that Mohammedanism ought to have a political as well as a religious existence?

If the latter question were answered in the affirmative, Arabia, Syria, and Mesopotamia were the only possible territories for an Arab Empire. If we took this standpoint we could say to our Moslem subjects that, as Turkey had handed itself over to the Germans, we had set up a new and independent Moslem State.

LORD CREWE said that two different views were taken in the India Office. The Military Department, who were in general agreement with the Viceroy of India, considered that Turkey in Asia ought to be made as strong as possible. The Political Department, on the other hand, thought that Turkey should be sacrificed and Arabia made as strong as possible.

LORD KITCHENER objected to the Military Department's plan. The Turks, he said, would always be under pressure from their strong Russian neighbour, with the result that the Khalifate might be to a great extent under Russian domination, and Russian influence might indirectly assert itself over the Mohammedan part of the population of India. If, on the other hand, the Khalifate were transferred to Arabia, it would remain to a great extent under our influence.

LORD CREWE agreed with Lord Kitchener.

THE PRIME MINISTER read an extract from a memorandum by Sir Theodore Morison, in which he stated the apprehension of some leading Moslems that they would become like the Jews—a people having a religion, but no country—and in which he expressed a hope that the Khalifate would obtain Syria and Mesopotamia.

LORD KITCHENER said that, if Mesopotamia was to be left undeveloped, it was all very well to leave it to the Arabs. But, if it was to be developed, we should only be creating trouble for ourselves by leaving it to them.

LORD HALDANE said there were two great questions of principle governing these questions:

1. Whether we wished to acquire more territory at all.
2. Whether we intended to leave the Germans and Turks crushed up at the end of the war. In the interests of a lasting peace, he urged that this should not be aimed at. Napoleon had failed in the attempt to crush nations, and since 1870 Germany had failed to crush the nationality out of Alsace and Lorraine. All experience showed that a permanent peace could not be obtained except by general consent.

MR. BALFOUR suggested that there was no comparison between our proposals and the Napoleonic plan of crushing nations. In Europe, he understood, there was a general consensus that divisions of territory should be by nationality. But in Asia we had to deal with countries which had been misgoverned by the Turks.

LORD KITCHENER said that India would expect some return for her effort and losses in Mesopotamia.

LORD CREWE said that all shades of opinion in the India Office agreed that the Basra Vilayet must form part of the British Empire. Some, however, thought that we ought to be content with a protectorate over the Baghdad Vilayet, which would be in a position somewhat similar to the Soudan.

LORD KITCHENER asked what object was to be gained by raising such difficulties for the future?

MR. CHURCHILL said that in this question of the partition of Turkey in Asia the main difficulty was likely to be between England and France, leaving out the question of the Christian Holy Places, in which Russia also was concerned. He suggested that the best plan would be to postpone our conversations with France on the subject. Consideration of the question was really premature. We should say to France outright that we had not made up our mind. We had been obliged to settle with Russia, because the question was urgent, but there was not the same urgency with France. Either France and we ourselves should both agree to a self-denying policy in regard to the acquisition of territory, or we should discuss the matter in detail, which would at present be inconvenient.

LORD CREWE said he would have preferred to postpone the whole question, if Russia had not suggested that we should formulate our desiderata.

SIR EDWARD GREY said that at present it was a question of making up our own mind, and not of discussing the matter with France.

MR. LLOYD GEORGE said that the Lord Chancellor's idea made the same appeal to him. We ought not to rule out the possibility of giving Germany a bone of some sort. She would always be a very powerful nation, and it might eventually even be desirable to have her in a position to prevent Russia becoming too predominant.

LORD CREWE agreed, but said it would be very dangerous to put the Germans back on the Baghdad Railway.

MR. CHURCHILL said that the whole question depended on whether we intended to divide Turkey. Surely, he suggested, we did not intend to leave this inefficient and out-of-date nation, which had long misruled one of the most fertile countries [in] the world, still in possession! Turkey had long shown herself to be inefficient as a governing Power, and it was time for us to make a clean sweep.

THE PRIME MINISTER said that he had great sympathy with Sir Edward Grey's first proposition that we have already as much territory as we are able to hold, but the fact was we were not free agents. Russia intended to take a good slice of Turkey. France, Italy, and Greece each demanded a piece. If, for one reason or another, because we didn't want more territory, or because we didn't feel equal to the responsibility, we were to leave the other nations to scramble for Turkey without taking anything ourselves, we should not be doing our duty.

MR. MCKENNA suggested that, in the meantime, we should put forward a suggestion that none of us take anything.

SIR EDWARD GREY suggested that our reply about our desiderata should be, in the sense, that our first requirement was the preservation of a Moslem political entity, and that we are pledged to the maintenance of the Moslem Holy Places. The first thing we had to consider was as to what that entity should include. We might base our first reply by taking up this line.

LORD CREWE said that we must have a political capital for the Mohammedan State, and that this could not be at Mecca, as no one except Mohammedans could go there.

(Conclusion)

A reply to be sent to Petrograd in the sense proposed by Sir Edward Grey, viz., that, after the Straits had been forced, and Constantinople had passed into the hands of the Allies, our first desideratum would be the establishment of a Moslem entity. It would have to include Arabia, and the question would arise as to what was to go with it. In the meantime, it would be premature to discuss the partition of Turkey.

[A telegram somewhat in this sense was sent on the 19th March.]

ALEXANDRETTA

MR. BALFOUR said that the French demand to control Cilicia as well as Syria, was excessive. He had expressed no views as regards the desirability of a British control over Mesopotamia, but he held strongly that Alexandretta and Mesopotamia should go together.

MR. MCKENNA pointed out that Sir Arthur Hirtzel, in his memorandum, did not share this view.

MR. LLOYD GEORGE said that he agreed with Sir Arthur Hirtzel.

LORD KITCHENER said that, if we did not take Alexandretta, it would be better not to take Mesopotamia.

[The discussion was adjourned.]

THE NEGOTIATIONS WITH THE ARABS

93. *(McMahon to Grey, 18 October 1915, F.O. 371/2486/34982)*

Please see my Despatch Confidential, No. 121, of October 12th, forwarding statements of Sherif-El-Faroki and also my telegram No. 623, conveying the purpose of letter from Sherif of Mecca. From further conversation with Faroki it appears evident that Arab party are at parting of the ways and unless we can give them immediate assurance of nature to satisfy them they will throw themselves into the hands of Germany who he says has furnished them fulfilment of all their demands. In the one case they seem ready to work actively with us which will greatly influence the course of Mesopotamia and Syrian campaigns while in the other Arabs will throw in their lot against us and we may have all Islam in the East united against the Allies.

Arab party say they cannot longer hesitate because they must act before Turkey receives further assistance from Germany. Matter therefore is urgent.

Decision presents great difficulties because unless care is taken it is quite possible that young Arab party may eventually prove as troublesome as young Turks. Unless however information in possession of His Majesty's Government removes anxiety regarding threatened Turco-German designs against Bagdad and Egypt we must take this risk in endeavour to get and keep Arabs on our side.

I understand Faroki in course of further conversations expresses opinion that Arab party would accept an assurance on the following lines:

England accepts principle of independent Arabia under British guidance and control within limits propounded by Sherif of Mecca, in so far as England is free to act without detriment to the interests of her present Allies (this refers to French in regard to whom see remarks on modification of north west limits of Arabia). England when situation admits will advise and help Arabs regarding establishment of such form of Government in territories concerned as may seem most suitable. In respect to above territory Arabs will recognise British and no other influence, will recognise British interests as paramount, and will work under British guidance and control. Arabs for this purpose will accept such British residencies, advisers and officials as may be necessary to ensure sound administration, but Arabian peninsula itself will remain under its own chiefs. England will recognise inviolability of Holy Places and guarantee them against unlikely [sic] aggression.

In regard to North Western boundaries proposed by Sherif of Mecca, Faroki thinks Arabs would accept modification leaving in Arabia purely Arab districts of Aleppo Damascus Hama and Homs, whose occupation by the French they would oppose by force of arms.

He also accepts the fact that British interests necessitate special measures of British control in Basrah Vilayet.

If we consider letter of Sherif of Mecca in the light of Faroki's views I do not think either Sherif or Arab party are likely to regard any less wide assurance as acceptable.

Faroki is anxious himself to visit Sherif and I propose to facilitate his doing so in due course.

In the meantime I would be glad of instructions how to reply to Sherif and what assurances to give Arab party through Faroki.

94. (*Minutes on McMahon to Grey, 18 October 1915, no. 623, F.O. 371/2486/34982*)

Sherif of Mecca

The question has two aspects, military and political, of which the military side is urgent.

We are told that not only the Arabs in Arabia, but also the Arab officers and men in the Turkish army are ready to work against the C.U.P. and the Turks, if we will accept their pretensions, while if we cannot come to terms they will definitely side with the Germans and Turks against us. The advantages of the one are as obvious as the dangers of the other, and I would venture to suggest that no time should be lost in getting officers from Egypt and the Dardanelles, with local knowledge and experience, and a representative of the French military authorities, to come to London to discuss the position and work out plans.

Politically, the first thing is to settle whether we are prepared to accept in principle the idea of Arabia—even an exaggerated Arabia such as the Sherif proposes—for the Arabs. If I may express my own view, it is, as I have held since the war began, that the best solution is an independent Arabia, looking to Great Britain as its founder and protector, and provided with territory rich and wide enough to furnish adequate revenues.

There are however two important limitations to the creation of such a State:

(i) French claims and ambitions.

(ii) Our own advance in Mesopotamia.

(i) It is difficult to challenge the position which France claims, and has to some extent secured by acquiring special interests, in the north-western portion of Arabia as now defined by the Arabs. But we cannot win the Arabs unless we can reconcile French and Arab claims, and the position must be clearly understood from both the French and the Arab side from the outset, or we shall be heading straight for serious trouble. It seems to me that the line to work on is, first, to impress on our Allies the urgency of the situation and to get them to accept us as our mouthpiece, at the same time impressing on the Arabs that we speak for the Allies as a whole: and, secondly, to be ready to recognize the priority of French commercial interests in the north-west.

(ii) Mesopotamia is primarily a question for India, but I do not think that a solution, which would provide for Arab independence and yet safeguard our vital interest, is necessarily impossible. Moreover, we shall have to be ready to resign acquisitions of territory in Mesopotamia if we are to get the French to give up their Syrian dreams.

There is a third difficulty, namely, who is, or are, to rule this Arab empire? Bin Saud can run Nejd, Sherif Hosein can govern the Hedjaz, then Idrisi or Imam Yahya may be master of the Yemen, but no one is indicated as Emir of Damascus or Caliph of Bagdad. This is however a question on which light can only be thrown when we reach the stage of discussion with the Arab representatives. But subject to any fresh considerations which may arise out of Sir H. McMahon's desp. No. 121, when we get it, I would submit that he should be told that H.M.G. agree in principle to the establishment of an independent Arabia and that we are ready to discuss the boundaries of such a State, and the measures to be taken to call into being, with qualified Arabian representatives without delay.

These are notes written in haste and I could have wished for more time for consideration, but even as it is I must apologize for the length of the minute, and I do not think that any amount of consideration would alter my belief that we should try to come to terms with the Arabs, for which purpose we should start negotiations forthwith.

G.R.C[lerk]

19–X–15

I doubt if it will be easy in view of conflicting rivalries and jealousies of the Arab chiefs to set up an 'independent Arab State' —but we might proceed on the lines suggested by Mr. Clerk.

A. Nicholson

95. (*Grey to McMahon, 20 October 1915, no. 796, F.O. 381/2486/ 34982*)

Your personal telegram of the 18th.
You can give cordial assurances on the lines, and with the reserve about our Allies, proposed by you. Stipulation that Arabs will recognise British interests as paramount and work under British guidance etc. should not be included unless it is necessary to secure Arab consent, as this might give rise to impression in France that we were not only endeavouring to secure Arab interests, but to establish our own in Syria at expense of French.

There is no difficulty in speaking without reserve about Arab peninsula and Holy Places. The general reserve you propose is however necessary more especially for North Western Boundaries.

As regards Mesopotamia proposed sphere of British control, namely, Basra Vilayet, will need extension in view of special interests in Bagdad province and area actually in our occupation. Our treaties with Arab chiefs will of course stand.

But the important thing is to give our assurances that will prevent Arabs from being alienated, and I must leave you discretion in the matter as it is urgent and there is not time to discuss an exact formula.

The simplest plan would be to give an assurance of Arab independence saying that we will proceed at once to discuss boundaries if they will send representatives for that purpose, but if something more precise than this is required you can give it.

You should keep Wingate informed.

SEPARATE PEACE WITH TURKEY

96. (*Grey to Buchanan, 16 November 1915, F.O. 800/75*)
We have been recently approached by various Turks opposed to the present régime, who stated that they were in a position to start a revolutionary movement in Constantinople and could upset the Government. They asserted that they were anxious for peace with the Allies, but their terms always included the integ-

rity of the Ottoman Empire and especially the retention of Constantinople in Turkish hands. In view of our pledges to Russia these terms were of course out of the question and it seemed very unlikely that those who put them forward were of sufficient standing to carry out their project. We have therefore never proceeded any further.

We have now received information that two British Officers have been released by the Turks and it seems possible that they may be bringing some message from the Turkish Government as there appears to be no other motive for their release.

The whole situation in the Near East is extremely critical. We may be forced either to withdraw our troops from Gallipoli: a step which can only be accomplished with very considerable loss of men and material, and which would undoubtedly greatly lower the prestige of the Allies throughout the East and all neutral countries or, if we hold on, we may be driven out, which would mean the loss of our entire force with still more disastrous consequences as regards prestige. If this occurs, we shall be faced with the necessity of employing very large forces to defend Egypt. These will have to come from the Western Front, which would make doubtful the possibility of the Allies undertaking the big offensive in the West which they hoped to take in the spring.

In all these circumstances, it seems to me to be worth consideration whether it would be possible to negotiate with the Turks if suggestions for a separate peace came from them. If the Turks were willing to conclude peace, the ultimate result of the war would be practically certain, as Germany would be ringed round and the effect on her internal position and prestige would be incalculable. I do not, of course, suggest that we desire to depart in any way from our pledges as regards Constantinople and the Straits, but if Turkey were willing to give binding assurances that the Straits should always remain open and unfortified, and even that there should be a Russian protectorate over the Straits, Russia holding the entrance to the Bosphorus, Constantinople remaining Turkish, it seems to me that Russia could afford to do without the actual possession of the town, as she would have secured all the practical advantages which are assured to her by our present agreement. There can be no question however, of our receding from the engagement to Russia unless she is really willing.

I fully realize the delicacy of the question but, in view of the immense issues involved, I should be glad of your views as to whether you think it possible to sound M.F.A. or the Emperor privately on this matter and also as to popular feeling in Russia and especially in Moscow on the subject. Please communicate with me before taking any action.

97. (*Buchanan to Grey, 17 November 1915, F.O. 800/75*)

Your private & secret telegram of yesterday.
I fear that for me to sound either the Emperor or M. Sazonof in the sense of the suggestion would produce a very bad impression, and that any such step would be foredoomed to failure.

When, in February last, overtures were made to Allies through M. Venizelos by the Commander of the First Turkish Army Corps the Minister for Foreign Affairs said that it would be impossible to give assurances that would tranquillise the anti-German Party without compromising the attainment of the end which Russia had in view, and that all that we could do was to reply that the longer the war lasted the more onerous would be the terms of peace (see my telegram, No. 168).

On March 1st, as reported in my telegram, No. 235, His Excellency said that, though he had been personally in favour of neutralising Constantinople, he had been obliged to yield to the demand of the Russian public for its actual possession.

In my telegram, No. 249, Secret, I recorded what the Emperor had said to the French Ambassador and General Pau, to the effect that he must insist on the incorporation of Constantinople in the Russian Empire, as he could not impose on his subjects the tremendous sacrifices entailed by the war without securing for them the realisation of their secular ambitions and when on the following day, the French Ambassador spoke by order of his Government against the annexation and fortification of both sides of the Straits, the Minister for Foreign Affairs said that if France and Great Britain did not sanction the settlement of the question of the Straits and Constantinople on terms desired by the Emperor the consequences would be incalculable, while he personally would be obliged to tender his resignation (see my telegram, No. 257).

On October 14th, M. Sazonof called the attention of the French Ambassador to an article in the 'Débats' hinting that Great

Britain and France would have to modify their agreement about Constantinople, and said that it would prove a potent weapon in the hands of the German agents in Russia, who were making a propaganda in favour of a separate peace. He was indeed so incensed that he even went so far as to say that an attempt to modify our agreement might lead to a termination of the Alliance.

Though the Minister for Foreign Affairs has not referred to the question of Constantinople and the Straits in our recent conversations, he discussed the question of our operations in Gallipoli with Captain George Lloyd on the eve of the latter's departure for London four days ago, and spoke very strongly against any withdrawal of our troops. It might be well if you could see Captain Lloyd on his arrival.

So far as I am able to gauge public opinion, I believe that the great majority of Russians have for some time past regarded the acquisition of Constantinople and the Straits as assured to them after the war. Idea of annexing Galicia or Posen for the purpose of creating a united Poland leaves them cold, and Constantinople, in their eyes, can alone compensate them for their enormous losses in the war. Were it to be known that we were inviting the Government to be contented with the possession of the entrance to the Bosphorus, and with perhaps the protectorate of the Straits, we should at once be accused of trying to thwart Russia's ambitions from selfish motives.

In Moscow, according to Mr. Lockhart's Reports, the feeling about the Straits is intense, and no price or sacrifice is considered too high to pay for their acquisition. Though in an industrial town like Moscow more prominence is given to the question of the Straits than to that of Constantinople, I have no reason to believe that the desire to see Constantinople incorporated in the Russian Empire is less strong in Moscow than elsewhere.

In view of the above considerations, I feel that the course which you suggest has no chance of success while it may seriously indispose the Russian Government and public against us. If the two British Officers bring us a message from the Turkish Government, all that in my opinion it would be safe to do would be to communicate it to M. Sazonof for his information, and I would then endeavour to draw him into conversation on the subject.

PERSIA AND TURKEY—LIMITATIONS ON POLICY

98. (*Minutes on the Aga Khan's Memoranda*[1] *on the Middle East, March 1916, F.O. 371/2731/3254*)

(a) Persia

That our position in S. Persia at present is at a low ebb cannot be questioned. It must however be seen whether Sir P. Sykes' mission may not improve matters if he manages to raise a police. The Zil has already been invited here and may soon go there. The suggestion, however, that he should be governor general of all Southern and Central Persia seems premature.

To unite Isfahan (in the Russian sphere) with Shiraz and Kerman (in the present neutral and British spheres respectively) into one governor generalship would be a very difficult business. Let us first see how the Zil shapes at Isfahan. I own to being strongly in favour of his return, all else having failed but I realize that the Legations and the Persian Govt. may all soon be exclaiming 'quantum mutatus!' It will be time enough to decide later.

(b) Turkey

The views put forward by H.H. are very widely held in this country: but I am far from being convinced of them.

Sir A. Hirtzel's recent and most interesting Memoranda on German designs in Asiatic Turkey and the commitments of H.M.G. regarding the future of Constantinople both illustrate the difficulty if not absolute impossibility of entertaining the idea in question. [i.e. a separate peace]

L. O(liphant) 24 March 1916.

The pledge to Russia as to Constantinople on the one hand, and the Arab arrangement on the other, evidently make it impossible to think of a peace with Turkey until she is completely vanquished.

(Austen) C(hamberlain)

I agree (a) that we should see what the Zil does before supporting a new sphere for him. For many years I have desired to see him got back; but it may be too late, if he is 'quantum mutatus a Zililo' of former days: and (b) that there is no money to put on the Turkish horse, it all being on the Cossack & Arab animals.

C(rewe) 26.III [1916]

---

[1] Not printed. Advocating peace with Turkey and supporting the Zil in Persia.

PAN-ISLAMISM

99. (*Memo. by Sir A. Hirtzel, Political Dept., India Office, dated 25 May 1916, Cab/42/16/1*)

Extract

The pan-Islamic danger is a real and permanent one. All the parties to the present war have to face it, except Germany. We cannot get rid of it altogether. But we have the opportunity now (if, in conjunction with Russia, we press the war to its natural conclusion) of immensely diminishing it by reducing to impotence the only existing organised Government that can further the pan-Islamic idea; and when we see the progress which that idea has made in India, under Turkish influence, in the last 10 years, does not common prudence require that we should do so? To leave a Moslem State that will count among the Governments of the world is simply to create a focus of which Germany (who will have nothing to lose) will fan the flame when it suits her—and we, in India and Africa, shall be the principal sufferers.

These considerations seem to point to this conclusion: For Great Britain the war with Turkey can never be a side issue. It is, of course, obvious that by defeating Turkey we have not defeated Germany, whereas if we succeed in defeating Germany, the collapse of Turkey's military power follows automatically. What is less obvious is why this will not suffice for our purpose. Great Britain is an Asiatic and a Moslem power, and what makes the war with Turkey rather a separate war than a mere episode in a world war, is the fact that we are waging it against another Moslem Power with the rest of the Moslem world for spectators. It is on Mesopotamia and not on Europe that attention is fixed in the Persian Gulf, as we heard the other day from Mekran. 'The intellect of the Arab is in his eyes,' and the Political Assistant at Aden recently expressed the opinion that a merely diplomatic defeat of Turkey will not count in Arabia. In Afghanistan (where Nasrullah Khan has been diligently retailing British defeats in Mesopotamia) it is to Enver Pasha, who is expected to arrive at the head of 200,000 Turks, that people are looking. In India itself the vernacular Press is loth to believe Russian victories, and loses no opportunity of admiring the feats of Turkish arms. With all these people we shall have to deal after the war, and to live with them on terms of moral supremacy. We shall have to govern

India itself—where, besides the Moslem problem, the fact has to be reckoned with that the educated Hindus, though they have thrown in their lot with us, are not averse to seeing British pride humbled, and humbled by an Asiatic Power—and to convince the peoples of India that a handful of white men can still control them, a task which will not have been rendered easier by indiscriminate eulogy of the exploits of the Indian troops in France. In the regions adjoining India, where for a variety of reasons the military prestige of Great Britain had suffered serious eclipse in the 10 years preceding the war, we shall have to rehabilitate it. To restore order on the frontier and maintain tolerable relations with Afghanistan; to conduct the business of everyday life in Persia; to keep order in the Gulf and control those Arab chiefs with whom we already have relations, and to whose number the very important Amir of Nejd has recently been added; and finally, if it should so turn out, to develop the resources of Mesopotamia: in all of which regions the Islamic self-consciousness will have been intensified. The Arabian policy of His Majesty's Government, so far from diminishing the difficulty of these tasks, will add to it, unless Turkey has been decisively defeated—and defeated by us, not merely by Russians or French. For while the Arabs are content to use us now for their own ends, it is certain that if and when those ends are attained their attitude will always be less antagonistic towards the Moslem Turk, whatever their grievances against him in the past, than towards the Christian; and if the former is believed to be the better soldier they will play him off against us to their heart's content. Indeed, the policy of fanning the Arab nationalist spirit to a flame is, as far as eastern Arabia and Nejd are concerned, a two-edged weapon of a very dangerous description—innocuous only if the Turk is beaten in the field, but otherwise likely eventually to result in acute antagonism between the Arabs and ourselves.

THE SYKES–PICOT AGREEMENT

100. (*Crewe to Bertie, 17 December 1915, Cab/42/6/11*)

Extract

There was a meeting of the War Committee yesterday, at which various questions relating to the War in the East were considered.

Sir Mark Sykes, who had written a memorandum on the subject, came and gave us his views. He was just back from a tour

which included rapid visits to India, to our forces in Mesopotamia, and to Egypt. I do not know whether you ever met him.
He has travelled a great deal in Asia and learnt much about the
people, knowing, I think, both Turkish and Arabic. He is certainly a very capable fellow, with plenty of ideas, but at the same
time painstaking and careful.

The whole question of the defence of Egypt is one of extreme
difficulty. It seems obvious to hold the line of the Canal, which can
be approached only across the desert; but it does not seem to be a
particularly defensible position in itself, and the effect on Egyptian
feeling, and on our prestige, of being obliged to fight with a very
large army on the edge of the country itself must be bad. There is
the other and very important aspect that, if the Turks advance
unchecked, everything behind them will be either won over or
destroyed. If you apply this to Arabia, it means that all hopes in
which we have indulged of exploiting the Arab dislike of Turkey,
and perhaps of creating an Arabian Federation under the Shereef
of Mecca, go by the board. The Shereef, who is friendly to us and
tolerates the French, will either be put to death or have to fly for
his life. If the Committee of Union and Progress get control of
Mecca, they might be able to declare a regular Jehad, probably
affecting Afghanistan and giving serious trouble in India. Consequently, if the passive defence of Egypt can be avoided, every
stage further back, whether it be Palestine or Syria, or right up to
Asia Minor, at which we could attack in force, would be so much
to the good. But then we come up against French susceptibilities
and claims, and any discussion becomes exceedingly delicate,
because the French always seem to talk as though Syria and even
Palestine were as completely theirs as Normandy. Only to-day,
when Cambon was here, he talked at length about the way his
Government have been kept in the dark concerning conversations with the Shereef of Mecca. These were carried on, as I may
tell you for your private information, without great wisdom by
McMahon in Cairo. I was able to reassure Cambon that we had
no intention of arranging that a new Arab State, if one could be
formed, would include the Lebanon or any part of the world to
which the French could lay distinct claim. I added, however, that
his Government would be wise to consider the situation in all its
bearings, because, if Arabia should be won over by the Young
Turks, the Syrian Christians, man, woman, and child, would

undoubtedly enjoy the fate of the Armenians during the last few months.

The War Committee concluded that the facts pointed to the desirability of some offensive operation, either from Egypt or the sea if opportunity should offer; but it was clear that an understanding with France was a necessary preliminary; and it must be remembered that, though the matter may be in one sense really urgent, yet immediate action does not seem possible, because the requisite force is not available, nor, if it were, could it be transported at once. But, so soon as the increased forces which the General Staff consider necessary if Egypt is to be defended on its frontier are ready to go there, an alternative operation will have to be borne in mind as a possibility, and it should be studied beforehand.

101. *(Memo. by Sykes, January 1916,*[1] *Cab/42/11/5)*

Arab Question.—(Received at Foreign Office January 5.)

Note

This memorandum was drawn up under the following circumstances: After the committee under the presidency of Sir A. Nicolson had met M. Picot twice, it became apparent that there were so many details which required separate consideration that either more time would have to be devoted to the work by the committee than the press of other business on its various members would permit, or that negotiations would be prolonged which, in view of the military and political situation in the Near East, was undesirable.

Sir A. Nicolson therefore suggested that M. Picot and I should examine the whole question so as to clear the ground of details and collaborate with him in drawing up a memorandum which would co-relate the various factors of the general problem.

M. S[ykes]

Memorandum

I.—*Preliminary Observation*

The main problem to be solved is to discover a middle course which will harmonise with the requirements of the various parties, which are as follows:

[1] The final agreements of May 1916 are printed in D.B.F.P. IV, pp. 241–8.

(*a*) France requires a settlement which (1) while compensating her for the inconvenience and loss attendant upon the disruption of the Ottoman Empire, will (2) safeguard her historic and traditional position in Syria, (3) assure her of full opportunity of realising her economic aspirations in the Near East.

(*b*) The Arabs require (1) recognition of their nationality, (2) protection of their race from alien oppression, and (3) an opportunity of re-establishing their position as a contributing factor in the world's progress.

(*c*) Great Britain requires (1) to assure her position in the Persian Gulf, (2) opportunity to develop Lower Mesopotamia, (3) (*a*) commercial and military communication between the Persian Gulf and the Mediterranean by land, (*b*) influence in an area sufficient to provide the personnel engaged in Mesopotamia irrigation work with suitable sanatoria, and hill stations, and containing an adequate native recruiting ground for administrative purposes, (4) to obtain commercial facilities in the area under discussion.

(*d*) Lastly, such a settlement has to be worked in with an arrangement satisfactory to the conscientious desires of Christianity, Judaeism, and Mohammedanism in regard to the status of Jerusalem and the neighbouring shrines.

II

To arrive at a satisfactory settlement the three principal parties must observe a spirit of compromise. This will be obvious when the various claims are regarded individually.

France

The French nation has the following direct interests:

1. Since the earliest times the French have been regarded as the champions and protectors of the Latin Christians in the Ottoman Empire generally, and the especial patrons of the Maronites in the Lebanon owing to the action of the French Government in 1860.

2. Owing to French scholastic effort the French have taken a prominent part in the intellectual development of both Christian and Moslem Arabs during the last century, this has especially been the case in the provinces of Aleppo, Beirout, Damascus and Mosul.

3. Based on the above facts, a strong public opinion has grown up in France favourable to French expansion in Syria and Palestine.

4. The development of French railway enterprises in Syria has confirmed this opinion, and has made it a permanent factor in the average French point of view.

5. The participation of French capital to the extent of 30 per cent. in the Bagdad Railway and the terms of the Franco-Ottoman Loan of 1914 have complicated the case by including in French interests certain areas which would not naturally come under consideration, were the subject-matter of discussion confined to the traditions and activities referred to in paragraphs 1, 2, 3, and 4 of this section.

6. Based on the foregoing, it may be said on the hypothesis that were there no other circumstances to be considered, the French Government might be expected to desire commercial and political predominance in an area bounded on the south by a line drawn from El Arish to Kasr-i-Shirin, and on the north by the main ridge of the Taurus and anti-Taurus, beginning in the vicinity of Cap Anamur and ending about Koshab.

The Arabs

1. Although divided by religion, custom, social habits, and geographic circumstances, there is a considerable desire for unity among the bulk of the peoples of Arabia proper, and the Arabic-speaking peoples of the Asiatic provinces of the Ottoman Empire.

2. The leaders of this movement recognise that a closely compacted Arab State is neither in harmony with the national genius of the Arabs nor feasible from the point of view of finance and administration; however, they are of opinion that if protection against Turkish and German domination is assured, a confederation of Arabic-speaking States could be formed which would satisfy their racial desire for freedom, and at the same time conform with their natural political customs.

3. The ideal of the Arab leaders would be to establish a confederation of States under the aegis of an Arabian prince, roughly approximating to the Arabian peninsula plus the Ottoman provinces of Basra, Bagdad, Jerusalem, Damascus, Aleppo, Mosul, Adana, and Diarbekir, with its littoral under the protection of

Great Britain and France. That such a State should agree to select its administrative advisers from subjects of the two protecting Powers, and that it should accord especial facilities to both Powers in matters of enterprise and industrial development.

Great Britain

1. In so far as Great Britain is concerned, her *desiderata* have already been stated in paragraph (*a*), Preliminary observation.

2. The ideal solution for Great Britain would be to have administrative control and priority of enterprise in an area bounded by the line Acre, Tadmor, Ras-ul-Ain, Jeziriret-ibn-Omar, Zakhu, Amaida, Rowanduz, combined with the possession of Alexandretta, with a suitable hinterland connecting the Euphrates Valley with the Mediterranean, and rights of railway construction connecting Alexandretta with Bagdad. Further, that Great Britain should have a veto on irrigation schemes likely to divert water from Lower Mesopotamia.

International Religious Interests

As regards Jerusalem and the Holy Places, the following must be borne in mind:

(*a*) The Latin and Orthodox religions require equal considerations in Palestine.

(*b*) The members of the Jewish community throughout the world have a conscientious and sentimental interest in the future of the country.

(*c*) The Mosque of Omar represents, next to Mecca, the most holy and venerable shrine in Islam, and it must be a *sine qua non* that the Mosque of Omar itself should be under the sole control of Moslems, and that the chief of the Arabian confederation should have an equal voice in the administration of Palestine.

The lines of the proposed settlement are as follows:

1. *Arabs.*—That France and Great Britain should be prepared to recognise and protect a confederation of Arab States in the areas (*a*) and (*b*) under the suzerainty of an Arabian chief. That in area (*a*) France, and in area (*b*) Great Britain, should have priority of right of enterprise and local loans. That in area (*a*) France, and in area (*b*) Great Britain, should alone supply advisers or foreign functionaries at the request of the Arab confederation.

2. That in the blue area France, and in the red area Great Britain, should be allowed to establish such direct or indirect administration or control as they desire.

3. That in the brown area there should be established an international administration, the form of which is to be decided upon after consultation with Russia, and subsequently in consultation with Russia, Italy, and the representatives of Islam.

4. That Great Britain be accorded (1) the ports of Haifa and Acre, (2) guarantee of a given supply of water from area (*a*) for irrigation in area (*b*). (3) That an agreement be made between France and Great Britain regarding the commercial status of Alexandretta, and the construction of a railway connecting Bagdad with Alexandretta.

5. That Great Britain have the right to build, administer, and be sole owner of a railway connecting Haifa or Acre with area (*b*), and that Great Britain should have a perpetual right to transport troops along such a line at all times.

G. P[icot]

M. S[ykes]

ITALY AND ASIA MINOR

102. (*Grey to Rodd, 21 September 1916, No. 192, Cab/37/155/33*)

When I spoke to the Italian Ambassador to-day about the Constantinople and Asia Minor Agreements, he raised no question about Constantinople and the Straits. Indeed he said he knew it was absolutely essential or else Russia would have made a separate peace and in any case it was concluded before Italy entered the war. But he continued to speak with great earnestness about the Asia Minor Agreements. He said that it had always been understood that Italy was to have a sphere in Asia Minor as large as that given to other Powers. If she did not receive it Baron Sonnino would be swept away for not having provided sufficiently for the interests of Italy when he entered the war. Mersina, in particular, had always been a great desire of Italy and by the agreement made with Italy it had been stipulated that she was to receive a sphere in territory neighbouring Adalia which must therefore include some territory not included in Adalia or it could not be described as neighbouring Adalia.

I pointed out that Italy had already been promised very large things in the Adriatic, and that everybody could not have exactly the same extent of gain everywhere. Up to the present moment the territory promised to Italy, the acquisition of which we were bound in the Agreement of September 1914, to which Italy subsequently became a party, to support, exceeded what we or other Allies had yet put forward on our own behalf. Italy having made that agreement with us was bound to receive sympathetically the first requests we and other Allies put forward to her to support claims of ours and theirs in the terms of peace. If two or more of the Allies would insist on claiming the same thing each for themselves no alliance could be worked. Public opinion in France must be considered as well as in Italy and it must be remembered that for two years France had had the Germans in her vitals so to speak. Her women and the population in the occupied territory had been abominably treated, she had suffered cruelly and the whole of her manhood for more than two years had been put into the war. I should be prepared, if public opinion here accused me of claiming too little for Great Britain and conceding too much to France, to combat public opinion here by these arguments. The Italian Ambassador did not seem to think that the Italian Government could combat public opinion and while not demurring to what I had said about France, he said that the Italian Government were in a different position because they could have avoided the war and their public opinion would say that as they deliberately entered the war on the side of the Allies they ought to have good terms.

I said that all this would have to be discussed later. For the moment the question was rather one of communicating the agreements to Baron Sonnino in a form that would satisfy him that the claims of Italy in Asia Minor would be formally discussed.

I assumed that Italy would receive a large sphere but two of the Allies must not each insist on claiming exactly the same part. I explained to the Italian Ambassador how the Asia Minor Agreements came to be made.

The Shereef of Mecca had communicated to the Egyptian authorities his desire to make himself independent but had insisted upon knowing whether we were prepared to recognise an independent Arab State. We were of course prepared to do that if he succeeded in establishing his independence, for all we were pledged to was that the Moslem holy places should remain in independent Moslem hands. We had no difficulty in agreeing to any boundaries which the Shereef wanted on the south but on the north the Shereef came up against Syria where we had always admitted French interest and the French would not make concessions to the Shereef of places like Damascus without knowing what the limits of their sphere were to be. Meanwhile Russia had advanced to Trebizond and Erzeroum and it became necessary to ascertain what eastern limit would satisfy Russia. This latter point had been discussed not here but between the French and Russians at Petrograd. In this way the question had grown to a definition of spheres of interest and when it had assumed this form it should be communicated to Italy but in discussion with the other Allies it had been felt that Italy was not a full Ally till she had declared war on Germany. That was constantly expected and we waited for that date.

103. (*Balfour to Rodd, 25 April 1917, no. 748(D), F.O. 371/3043/ 1142*)

You should make the following communication to the Italian Minister for Foreign Affairs.

The War Cabinet have had under consideration the claims put forward by the Italian Government, under Article 9 of the Treaty of April 26th, 1915, to an equitable share of territory in the region of the Mediterranean adjoining the Province of Adalia, in the event of the complete or partial partition of the territories of Turkey in Asia.

Although the partition of these regions is one of the aims of the Allies in this war it is still far from realisation. Nevertheless subject to the consent of the Russian Government the War Cabinet agree conditionally to the zones of occupation and of interest respectively to be attributed to Italy, as defined in the Conference held at St. Jean de Maurienne on the 19th April as shown in the map. It is understood by the War Cabinet that if at the time when peace is declared the total or partial possession of the territories contemplated in the agreements come to between Great Britain, France, Italy and Russia, as to the disposal of part of the Ottoman Empire cannot be fully accorded to one or more of these Powers, then the interests of the Powers concerned will be again taken into equitable consideration having regard to the efforts made by each of the Powers.

The War Cabinet desire, however, to point out to the Italian

Government that the allocation to Italy of such large territories of the Ottoman Empire can hardly be regarded as justified by the effort hitherto made by Italy in the war as compared with the sacrifices already made by Great Britain, France and Russia, more particularly in their conflict with Turkey, in which no Italian forces have so far taken part.

While a considerable French Naval and Military force co-operated with British ships and troops in the attacks on the Dardanelles, Great Britain has during the past $2\frac{1}{2}$ years maintained a force of more than 300,000 men in operations undertaken against the Turks on the confines of Egypt and in Mesopotamia, while Russia, during the same period, has carried on a successful campaign in Eastern Asia Minor, and inflicted serious losses upon Turkey of territory, men and material. The exhaustion of Turkey, which alone could render such a partition as now contemplated possible will, if realised, be chiefly due to efforts of the Allies not shared by Italy. Under these circumstances, the War Cabinet strongly urge the Italian Government to make an increased effort to co-operate with the Allies against the common enemy, and they trust that they will understand that the achievement of Italian aspirations in Asia Minor must be conditional on such an effort being made.

The War Cabinet also make a reservation to their assent to the eventual cession of Smyrna that the port shall be free.

Zionism

104. (*War Cabinet 245, 2 October 1917, Cab/23/4*)

With reference to War Cabinet 227, Minute 2, the Secretary of State for Foreign Affairs stated that the German Government were making great efforts to capture the sympathy of the Zionist Movement. This Movement, though opposed by a number of wealthy Jews in this country, had behind it the support of a majority of Jews, at all events in Russia and America, and possibly in other countries. He saw nothing inconsistent between the establishment of a Jewish national focus in Palestine and the complete assimilation and absorption of Jews into the nationality of other countries. Just as English emigrants to the United States became, either in the first or subsequent generations, American nationals, so, in future, should a Jewish citizenship be established in Palestine, would Jews become either Englishmen, Americans,

Germans, or Palestinians. What was at the back of the Zionist Movement was the intense national consciousness held by certain members of the Jewish race. They regarded themselves as one of the great historic races of the world, whose original home was Palestine, and these Jews had a passionate longing to regain once more this ancient national home. Other Jews had become absorbed into the nations among whom they and their forefathers had dwelt for many generations. Mr. Balfour then read a very sympathetic declaration by the French Government which had been conveyed to the Zionists, and he stated that he knew that President Wilson was extremely favourable to the Movement.

Attention was drawn to the contradictory telegrams received from Colonel House and Justice Brandeis (Papers G.T.-2015 and G.T.-2158).

Mr. Montagu urged strong objections to any declaration in which it was stated that Palestine was the 'national home' of the Jewish people. He regarded the Jews as a religious community and himself as a Jewish Englishman. He based his argument on the prejudicial effect on the status of Jewish Britons of a statement that His Majesty's Government regarded Palestine as the national home of Jewish people. Whatever safeguarding words might be used in the formula, the civil rights of Jews as nationals in the country in which they were born might be endangered. How would he negotiate with the peoples of India on behalf of His Majesty's Government if the world had just been told that His Majesty's Government regarded his national home as being in Turkish territory? He specially urged that the only trial of strength between Zionists and anti-Zionists in England had resulted in a very narrow majority for the Zionists, namely, 56 to 51 of the representatives of Anglo-Jewry on the Conjoint Committee. He also pointed out that most English-born Jews were opposed to Zionism, while it was supported by foreign-born Jews, such as Dr. Gaster and Dr. Herz, the two Grand Rabbis, who had been born in Roumania and Austria respectively, and Dr. Weizmann, President of the English Zionist Federation, who was born in Russia. He submitted that the Cabinet's first duty was to English Jews, and that Colonel House had declared that President Wilson is opposed to a declaration now.

Lord Curzon urged strong objections upon practical grounds. He stated, from his recollection of Palestine, that the country was, for the most part, barren and desolate; there being but sparse cultivation on the terraced slopes, the valleys and streams being few, and large centres of population scarce, a less propitious seat for the future Jewish race could not be imagined. How was it proposed to get rid of the existing majority of Mussulman inhabitants and to introduce the Jews in their place? How many would be willing to return and on what pursuits would they engage?

To secure for the Jews already in Palestine equal civil and religious rights seemed to him a better policy than to aim at repatriation on a large scale. He regarded the latter as sentimental idealism, which would never be realised, and that His Majesty's Government should have nothing to do with it.

It was pointed out that during recent years before the War, Jewish immigration into Palestine had been considerably on the increase, and that several flourishing Zionist colonies were already in existence.

Lord Milner submitted an alternative draft declaration, as follows:

'His Majesty's Government views with favour the establishment in Palestine of a National Home for the Jewish Race, and will use its best endeavours to facilitate the achievement of this object; it being clearly understood that nothing shall be done which may prejudice the civil and religious rights of the existing non-Jewish communities in Palestine, or the rights and political status enjoyed in any other country by such Jews who are fully contented with their existing nationality and citizenship.'

The War Cabinet decided that—

Before coming to a decision they should hear the views of some of the representative Zionists, as well as of those who held the opposite opinion, and that meanwhile the declaration, as read by Lord Milner, should be submitted confidentially to—

(*a*) President Wilson.
(*b*) Leaders of the Zionist Movement.
(*c*) Representative persons in Anglo-Jewry opposed to Zionism.

105. (*Cecil to Balfour, 24 October 1917, F.O. 371/3054/84173*)

I understand that consideration by the War Cabinet of the assurance to be given by His Majesty's Government to the Zionists is again being postponed. I beg respectfully to submit that this further delay will have a deplorable result and may jeopardise the whole Jewish situation. At the present moment uncertainty as regards the attitude of His Majesty's Government on this question is growing into suspicion, and not only are we losing the very valuable co-operation of the Zionist forces in Russia and America, but we may bring them into antagonism with us and throw the Zionists into the arms of the Germans who would only be too ready to welcome this opportunity. As Mr. Balfour is aware the German Press has already taken up the question of Zionism and the danger to Germany of allowing the Zionists to depend on the support of the Allies. We might at any moment be confronted by a German move on the Zionist question and it must be remembered that Zionism was originally if not a German at any rate an Austrian idea.

The French have already given an assurance of sympathy to the Zionists on the same lines as is now proposed for His Majesty's Government, though in rather more definite terms. The Italian Government and the Vatican have expressed their sympathy and we know that President Wilson is sympathetic and is prepared to make a declaration at the proper moment.

Information from every quarter shows the very important role which the Jews are now playing in the Russian political situation. At the present moment the Jews are certainly against the Allies and for the Germans, but almost every Jew in Russia is a Zionist and if they can be made to realise that the success of Zionist aspirations depends on the support of the Allies and the expulsion of the Turks from Palestine we shall enlist a most powerful element in our favour.

Mr. Tschlenoff, the Chief of the Russian Zionists, is now on his way to England and is likely to arrive shortly. Special facilities for his journey from Bergen have been granted to him. It is most desirable that the assurance from His Majesty's Government should be given before his arrival.

The moment this assurance is granted the Zionist Jews are prepared to start an active pro-Ally propaganda throughout the world. Dr. Weizmann, who is a most able and energetic propagandist, is prepared to proceed himself to Russia and to take charge of the campaign. Propaganda in America is also most necessary. I earnestly trust that unless there is very good reason to the contrary the assurance from His Majesty's Government should be given at once.

It has been contended that the feeling of the British Jews is against Zionism but I would call attention to the fact that within the last week 300 representative Jewish bodies have forwarded unanimous resolutions in favour of the movement.

106. (*War Cabinet 261, 31 October 1917, Cab/23/4*)

12. With reference to War Cabinet 245, Minute 18, the War Cabinet had before them a note by the Secretary (Paper G.-164) and also a memorandum by Lord Curzon (Paper G.T.-2406) on the subject of the Zionist movement.

The Secretary of State for Foreign Affairs stated that he gathered that everyone was now agreed that, from a purely diplomatic and political point of view, it was desirable that some declaration favourable to the aspirations of the Jewish nationalists should now be made. The vast majority of Jews in Russia and America, as, indeed, all over the world, now appeared to be favourable to Zionism. If we could make a declaration favourable to such an ideal, we should be able to carry on extremely useful propaganda both in Russia and America. He gathered that the main arguments still put forward against Zionism were twofold:

(*a*) That Palestine was inadequate to form a home for either the Jewish or any other people.

(*b*) The difficulty felt with regard to the future position of Jews in Western countries.

With regard to the first, he understood that there were considerable differences of opinion among experts regarding the possibility of the settlement of any large population in Palestine, but he was informed that, if Palestine were scientifically developed, a very much larger population could be sustained than had existed during the period of Turkish misrule. As to the meaning of the words 'national home', to which the Zionists attach so much importance, he understood it to mean some form of British, American, or other protectorate, under which full facilities would be given to the Jews to work out their own salvation, and to build up, by means of education, agriculture, and industry, a real centre of national culture and focus of national life. It did not necessarily involve the early establishment of an independent Jewish State, which was a matter for gradual development in accordance with the ordinary laws of political evolution.

With regard to the second point, he felt that, so far from Zionism hindering the process of assimilation in Western countries, the truer parallel was to be found in the position of an Englishman who leaves his country to establish a permanent home in the United States. In the latter case there was no difficulty in the Englishman or his children becoming full nationals of the United States, whereas, in the present position of Jewry, the assimilation was often felt to be incomplete, and any danger of a double allegiance or non-national outlook would be eliminated.

Lord Curzon stated that he admitted the force of the diplomatic arguments in favour of expressing sympathy, and agreed that the bulk of the Jews held Zionist rather than anti-Zionist opinions. He added that he did not agree with the attitude taken up by Mr. Montagu. On the other hand, he could not share the optimistic views held regarding the future of Palestine. These views were not merely the result of his own personal experiences of travel in that country, but of careful investigations from persons who had lived for many years in the country. He feared that by the suggested declaration we should be raising false expectations which could never be realised. He attached great importance to the necessity of retaining the Christian and Moslem Holy Places in Jerusalem and Bethlehem, and, if this were to be effectively done, he did not see how the Jewish people could have a political capital in Palestine. However, he recognised that some expression of sympathy with Jewish aspirations would be a valuable adjunct to our propaganda, though he thought that we should be guarded in the language used in giving expression to such sympathy.

The War Cabinet authorised—

The Secretary of State for Foreign Affairs to take a suitable opportunity of making the following declaration of sympathy with the Zionist aspirations:

'His Majesty's Government views with favour the establishment in Palestine of a national home for the Jewish people, and will use its best endeavours to facilitate the achievement of this object, it being clearly understood that nothing shall be done which may prejudice the civil and religious rights of existing non-Jewish communities in Palestine, or the rights and political status enjoyed by Jews in any other country.'

ZIONISM AND THE ARABS

107. (*To Wingate, 4 January 1918, no. 24, F.O. 371/3054/86526*)
Your telegram No. 1418 (of 31st December).

(I) The following formulas would be best.

(II) That the Entente Powers are determined that the Arab race shall be given full opportunity of once again forming a nation in the world. That this can only be achieved by the Arabs themselves uniting, and that Great Britain and her Allies will pursue a policy with this ultimate unity in view.

(III) That so far as Palestine is concerned we are determined that no people shall be subjected to another, but that in view of the fact

(a) That there are in Palestine shrines, Wakfs and Holy Places, sacred in some cases to Moslems alone, to Jews alone, to Christians alone, and in others to two or all three, and inasmuch as these places are of interest to vast masses of people outside Palestine and Arabia, there must be a special régime to deal with these places approved of by the world.

(b) That as regards the Mosque of Omar it shall be considered as a Moslem concern alone and shall not be subjected directly or indirectly to any non-Moslem authority.

(IV) That since the Jewish opinion of the world is in favour of a return of Jews to Palestine and inasmuch as this opinion must remain a constant factor, and further as His Majesty's Government view with favour the realisation of this aspiration, His Majesty's Government are determined that in so far as is compatible with the freedom of the existing population both economic and political, no obstacle should be put in the way of the realisation of this ideal.

In this matter it should be pointed out to the King that the friendship of world Jewry to the Arab cause is equivalent to support in all States where Jews have a political influence. That the leaders of the movement are determined to bring about the success of Zionism by friendship and co-operation with the Arabs, and that such an offer is not one to be lightly thrown aside.

The King should be urged to capture Medina.

LLOYD GEORGE REJECTS THE SYKES–PICOT AGREEMENT

108. (*War Cabinet 482A, 3 October 1918, Cab/23/14*)

Extract

The Prime Minister said he had been refreshing his memory about the Sykes–Picot Agreement, and had come to the conclusion that it was quite inapplicable to present circumstances, and was altogether a most undesirable agreement from the British point of view. Having been concluded more than two years ago, it entirely overlooked the fact that our position in Turkey had been won by very large British forces, whereas our Allies had contributed but little to the result. As an objection of detail he pointed out that if General Marshal were to advance to Mosul this place would be treated as though it were part of Syria and in the French sphere. He thought that the whole question ought to have been discussed at the War Cabinet before the Conference took place at the Foreign Office.

Lord Curzon pointed out that one ground for revising the Report was that Russia had been an important party to the agreement, and was now not in a position to fulfil her share of it.

Mr. Balfour said that the reason why he favoured an armistice with Turkey rather than a separate peace at the present time was precisely owing to the difficulties in regard to the Sykes–Picot Agreement, and the present discussion only confirmed his view. He pointed out that the Italians might be even more difficult to deal with in regard to Turkey than the French.

The Prime Minister said it would not be possible for the British to go on fighting the Turks simply because the French wanted Syria or Armenia or the Italians wanted Adalia. He felt very doubtful whether M. Clemenceau or M. Orlando would press the question, and he was inclined to sound them at his forthcoming Conference.

Mr. Balfour reminded the War Cabinet that the original idea had been that any territories that the Allies might acquire should be pooled and should not be regarded as the property of the nation which had won them. The theory had been that the fighting in one theatre of war, where there was little to gain, might be just as important a contribution to the cause of the Allies as much easier fighting in other theatres where great successes were achieved. He believed that some statement of this kind had been made.

Mr. Bonar Law confirmed this view and pointed out that the provisional arrangement with the French in regard to the West African Colonies had been decided by the Cabinet on these grounds, in spite of the objections of the Colonial Office.

Chapter 3

War Aims and Peace Terms

SITUATION IN AMERICA

109. (*Spring Rice to Grey, 21 July 1915, Cab/37/131/31*)

Extract

The elements of the situation as regards us are—

1. The monied interests are affected by our blockade. They desire to trade with Germany; we prevent them. Thus there is a solidarity of interests between them and Germany, which Germany is urging with all her skill. These interests are mainly—(*a*) the Packers, controlling the middle States; (*b*) the Cotton people, controlling the South and the Democratic party; and (*c*) the Oil interests, which have great influence in New York.

2. On the other hand, other monied interests are strongly affected by the war orders and are very anxious to maintain freedom of manufacture and export to the Allies. They are powerful in New England, where, however, we should in any case have many friends.

3. The Irish and German organisations, assisted by the Catholic Church, are working together and bringing very strong pressure to bear on Congressmen and Senators.

The Jews are, as a rule, with them, and are able through their financial and journalistic influence to help the Germans greatly. The political combination (unless the American citizens connected by race with the Allies are politically organised) is a very strong and formidable one, and greatly to be feared.

4. Congress will represent, as usual, not the nation, but the sectional interests alone, and it happens that the most prominent and influential members are under German influence as a rule. Therefore, although philosophically speaking the great bulk of the American people sympathise with the Allies, their pockets speak a different language. Most people want German trade, and are angry because we came in their way. Their present policy is to

bring pressure on the Administration to call Congress, and then when Congress is called they will urge the President to impose an embargo on arms and ammunition unless the Allies consent to allow cotton and meat to go freely into Germany. Opinions are divided as to whether this will succeed, but there is no doubt of the danger of the situation. If we are dependent on this people for supplies and for money, it is hard to avoid the conclusion that if blackmail is insisted on, some must be paid unless the price is too heavy. The best means would seem to be to insist firmly on our rights, and at the same time to offer some sort of compromise satisfactory to the threatened interests *i.e.,* to keep up the price of cotton by some sort of pre-emption. This is being considered.

I fear this letter is much too long, but the situation is not simple. To resume it, I can only repeat that if Germany insists on war she can have it. There are bounds to the patience of this people. But if she is conciliatory, and appeals to the American pocket, she can form a sort of alliance of important interests against us. The dollar against honour; and, after all, the passengers on the 'Lusitania' are dead, and the cotton people very much alive. Dead people have no votes and no pockets. We have not threatened either the honour or the lives of Americans, but we have threatened, and are threatening, their pockets. And whatever be the sentimental or moral sympathy of the mass of the people, we cannot afford to ignore this.

The same argument under similar cases would no doubt apply to our own people.

110. (*Spring Rice to Grey, 15 September 1916, Cab/37/155/20*)

Extract

The elections are now entering the critical stage, and it is evident that things are working up for trouble with the Allies or, at any rate, with England. I quite understand that we must maintain our belligerent rights, and that if we make war at all we must make it effectively. I would not dare to interfere in any way, even in a discussion of war measures. But I think it my duty to make it as clear as I can that from now on until the election the interest of both political parties, certainly of the political party now in power, is to have trouble with England. Germany seems to be counting on this, and to have made all her plans on the supposition that relations between the United States and Great Britain will be strained, and that the President can be induced to make an offer of mediation on the basis of an armistice with a partial withdrawal of the German troops.

There certainly seems to be an impression among our friends here that many of our measures are taken as much with the object of promoting our own trade at the expense of the trade of neutrals as for injuring the enemy. Lloyd George's speech is very much quoted as confirming this impression. There are also incidents which I have brought to your attention which give some support to the allegations of our enemies. It would be very dangerous for us if it appeared that our assurances with regard to our policy towards neutrals were not borne out in fact. I daresay many people are telling you, first, that the United States does not matter because she has no army or navy; second, that it does not matter what you do to her because she will in any case be your friend. With regard to the first, there is an immediate danger of the United States heading a league of neutrals. There is also the question of what is to come in the future. Who is to help us financially during and after the war? With whom will the United States have the closest financial and commercial relations? Second, it is not true that you can count upon the friendship of the people of the United States in any and every case. You will be very much misled if you believe this. You would draw a cheque which would not be honoured. Your account here is not of that nature. You cannot draw on it on demand. It can very easily be dissipated. Of course you will hear from Americans in London, and others, that the United States is in your favour by an enormous majority. That may be so now, but this situation could be changed by a single incident. Until the date of the election every effort will be made to bring the incident about, and to magnify it when made. Every effort will be made to damage our reputation and misconstrue our motives. We must be prepared for this; and although we were as chaste as snow and as pure as ice we should not escape calumny. Unfortunately, as I said above, certain incidents are occurring at the present moment which are being used greatly to our disadvantage. I think we should exercise the greatest possible care. We should also be prepared for the worst, because a serious crisis might possibly occur. It seems to me that as the President is empowered to use the armed forces of the Republic against the Allies under certain circumstances, we should, if the case arose, make an appeal to the

Bryan treaty and ask that the matter should be referred to a commission.

U.S. POLICY UNRELIABLE

111. (*Minutes on Spring Rice to Grey, 6 October 1916, no. 804, F.O. 371/2796/63430*)

I believe Mr. Root's strictures of President Wilson's policy are merited. I also believe that the tendencies which President Wilson's policy embodies are largely representative of the United States as a nation. I would like, if I may venture to do so with all respect, utter a word of warning against the danger of entrusting the United States with any large measure of influence over the affairs of other nations and over any machinery that may be devised for dealing with and settling international disputes.

The U.S. Government during this war has abundantly proved —what was not unknown to students of American policy before— that there is nothing so sacred in national and international law, no consideration of right and wrong, of honour, of duty to self-proclaimed ideals, of principle embodied in conventions over American signatures, that it is not subordinated, without a semblance of shame or hesitation, to the party calculations of a presidential election. We should at least be forewarned. We may be quite certain that questions which may affect the existence and the most cherished principles of government of nations, if they come before a tribunal over which American governments will have sway or influence, will be decided solely and shamelessly according to the exigencies of the party-game in American elections.

Though the above minute is expressed rather more emphatically than will commend itself to everyone I believe in substance it is true. The American constitution and still more the American lack of knowledge of European international affairs makes them act sometimes with a frivolity which renders them worse than useless as arbitrators in international disputes. It does not however unfit them for taking part in international conferences.

PEACE NEGOTIATIONS REJECTED

112. (*War Committee, 21 March 1916, Cab/42/11/6*)

SIR EDWARD GREY referred to conversations he had had with

Colonel House, who had recently visited England, France, and Germany. A record of these conversations had already been circulated to the Cabinet Ministers who were also members of the War Committee. The general tenor of this record had been that, according to Colonel House, President Wilson, if desired by Great Britain and France, was prepared to propose a peace Conference, and, if the proposal was accepted by the parties to the war, to conduct it in a manner generally sympathetic to the Allies. Further, if the Central Powers refused to take part in the Conference, or to agree to terms reasonably favourable to the Allies, there was every prospect that the United States would intervene on the side of the Allies. A telegram had now been received from Colonel House to the effect that President Wilson had read and confirmed Sir Edward Grey's record of these conversations. M. Briand had also made his own record of his conversations with Colonel House during the stay of the latter in Paris and he might also have heard from Colonel House or might raise the subject at Paris. There were two points on which Sir Edward Grey wished to consult the War Committee:

(a) What attitude should he adopt if M. Briand raised the question during his forthcoming visit to Paris?

(b) Ought we to sound M. Briand as to his views on the question?

It appeared to him that our attitude should depend very largely on the views of our naval and military prospects taken by the responsible naval and military advisers of the Government. If in the next six months, the allies were likely to be able to dictate their own terms to Germany or to improve considerably their military position it was certain that we could get better terms then with or without the intervention of the United States than could be obtained now, and it would be better not to consider President Wilson's proposals. But if there was a prospect of a deadlock at the end of six months, when he gathered our financial and economic power to meet the demands of our allies would be less than at present; or if there was any prospect of the weakening of the relative position vis-à-vis the enemy of the allies by (say) the defeat of one of the allies (Russia for example)—in either of these eventualities it might be worth while or even imperative to consult the French Government as to the expediency of making use of President Wilson's suggestion now. He presumed also that it would be considered if either France or Russia intimated that it could not continue the struggle.

He said he had felt that he must share his responsibility with the War Committee. He did not press for an immediate decision, but would like the First Sea Lord and the Chief of the Imperial General Staff to know what the situation was and if necessary be asked by the Ministers of the War Committee to express an opinion upon the prospects of the war.

MR. BALFOUR asked whether Colonel House had not stated that the offer would be repeated, and, if not convenient at the moment, might be taken advantage of at some later date.

SIR EDWARD GREY agreed that this was correct but the offer might not be renewed indefinitely.

THE PRIME MINISTER asked Sir William Robertson if he had anything to say at this stage.

SIR WILLIAM ROBERTSON said he was not in a position to give a definite statement as to our military prospects at present. He knew our own position but it was difficult to know or form a judgement as to that of our allies, particularly in the moral aspects of the question in regard to their endurance and staying power. He could give a better answer if he could discuss the matter with General Joffre. At present however all his own instincts were opposed to availing ourselves of Col. House's suggestion.

MR. BONAR LAW said that at the present time the only result of peace negotiations must be based on the *status quo* before the war, and in the present state of public opinion the Government could not enter into negotiations on such a basis, which would be equivalent to defeat for the allies.

THE PRIME MINISTER considered that the proposal ought to be put aside for the present. Personally he doubted whether President Wilson's position was strong enough to enable him to carry through this policy.

SIR EDWARD GREY thought President Wilson would have the support of the whole nation of the United States in a proposal to end the war by a Conference if the Allies agreed to it.

MR. BALFOUR said that at present the proposal was not worth five minutes' thought. No doubt, if carried out, it would get the President of the United States out of political difficulties. If he could bring about peace his prestige in the United States would be greatly enhanced.

SIR EDWARD GREY said that, so far as his information went hitherto, the French would not wish to avail themselves of this offer.

MR. BALFOUR asked whether there was any dark spot in the situation except money and ships?

MR. LLOYD GEORGE added the Russian military situation. He would like to know the views of the military advisers as to whether the Russian army could withstand a German attack in the spring.

SIR WILLIAM ROBERTSON said that according to his information the Russians themselves wished to take the offensive.

LORD KITCHENER said that he always felt some hesitation in accepting Russian estimates of their own strength, but he was satisfied that General Alexeieff felt confident of holding up the Germans on the Riga front.

MR. LLOYD GEORGE pointed out that the position of the Russian army in regard to munitions was not such as to justify hopes of a successful offensive.

MR. MCKENNA said that in regard to the financial position we were perfectly safe as to the American exchange situation until July. On the side of internal finances the position depended mainly on our maintenance of credit, and this in turn depended on our supplies of labour. If expenditure exceeds the means of paying, credit disappears. The assistance required for labour is not really very great. All that is required is time. The Minister of Munitions had rendered inestimable services in stimulating production by women's labour, and this process of dilution would be carried much further, though time was necessary, and the Army must not withdraw labour too rapidly.

MR. BONAR LAW pointed out that credit depended on success, and this could only be achieved by withdrawing the manhood of the country in sufficient volume to ensure success this year, which was inconsistent with Mr. McKenna's plea for a gradual withdrawal when the time required for military training was taken into consideration.

MR. MCKENNA questioned the soundness of this theory. He pointed out that although we had won no victories our credit was splendid.

THE PRIME MINISTER said that the discussion was now passing rather beyond the scope of Sir Edward Grey's point.

113. (*Grey to Buchanan, 15 May 1916, Cab/37/147/40*)

I had a long talk this morning with M. Miliukof, who came to see me.

He asked me what were our ideas about the future of Armenia.

I said our interest in the Armenians was that of philanthropy and sentiment. It would no doubt be welcome to people here if Russia gave an autonomy to Armenia, but we should not put forward any claims of our own. Our aspirations in Asia Minor did not go beyond a sphere of influence in Mesopotamia, which would not go far enough north to affect Russian interests.

M. Miliukof asked me whether I favoured an International Act for Poland, and what opinions were held here about Poland.

I said it was hardly for us to make suggestions about Poland. I hoped Russia would fulfil, in a liberal spirit, the proclamation of autonomy that she had issued at the beginning of the war. I was sure there would be disappointment here if that was not done. But I thought that, if matters which specially concerned one country and its internal affairs became the subject of an International Act, that Act was likely to remain a dead letter or to give rise to friction between the different parties to it, in which all sight was lost or obscured of the original purpose of the Act.

M. Miliukof told me that M. Sazonof wished the Slav element to be retained in Austria to neutralise the German element.

I said personally I had favoured the liberation of the Slav element. I did not much fear the absorption of the South German element of Austria in Germany, as it would tend rather to neutralise Prussian influence, but, as regards these Slav questions affecting Serbia, it was rather for Russia to take the initiative.

M. Miliukof asked me what was meant by 'crushing Prussian militarism', and whether we should impose direct limitation of armaments.

I said, of course, if the Allies dictated peace in Berlin they could impose what conditions they liked, but Prussian militarism would cease to dominate Germany if the German people were convinced that the war had been a mistake. Prussian military policy being entirely devoid of all moral right, its only justification was success, and if it was not successful I believed it would cease to dominate Germany.

M. Miliukof asked me whether we should not retake Heligoland, and what would happen to the German fleet.

I said these were things that could only be considered at a time of very complete victory. The one condition which we put, for the sake of honour and justice, in the first rank, was the full restoration of the independence of Belgium. France, I presumed, would put Alsace-Lorraine in the first rank as a question more important to her than German colonies. Russia, presumably, would put the possession of Constantinople and the Straits, and thereby an outlet to the sea, as her first great object.

M. Miliukof said this was so. Indeed, he had already begun to say so before I had expressed it.

I suggested that it would be time enough to consider other conditions of peace when we had reached a point at which Germany was prepared to concede these first elementary conditions. As to future reduction of armaments, I said, in reply to questions, that it had been found exceedingly difficult to secure this by direct limitation, but, if the effect of this war upon mankind was to produce a determination amongst nations to side against any Power which disturbed the peace by aggressive war, one of the consequences might be the reduction of the expenditure on armaments. To secure that, nations wanted to feel that they were secure from aggression, and that if aggression was made upon them they would have plenty of support.

WAR AIMS, 1916

114. (*General Staff Memorandum submitted in accordance with the Prime Minister's Instructions. Robertson, 31 August 1916, Cab/41/18/10*)

Extract

Although the end of the war is yet by no means in sight, negotiations for peace, in some form or other, may arise any day, and unless we are prepared for them we may find ourselves at a great disadvantage, not only as compared with our enemy but also as compared with our Allies. It is not unlikely that M. Briand already possesses very decided views on the subject, carefully worked out for him under his general direction by the clever people who serve him, and who do not appear on the surface of political life. At a hastily summoned council we should have no chance against him, armed with a definite policy to which he may beforehand, and unknown to us, have committed the Russians and perhaps other Powers of the Entente. If this should happen, the Germans might take advantage of it to drive in a wedge between us and the other Entente Powers, with the result that we might find ourselves without support in those claims which we may be compelled to make, more especially in regard to the disposal of the captured German Colonies. We need therefore to decide, without loss of time, as to what our policy is to be; then place it before the Entente Powers and ascertain in return what are their aims, and so endeavour to arrive at a clear understanding before we meet our enemies in Conference.

2. For centuries past—though unfortunately by no means continuously—our policy has been to help to maintain the balance between the Continental Powers, which have always been divided by their interests and sympathies into opposing groups. At one time the centre of gravity has been in Madrid, at another in Vienna, at another in Paris, at another in St. Petersburg. We have thwarted or helped to thwart, each and every Power in turn which has aspired to Continental predominance; and concurrently as a consequence we have enlarged our own sphere of Imperial ascendancy. As part of this traditional policy we have aimed at maintaining British maritime supremacy, and at keeping a weak Power in possession of the Low Countries. In more recent years a new preponderance has been allowed to grow up, of which the centre of gravity has been in Berlin, and the result of it is the present war.

3. It is submitted that the basis of peace negotiations must be the three principles for which we have so often fought in the past and for which we have been compelled to fight now, namely:

(*a*) The maintenance of the balance of power in Europe.
(*b*) The maintenance of British maritime supremacy, and
(*c*) The maintenance of a weak power in the Low Countries.

4. If and when these general principles, and such others as are deemed necessary, are accepted by His Majesty's Government it will be possible to formulate the conditions upon which, and upon which only, we would be prepared to negotiate. No useful purpose would be served by discussing these conditions until the general principles have been settled, but some of the many questions demanding examination may be mentioned by way of showing how important it is to commence investigation with as little delay as possible. It may be added that this paper is written mainly from a military standpoint, and in this connection it can-

not be too often remembered that the conditions upon which peace is concluded will govern, or at any rate ought to govern, the size and nature of the Army subsequently required by us.

5. If the balance of power in Europe is to be maintained it follows that the existence of a strong Central European Power is essential, and that such a State must be Teutonic, as a Slav nation, the only other alternative, would always lean towards Russia, which would accordingly obtain a preponderant position and so destroy the very principle which we desire to uphold. On the other hand, as Germany is the chief European competitor with us on the sea, it would be advantageous to make such terms of peace as would check the development of her navy and of her mercantile marine. In other words, it would be to the interests of the British Empire to leave Germany reasonably strong on land, but to weaken her at sea. The full extent to which His Majesty's Government have already been committed is not known to the General Staff, but apparently it is the intention to break up Austria-Hungary. By the Rumanian Political Convention a large part of Eastern Hungary will be transferred to Rumania; Italy will no doubt insist on retaining Trieste with Istria and some of the neighbouring districts; and Serbia is to be given part at least of Herzegovina, Bosnia and Slavonia. The chief problems to be determined are the disposal of Austria proper, of the Magyar districts of Hungary, of the Northern Slav provinces of Bohemia, Moravia and Galicia, and finally, whether there shall be access to the Adriatic from the north otherwise than through Italian or Serbian territory. It is clear that all these provinces cannot become independent states. Galicia may be absorbed in a new Polish kingdom, but Bohemia and Moravia on the one side and Hungary on the other will be difficult of disposal. Acting on the principle of maintaining a strong Germany it might be advantageous if Austria proper were incorporated in that Empire, more especially as thereby 10 millions South Germans would be brought in as a counterpoise to Prussia. The other alternative, which has the advantage of settling the question of the disposal of the various provinces, is to maintain a diminished Austria-Hungary, and in that case an Adriatic port, Fiume for choice, should be allotted to it. This new Austria-Hungary would very probably form a very close union with Germany, but such a union might be not altogether to our disadvantage on land as limiting the power of

Russia and the Slav States, and on sea as preventing the Mediterranean from becoming a French and Italian lake.

THE PEACE SETTLEMENT IN EUROPE

115. (*Memo. by Balfour, 4 October 1916, Cab/37/157/7*
Extract

The Prime Minister asked the members of the War Committee to express their views on the peace settlement; and the present paper is an attempt—a very tentative and halting attempt—to comply with this request.

Even the most tentative suggestions must, however, proceed upon some hypothesis with regard to the military position of the combatants at the end of the war. What this will be no human being can foresee with any assurance. But inasmuch as it is convenient to proceed upon a hypothesis which is clear and determinate, I shall assume in what follows, though merely for the sake of argument, that the Central Powers, either through defeat or exhaustion, have to accept the terms imposed upon them by the Allies.

Let me add this further preliminary observation. The number of questions which will have to be discussed at any Peace Conference is obviously very large. In what follows I desire to do no more than to offer some stray reflections upon the most important group of these questions—that which is concerned with the redistribution of population in the European area. By this limitation will be excluded not merely such subjects as the restriction of armaments, the freedom of the seas, and the revision of international law, but also Heligoland, the Kiel Canal, strategic modifications of frontiers,[1] and the extra-European problems connected with Asia Minor and Germany's Colonial Empire.

On some of these subjects I may perhaps trouble the Committee at a later date.

The principal object of the war is the attainment of a durable peace, and I submit that the best way of securing this is by the double method of diminishing the area from which the Central Powers can draw the men and money required for a policy of aggression, while at the same time rendering a policy of aggres-

---

[1] Of course such strategic modifications might involve transfers of population, which could not properly be described as negligible. But their object would not be to acquire territory, but to increase security by making frontiers more defensible.

sion less attractive by rearranging the map of Europe in closer agreement with what we rather vaguely call 'the principle of nationality'.

The second of these methods, if successfully applied, would secure many objects which are universally desired by the Allies. It would give Belgium her independence, restore Alsace and Lorraine to France, provide some kind of home rule for Poland, extend the frontiers of Italy, and establish a Greater Serbia and a Greater Roumania in South-East Europe. I should greatly like to see it applied to Bohemia also. To Bohemia Germanic civilisation is profoundly distasteful. The Czecs have been waging war against it for some generations, and waging it under grave difficulties with much success. Whether an independent Bohemia would be strong enough to hold her own, from a military as well as from a commercial point of view, against Teutonic domination—surrounded as she is at present entirely by German influences—I do not know; but I am sure the question deserves very careful consideration. If the change is possible it should be made.[1]

Now, a map of Europe so modified would not only carry out the second of the two methods of preserving peace which I have described above, but would also help to carry out the first. The resources of men and money on which the Central Powers could draw for purposes of aggressive warfare would be greatly diminished. Alsace-Lorraine, Austrian Poland, with (possibly) parts of German Poland, Transylvania, Italian Austria, Bosnia and Herzegovina would cease to be recruiting grounds for supplying German or Austrian armies; and the men of military age thus withdrawn from the Central armies would be added to the nations with which the Central Powers are now at war; thus, as it were, counting two on a division.

The populations thus transferred would, I suppose, be more than 20 millions. I take no account in this argument of the non-Italian population which Italy will no doubt obtain if the Allies are successful; nor do I discuss the uncontested zone coveted by Bulgaria. If the principle of nationality be rigidly applied, I suppose that, without doubt, Bulgaria ought to have it. Whether she deserves it, and whether, in view of Serbian sentiment, we can give it her, is quite another question.

[1] I presume that arrangements will be made by which the frontier of Bohemia would, to some small extent at least, become coterminous with the New Poland.

I conceive that this general scheme is, broadly speaking, what public opinion in this country would desire to see carried out. The point on which there might be most difference of opinion would perhaps be the fate of Poland—since the fate of Constantinople and the Banat is already settled so far as the Allies can settle it. Almost the only thing on which Russia and Germany seem to be agreed is that the status of Poland should be altered by the war, and that, while receiving some measure of autonomy, it should remain dependent upon one of its two great neighbours. But as to what the limits of the new Poland should be, and on which of its two great neighbours it is to be dependent, there is, it need hardly be said, a fundamental divergence of opinion between Petrograd and Berlin.

Looking at the Polish question from a purely British point of view, I should like to see the new State include not merely Russian Poland, but as much of Austrian and German Poland as possible. This, of course, is in strict accord with the two principles laid down earlier in the paper. But I should *not* like to see the old Kingdom of Poland restored. I should fear that the new Poland would suffer from the diseases through which the old Poland perished; that it would be a theatre of perpetual intrigues between Germany and Russia; and that its existence, so far from promoting the cause of European peace, would be a perpetual occasion of European strife.

Moreover, even if such a Poland were capable of playing the part of an efficient buffer State (which I doubt) I am not sure that a buffer State between Germany and Russia would be any advantage to Western Europe. If Germany were relieved of all fear of pressure from Russia, and were at liberty to turn her whole strength towards developing her western ambitions, France and Britain might be the sufferers; and I am not by any means confident that cutting off Russia from her western neighbours might not divert her interests towards the Far East to an extent which British statesmen could not view without some misgivings. The more Russia is made a European rather than an Asiatic Power the better for everybody.

I therefore conclude that the solution of the Polish question which would best suit our interests would be the constitution of a Poland endowed with a large measure of autonomy, while remaining an integral part of the Russian Empire—the new State or province to include not only all Russian Poland, but also Austria's and (part at least) of Prussia's share in the plunder of the ancient kingdom.

116. (*Memo. by R. Cecil, 6 November 1916, Cab/42/23/7*)

With reference to the memoranda circulated on the 1st November, relative to our dependence on the United States, the annexed memoranda originally drawn up by various Departments for the use of the Inter-departmental Conference which considered the subject, are now circulated for the information of the War Committee of the Cabinet.

R.C.

November 6, 1916.

[Treasury.

THE FINANCIAL DEPENDENCE OF THE UNITED KINGDOM ON THE UNITED STATES OF AMERICA

Of the 5,000,000*l*. which the Treasury have to find daily for the prosecution of the war, about 2,000,000*l*. has to be found in North America.

There is no prospect of any sensible diminution in this amount without a radical change in the policy and activities of the War Departments, both of this country and of the other Allies.

During recent months about three-fifths of the sums required have been obtained by the sale of gold and securities, and about two-fifths by loans. The former resources are nearly independent of any action that the American executive is able to take, except that the Assay Office could put practical difficulties in the way of the sale of the gold at a sufficient rate. But the extent to which such resources can be used in the future will be greatly inferior to what it has been recently, and they cannot be relied on to supply more than one-fifth of the total requirements during the next six months.

Thus, to the extent of four-fifths of their needs, the Allied Powers must depend upon the issue of public loans. A statement from the United States Executive deprecating or disapproving of such loans would render their flotation in sufficient volume a practical impossibility, and thus lead to a situation of the utmost gravity.

It is not necessary, however, that matters should go so far as an overt act of the executive, in order that the financial arrangements of the Allies should be prejudiced. Any feeling of irritation or lack of sympathy with this country or with its policy in the minds of the American public (and equally any lack of confidence in the military situation as interpreted by this public) would render it exceedingly difficult, if not impossible, to carry through financial operations on a scale adequate to our needs. The sums which this country will require to borrow in the U.S.A. in the next six or nine months, are so enormous, amounting to several times the entire national debt of that country, that it will be necessary to appeal to every class and section of the investing public.

It is hardly an exaggeration to say that in a few months' time the American executive and the American public will be in a position to dictate to this country on matters that affect us more nearly than them.

It is, therefore, the view of the Treasury, having regard to their special responsibilities, that the policy of this country towards the U.S.A. should be so directed as not only to avoid any form of reprisal or active irritation, but also to conciliate and to please.

J. M. KEYNES.

October 10, 1916.

Memorandum indicating Position of the Ministry of Munitions with reference to dependence upon Deliveries of certain Essential Munitions of War from U.S.A.

Guns

Of the total number of guns and howitzers ordered to meet the War Office programme, but not yet delivered, the proportion due from America is roughly as follows:

	From U.S.A. Per cent.
9·2-inch howitzers	50
8-inch	20
4·5-inch	25
18-pr.	20
13-pr.	100

Shells

The proportion of the whole shell programme due to come from U.S.A. by the 31st December is as follows:

	From U.S.A. Per cent.
Large shell: 15-inch, 12-inch, 9·2-inch, 8-inch and 6-inch	30
Medium shell: 60-pr., 4·7-inch, and 4·5-inch .	8
Small shell: 18-pr. and 13-pr.	15

N.B.—It is expected that in 1917 the number of small shell to be obtained from U.S.A. will be decreased very substantially; on the other hand, the weekly delivery of large shell from U.S.A. is expected to rise in 1917 to 33 per cent. of the whole programme.

Shell Components

The position with regard to some of the most important of these for the period from the 1st October to the 31st December is as follows:

	Per cent.
Fuzes (proportion of whole supply to come from U.S.A.)	30
Cartridge cases (proportion of whole supply to come from U.S.A.)	10
Primers (proportion of whole supply to come from U.S.A.)	10
Shell forgings (proportion of whole supply to come from U.S.A.):	
12-inch	25
9·2-inch	25
8-inch	20
6-inch	5
4·5-inch	7

N.B.—In 1917 it is expected that the supply of cartridge cases from U.S.A. can be very substantially decreased; it is probable that the supply of fuzes will be reduced; the supply of primers from U.S.A. will probably cease; the supply of forgings will probably have to be maintained at the present level at least.

Rifles

We are still expecting to receive on our contracts 1,350,000 rifles of U.S.A. manufacture, but are endeavouring to cancel a larger number which would be delivered too late to be of much use.

117. (*Memo. by Lansdowne, 13 November 1916, Cab/37/159/32*)
Extract

The members of the War Committee were asked by the Prime Minister some weeks ago to express their views as to the terms upon which peace might be concluded. I do not know whether there has been a general response to this invitation, but the only reply which I have seen is one written last month by the First Lord of the Admiralty, in which he deals at some length with the problems which might have to be discussed at any Peace Conference. Mr. Balfour observes truly that these questions cannot be profitably examined except upon an agreed hypothesis as to the military position of the combatants at the end of the war, and he proceeds to assume, though merely for the sake of argument, that the Central Powers, either through defeat or exhaustion, have to accept the terms imposed upon them by the Allies.

I venture to suggest that the attention of the War Committee might with advantage be directed to a somewhat different problem, and that they should be invited to give us their opinion as to our present prospects of being able to 'dictate' the kind of terms which we should all like to impose upon our enemies if we were in a position to do so.

We are agreed as to the goal, but we do not know how far we have really travelled towards it, or how much nearer to it we are likely to find ourselves even if the war be prolonged for, say, another year. What will that year have cost us? How much better will our position be at the end of it? Shall we even then be strong enough to 'dictate' terms?

It seems to me almost impossible to overrate the importance of these considerations, because it is clear that our diplomacy must be governed by an accurate appreciation of them.

We have obtained within the last few days from the different Departments of the Government a good deal of information as to the situation, naval, military, and economic. It is far from reassuring.

What does the prolongation of the war mean?

Our own casualties already amount to over 1,100,000. We have had 15,000 officers killed, not including those who are missing. There is no reason to suppose that, as the force at the front in the different theatres of war increases, the casualties will increase at a slower rate. We are slowly but surely killing off the best of the male population of these islands. The figures representing the casualties of our Allies are not before me. The total must be appalling.

The financial burden which we have already accumulated is almost incalculable. We are adding to it at the rate of over 5,000,000*l*. per day. Generations will have to come and go before the country recovers from the loss which it has sustained in human beings, and from the financial ruin and the destruction of the means of production which are taking place.

All this it is no doubt our duty to bear, but only if it can be shown that the sacrifice will have its reward. If it is to be made in vain, if the additional year, or two years, or three years, finds us still unable to dictate terms, the war with its nameless horrors will have been needlessly prolonged, and the responsibility of those who needlessly prolong such a war is not less than that of those who needlessly provoked it.

Many of us, however, must of late have asked ourselves how this war is ever to be brought to an end. If we are told that the deliberate conclusion of the Government is that it must be fought until Germany has been beaten to the ground and sues for peace on any terms which we are pleased to accord to her, my only observation would be that we ought to know something of the data upon which this conclusion has been reached. To many of us it seems as if the prospect of a 'knock out' was, to say the least of it, remote. Our forces and those of France have shown a splendid gallantry on the western front, and have made substantial advances; but is it believed that these, any more than those made in 1915 with equally high hopes and accompanied by not less cruel losses, will really enable us to 'break through'? Can we afford to go on paying the same sort of price for the same sort of gains?

118. (*Memo. by Grey, 27 November 1916, Cab/37/160/20*)

There is much in Sir William Robertson's Paper[1] which moves me to sympathy and even admiration. I am especially in sympathy with the plea that sacrifices should be required of every member of the community in the common interest; and I long to see this done, particularly by a food ration, which shall prevent waste, husband our resources, and add to the endurance of the community as a whole.

[1] Not printed. Dated 24 November 1916, copy in Cab. 37/160/15.

But there are two things in his Paper which need a reply:

1. The first is that: 'Since the war began, diplomacy seriously failed to assist us with regard to Bulgaria and Turkey.'

Diplomacy in war is futile without military success to back it. In time of war, military success is to diplomacy what heavy artillery, with plenty of munitions, is to an army in the field. Till the offensive began on the Somme this year, diplomacy has had to strive without the essential condition of military success, which was necessary to secure results. It has been required to exert the maximum pressure of blockade upon Germany, without giving offence to neutrals; a most delicate and difficult task, which, thanks to Lord Robert Cecil and his Department, has been achieved with, I believe, the maximum of success that was possible without a disastrous quarrel with the neutrals; but a task most difficult when things were going against the Allies in military operations, and when the neutrals believed that Germany was going to win.

As to Bulgaria and Turkey, is it seriously contended that diplomacy could have prevented the 'Goeben' and 'Breslau' from getting to Constantinople? Once there the situation was hopeless, unless the Allies could obtain military successes that would make the Turks doubt of an ultimate German victory. Diplomacy, in the person of Sir Louis Mallet, did most skilfully all that was possible to delay the entry of Turkey into the war. But, in face of the great German successes in Belgium and France, which were only stopped and not cancelled by the Battle of the Marne, in face of the fall of Antwerp, and the Russian disaster in the region of Tannenberg, how could diplomacy have been expected to prevent Turkey from entering the war on the side of Germany? Once Turkey had entered the war, and the military situation had become more favourable to the Allies, we could only, as far as diplomacy was concerned, have detached Turkey from Germany by assuring Turkey of the possession of Constantinople, and this would have alienated Russia. Russia would never have stood five months of reverses in 1915, but for the hope of Constantinople. Even now, the assurance of it is absolutely essential to keep Russia up to the mark.

If it is contended that we should have done better to let Russia go on the chance of thereby detaching Turkey and Bulgaria from Germany after they had joined her, I will admit that diplomacy neglected a chance, though I think a doubtful chance. But, unless Sir William Robertson considers that we ought to have done this, diplomacy is not open to reproach.

As to Bulgaria, I understood throughout the war that the military authorities considered it impossible to send sufficient force into the Balkans to save Serbia if she were attacked both by the Central Powers and by Bulgaria, though we were prepared to help Greece to help Serbia. I therefore strove, in concert with the Allied Governments, to avert such an attack, by urging Serbia to make to Bulgaria the concessions that alone might have satisfied Bulgaria. Serbia either would not or could not see the danger and the necessity. I consider that, after the disastrous Russian reverses began in May 1915, Bulgaria would have joined the Central Powers even earlier than she did, but for the fact that she was deterred by the prospect or the possibility of a British success at the Dardanelles. When it was clear that this success was not forthcoming, Bulgaria joined the Central Powers, and diplomacy had as much chance of stopping her as a man with a walking-stick would have against a machine-gun.

Now let me put a converse case: Supposing the Foreign Office had urged upon the military authorities that, for diplomatic reasons, it was necessary that a General in the field, without heavy artillery and munitions, should continue to attack an enemy possessed of these advantages, or even should continue to defend positions that he thought it hopeless to hold without artillery and munitions; and supposing, when many months of effort on the part of the General to do what from the beginning he knew to be hopeless had resulted in failure and defeats, the Secretary of State for Foreign Affairs had circulated a memorandum in which he had coldly remarked 'The Army has seriously failed to assist us,' would not Sir William Robertson, taking the soldier's part, have felt the reproach to be not only ungenerous, but unfair and unjust?

At least once, while the attitude of Bulgaria was doubtful, I said how hopeless it was to do anything without military success; but rather than be open to the reproach of not trying, I did, in concert with the Allies, what could be done. It was thankless work; it has been criticised in newspapers that are both biassed and ignorant; but I do not think that it should be the subject of reproach from the War Office.

2. Sir William Robertson says, 'Our policy was sadly out of step with our military preparations before the war.'

I think that this opinion is due to a failure to appreciate what the political conditions, both inside this country and in Europe, were during the ten years that preceded the war. But this concerns other Departments as well as the Foreign Office, and I reserve the justification of my comment upon Sir William Robertson's statement for a separate memorandum when there is time to prepare one.

3. On the general question of peace, I will make the following reflections:

It is a question, not of sentiment nor of rhetoric, but of cold, hard fact. It should be examined as far as possible without emotion, certainly without sentiment, and without rhetoric. I think that everyone must feel that this is the temper in which Lord Lansdowne has examined it. I submit four observations as preliminary to a discussion:

(i) As long as the naval and military authorities believe that Germany can be defeated and satisfactory terms of peace can eventually be dictated to her, peace is premature, and to contemplate it is to betray the interests of this country and of the Allies. I accept, and my own judgment, for what it is worth, agrees with the opinion of Sir William Robertson and Sir Douglas Haig on the military prospect, provided the Allies can continue the war with full vigour through next year, or even for the first eight months of next year. There have been but three factors, of unknown value at the beginning of the war, which have ever made me doubt of our power to outlast Germany: they were the Zeppelin, the mine, and the submarine. The Zeppelin I believe, for offensive purposes, to be a complete failure, and I have ceased to be anxious about it. The mine, though a great inconvenience, appears to be so controlled by the Admiralty that it cannot be a decisive factor in this war. There remains the submarine, which is not mastered, and for the present seems to be getting more and more beyond our control. The military authorities have expressed their opinion as to the prospect of defeating Germany. It remains for the naval authorities, with perhaps the Board of Trade and Lord Curzon's Committee, to estimate whether a breakdown in shipping, sufficient to paralyse ourselves or the Allies, is likely to bring us to our knees before military operations in the field can bring Germany to her knees. The future of this country depends upon our giving a correct answer to this question.

(ii) As long as the military and naval authorities consider that the position of the Allies is likely to improve, even though it may not result in the ultimate and complete defeat of Germany, it is premature to make peace.

(iii) If the military and naval authorities were of opinion that the position of the Allies was not likely to improve, that a year hence we should be able to secure terms of peace not more favourable than at present, it is obvious that it would be better to wind up the war on the best terms now obtainable, unless another year of war, while leaving Germany equally strong in the field, would have weakened her internally more than the Allies and made her recovery more difficult than theirs.

(iv) If the time arrived when either the military or the naval authorities considered the chances to be that the situation would change in the course of the next few months to the disadvantage of the Allies and would progressively deteriorate, then it would be incumbent on the Governments of the Allies to wind up the war at once on the best terms obtainable, presumably through the medium of not unsympathetic mediation; and, if they did not do so, they would be responsible for future disaster to their countries.

We have had a Paper from Sir William Robertson and from Sir Douglas Haig on the military situation. We ought to have one from the naval authorities on the naval, and more especially on the merchant shipping, situation. They alone can estimate what the losses of merchant shipping are likely to be during the next few months, and how far these losses can be relieved by releasing ships now requisitioned. On this latter point, of course, the opinion of the military, as well as of the naval authorities, must be obtained. The President of the Board of Trade and Lord Curzon have already given valuable contributions to the prospect. We have had from the War Office (I think) some figures of shipping required for Salonika.

Without drawing any conclusions of my own—which, indeed, I have not at present sufficient data to do—I would venture to say, with all respect both to Lord Lansdowne and to Sir William Robertson, that Lord Lansdowne has performed a faithful and courageous act in submitting a Paper that obliges these questions to be examined.

119. (*Memo. by Cecil, 22 December 1916, Cab/37/162/12*)

Proposed Action in regard to American Note.[1]

Two lines of reply seem open to us in dealing with the American note. We may either inform the Americans that we are not prepared to make any statement as to terms of peace at present; that Germany was the aggressor, and it is for her, if she wishes to do so, to make any proposals in the direction of peace; and that we cannot admit in any way the doctrine that the aims of the belligerents are identical or similar, or that at this stage any good purpose would be served by admitting the intervention of a neutral Government.

The advantage of a reply on some such lines as that would be that it would emphasise the impossibility of considering any peace terms at present, and that it would put heart into the most determined parts of the Allied populations, and that it might stifle the protests of those who are inclined to look about for some means of putting a stop to the war.

On the other hand it has considerable disadvantages. It would certainly strengthen the position of the military party in Germany —they would be able to say with some plausibility that nothing remained for any decent German but to fight until he was killed. Then its effect on the Allied pacifists is at least doubtful; it might be just the reverse of what we wish; it might induce them to say that there is no hope for peace under the existing leadership, and the only thing is to insist on an immediate cessation of war. They might argue that if our terms were at all moderate or defensible we should have been only too glad to state them, and the fact that we refuse to state them shows that we know them to be utterly inacceptable to all moderate men. In this country particularly any irreconcilable attitude is apt to be unpopular. Englishmen do not mind doing violent things, but they like to persuade themselves that they are all the while models of moderation. I confess that I should be a little afraid of the effect of the above reply upon English public opinion. Its effect on neutral opinion could scarcely be anything but bad. There would no doubt be a certain

[1] Cecil's 'Note on the German Offer of Peace' is not printed as it is substantially similar. It will be found in W.C. 10 of 18 December 1916, App. IV, Cab. 37/161/38.

number of people in the Eastern States of America who would applaud anything which had the appearance of strength, but unfortunately the East of America is of very little political importance at present. The President was elected by the votes of the West and South, and it is scarcely too much to say that any action warmly applauded by Eastern capitalists is on that very account likely to be disapproved by Western opinion. The President himself would evidently be much disappointed, to put it mildly, and though, on reflection, I think it very unlikely that he would proceed to directly hostile measures against the Allies, undoubtedly he would look about for means to make them feel his displeasure. He would very possibly stir up again the agitation about the black list; he might go so far as to exercise the powers given to him in the last Session of Congress to hold up ships which refuse black-listed cargo. The mails question would be, of course, raised again, and he might then go so far as to enter into correspondence with the Swedish and perhaps the Dutch Governments with the object of enforcing their views as to the illegality of our blockade operations. Very little encouragement from America would make the Governments of Sweden and Holland impossible to deal with. When an atmosphere of irritation had been created by methods of this description, it is not at all impossible that the President would feel himself strong enough to proceed to much more drastic measures.

The other line which we might take would be to protest in the strongest way against the American assumption that both sides were fighting for the same objects; and state again with vigour and directness the origin and purpose of the war as we understand it. There might then be a reference to the American claim to humanity, with an expression of regret that it had so far produced little active results, enumerating the various occasions in which they had failed to interfere to check or punish German outrages or atrocities. We should then go on to say that the general objects of the war, as far as we were concerned, had often been stated, and were quite well known; that we had no objection to restate them in a somewhat fuller form. We should then reiterate that we required restoration and repatriation for Belgium and Serbia, the evacuation of all occupied territory of the Allies in France, Russia and Roumania. Beyond that we should say that we looked for some territorial settlement that would have a chance of permanence; that it would and must be based on principles accept-able to human feeling, such as nationality and security. On these grounds France would be entitled, in our view, to such a re-arrangement of her eastern frontier as would render impossible such an unprovoked attack as she had been the victim of in the present war, and also should have given back to her those provinces which were ethnologically French. In Russia we should look for the formation of a real Poland, including all Poles, whether before the war Germans, Russians, or Austrians, auto-nomous in government, but under the protection of the Russian Emperor.

The same principles would be applied to Italy, including such alterations of territory as would give to her security in the Adriatic. As to the South-East of Europe, which has long been the breeding-place of European disturbances, a settlement on sound national lines is, in our view, essential; the details of it cannot be laid down at present, but they would include the libera-tion of Slav peoples from German domination. Not less im-portant is the final settlement of the Turkish question, and when we came to this point I think we should speak very strongly. We should insist that Turkish action during the present war had made it finally impossible for her to be allowed to have under her control any population which was of other than Ottoman nation-ality, or allow her to remain as one of the European Powers. She must in fact be relegated to Asia. We should then explain that in our view, both on commercial and political grounds, it was essen-tial that Russia should have control of Constantinople, with proper safeguards for free navigation of the Bosphorus and Dardanelles.

Further than this we should explain that we could not go. To ask us to lay down terms of peace in detail would be, in the Prime Minister's phrase, to ask us to put our heads into a noose. The general principles we had explained in sufficient detail to make them quite clear. But the manner in which these principles should in each case be worked out and the subsidiary provisions neces-sary for reparation and indemnity we could not discuss until the time for peace came. And then we could add any necessary peroration as to our determination to continue the war.

Without expressing any final opinion as to the desirability of either of the two courses which I have sketched, I cannot help feeling that the second would give us an opportunity of explaining vigorously and effectively to the Americans and other neutral nations, as well as to our own people and the Germans, that our aims are really based on justice and liberty, and that when we use those phrases we have something definite in mind beyond mere verbiage. It would also enable us to put on a proper footing the Constantinople question, which will assuredly be one of our great difficulties in the near future.

As to the league of nations for the prevention of war, our course is tolerably clear, whatever line we adopt on other questions. We should express the utmost sympathy with the proposal, and should ask what was exactly meant by the promised support of the United States. Did it mean that the United States Government had the will and the power to give armed support to the decisions of any such league? And we should refer to Senator Stone's recent speech on the subject. We should further enquire whether the province of the league was to extend to the American continent, and profess our readiness to enter more fully into the subject when we had been satisfied on these points.

BALFOUR CRITICAL OF FRENCH WAR AIMS

120. (*Balfour to Bertie, 2 July 1917, no. 483, F.O. 371/2937/11293*)
In the course of a long conversation which I had with M. Cambon this afternoon, he introduced the subject of Alsace-Lorraine and the French terms of peace. It had been made a matter of comment, he said, that, in his speech in Glasgow last week, the Prime Minister had not referred to this subject, although the omission was remedied in Dundee. M. Cambon thought it well to insist quite explicitly that this was a matter on which no French Government, and certainly not the present French Government, could make any concessions. He then asked me to read a memorandum which had been given him for his guidance last January, while M. Briand was in office, but which M. Ribot had read and accepted as representing the views of M. Briand's successors. The document was a confidential one, supplied to M. Cambon as a guide in his conversation with me, and he was not empowered to leave me a copy. But the following are the points which, on a hasty perusal, seem to me most worthy of attention:

As regards Africa, the French expect to obtain, in the

Cameroons and Togoland, the area which we have provisionally handed over to them for purposes of administration.

In Europe they expect to get back the whole of Alsace-Lorraine, but with the frontier rectified in their favour, so as to coincide with that which existed before 1790, and not that which was fixed after 1815 by the Congress of Vienna.

Alsace and Lorraine constitute the only additions to existing French possessions which France desires in Europe, and the French are very particular to describe this, not as the acquisition of new territory, but as a restitution of old territory of which they have been unjustly robbed.

To Luxembourg, famous in the diplomacy that preceded the war of 1870, they make no claim of any sort; nor are they prepared to yield to the clamour of a section of their politicians who demand that the old ambitions of France should be revived, and that her frontier should be extended to the left bank of the Rhine. They do, however, desire to see the territory to the west of the Rhine separated from the German Empire and erected into something in the nature of a buffer State.

I said nothing to encourage this rather wild project, and I do not think that M. Cambon himself had much belief in it.

As regards Alsace-Lorraine, I expressed my own personal desire to see it restored to France in its entirety; nor, if the war ended in favour of the Allies, did I see any difficulty in the way, save one: I reminded him that the Allies had been announcing with unwearied iteration that a governing consideration in the allocation of territory was the wish of the inhabitants; and questions were frequently asked implying that the only conclusive method of determining what that wish was consisted in putting the question to the vote. I had some doubt as to what the result of such a plebiscite would now be in the case of the lost provinces of France.

M. Cambon evidently shared this doubt to the full. In fact, he gave me to understand that a solution of this question by plebiscite was not one that could be accepted. The French had been driven out of the area in large numbers, and large numbers of Germans had been introduced; and, although French character and sympathies would rapidly revive, no plebiscite taken immediately after the war could be relied on to give a fair verdict.

I asked him to supply me with a memorandum dealing with

this aspect of the problem, which was, I thought, destined to give some little trouble in the future.

GERMAN PEACE PROPOSALS

121. (*War Cabinet 238A, 24 September 1917, Cab/23/16*)

MR. BALFOUR informed the War Cabinet that definite approaches had been made by Germany for discussion on terms of peace. He had not yet informed his colleagues of these, as Mr. Bonar Law had considered that the Prime Minister, who was away at the time, should be informed before the question was discussed at the War Cabinet. The approaches had been made both to the French and to ourselves, although the latter had been of a more official character.

The German approaches to the French, which had been communicated to him most secretly by M. Cambon, had been made through the intermediary of a certain von Lancken. This individual had been first secretary to the German Embassy in Paris before the war, and had subsequently been sent to Belgium where he was supposed to have played a somewhat sinister part in the Nurse Cavell affair. Under orders from von Kühlman, von Lancken had made approaches to M. Briand through a lady who was half French and half German and personally acquainted with M. Briand, who had quite properly communicated the information to M. Painlevé, who had forwarded it to Mr. Balfour through M. Cambon, the French ambassador. The suggested terms were so favourable to the British and French as to arouse suspicion that their object must be sinister. The suggested terms included the following:

> Cession of Alsace-Lorraine by Germany
> Restoration of Serbia
> Territorial Concessions to Italy
> Colonial Concessions to Great Britain
> Restoration of Belgium.

The significant feature in the terms however was that neither Russia nor Roumania were referred to. M. Cambon had expressed the apprehension that, if once it became known in France that the the cession of Alsace-Lorraine was included in the offer, it would be very difficult to keep France in the war.

If Russia and Roumania thought that we were discussing a

peace on these lines, they would probably themselves make a separate peace at once.

Beyond the above no details had been given and the available information was absolutely vague. However, this approach was of an entirely informal character.

The approach to us, Mr. Balfour continued, was through a formal channel, having been sent by the British Ambassador at Madrid, who himself received it from the Spanish Government who had received it from Germany through official channels, it was said from a most exalted quarter. Mr. Balfour was quite confident that it constituted a genuine approach. In this case no indication was given of Germany's terms and the message merely indicated that the German Government would like to discuss terms of peace and inquired whether the British Government would be willing to listen to them. Mr. Balfour said that he had sent a Memorandum to the Prime Minister giving his own views of what we ought to do. It was absolutely necessary for us to give some reply, and the question was what that reply should be. In this aspect our case differed from that of M. Briand, who was not bound to reply at all. Mr. Balfour's own view was that we should adopt a policy of absolute candour and openness towards our larger allies. The alternatives open to us were as follows:

(a) To decline to listen to the German proposals.
(b) To accept on our own behalf alone.
(c) To accompany an acceptance by stating that we could only consider the proposals in consultation with our five largest allies.

If the latter course, which he himself recommended, was adopted, he proposed to summon the ambassadors of France, Russia, the United States, Italy and Japan, and inform them of the action he intended to take, namely that we were willing, to hear what offer Germany was prepared to make.

MR. BONAR LAW suggested that in any case action should be postponed until the Prime Minister had had a talk with M. Painlevé. Russia as an ally was now practically useless. We could not tell what might happen in Russia the day after tomorrow. In these circumstances he felt that we ought not entirely to reject the German proposal until the question of the effect on the military situation of Russia dropping out of the war had been investigated.

THE PRIME MINISTER said that the first thing we ought to do was to ascertain what the position would be if Russia dropped out. For this reason he had seen the Chief of the Imperial General Staff, who hoped to be in a position to give him a considered opinion on this subject later in the day, when the War Cabinet might meet again. If Sir William Robertson should inform the War Cabinet that the position in the event of a Russian collapse would be hopeless so far as our projects of achieving our main desiderata by force of arms are concerned, then we should have to consider whether with Russia out of the war we could achieve our object by means of a blockade. Finally we should have to form an opinion as to the probability of a Russian collapse, a matter on which the War Cabinet was as competent to form an opinion as anyone else.

If we came to the conclusion that the Soviet was going to destroy our prospects of success, then Russia ought to pay the penalty. We could then consider the terms offered to the French in a different light. He had read in the *Daily Chronicle* that the Leninites were proposing peace on terms practically identical with those proposed to M. Briand.

He himself felt no doubt that Germany proposed to acquire Courland and Lithuania, and to make some arrangement in regard to Poland as her spoils of war. The strength of her attacks on the Riga front indicated this.

Before we could discuss the question with our allies at a Conference we must ascertain what the Germans had to propose. He did not agree therefore, in the proposal to communicate with the allies at this stage.

SIR EDWARD CARSON suggested that the best plan would be, not to consult or communicate with our allies at the moment, but to ask Sir Arthur Hardinge to obtain details and to add that we would then discuss the matter with our allies, if there was anything to lay before them. Our first step should be to ascertain whether the Germans meant business.

MR. BARNES and GENERAL SMUTS agreed in this view and suggested that we were entitled to learn the nature of the offer before we ever discussed it with our allies.

L[ORD] CURZON after reading an excerpt from Sir Arthur Hardinge's telegram, expressed similar views.

THE PRIME MINISTER was inclined rather to pursue the informal negotiation opened with the French Government, which could be repudiated, if necessary.

SIR EDWARD CARSON urged that, if anything were said by our allies afterwards, we ought to be in a position to show that we had discussed nothing behind their backs. We should merely hear what the Germans had to say.

MR. BALFOUR said that he himself differed from the view expressed by the majority of the War Cabinet, that we should be on the thinnest ice, if we put Germany in a position to say that we had discussed the question without first consulting our allies.

LORD MILNER suggested that the Prime Minister should inform M. Painlevé of the German approach, and we should reply to Spain that we were prepared to learn what they had to say, but we were not prepared to discuss their proposals without consultation with our allies.

THE PRIME MINISTER suggested that we might instruct Sir Rennell Rodd, who was in England, to inform Baron Sonnino personally on his return.

SIR EDWARD CARSON repeated his view that our reply should be that we are willing to hear what the German terms are, and if business is intended, to communicate with our allies.

THE PRIME MINISTER pointed out that this would involve communicating with Russia at the very moment when an important section in that country (the Bolsheviks) were discussing whether they should abandon us.

MR. BONAR LAW pointed out the impossibility of discussing every point with five great Powers. The moment you told them what you are doing they would all want to have a voice.

MR. BALFOUR urged that we should be in a very difficult position if it were to leak out that we had acted without consulting our allies. The German newspapers were already saying that we had entered into negotiations for peace.

MR. BONAR LAW suggested that we should not take umbrage if France, in corresponding circumstances, were to act as we proposed to do.

LORD CURZON reminded the War Cabinet that any of the allies were entitled to hear any proposal.

MR. BARNES suggested that, if Russia got to know, she would probably use it as a pretext to get out of the war.

THE PRIME MINISTER said that it was no use to regard the present situation as the same as it was when we entered into agreement with Russia. The fact was that Russia had let us down. Some of the most important influences in Russia were discussing the possibility of a separate peace on the basis of the surrender of the western provinces.

[At this point there was a discussion on the subject of the ethnography of Courland and Lithuania, Lord Milner pointing out that the population was Slavonic, but not Russian.]

THE PRIME MINISTER pointed out that, if Germany secured Courland and Lithuania, two great Empires would emerge from the war, namely the British Empire and Germany.

LORD MILNER said it would mean Germany coming out of the war more powerful than she entered it, and another war in 10 years' time.

MR. BONAR LAW said that, if there were reasonable grounds for holding out, he would do so.

GENERAL SMUTS suggested that Courland, Lithuania and Poland should be formed into buffer states.

MR. BALFOUR called attention to a review in *The Times* of even date of a book by the German Deputy Chief of Staff in which it had practically been admitted that Germany could not win the war, and another war had been forecasted.

THE PRIME MINISTER regarded this book as an attempt to prepare German public opinion for a bad peace.

MR. BARNES expressed himself in favour of holding out.

THE PRIME MINISTER agreed, but only provided that the Chief of the Imperial General Staff could advise that we could smash Germany, with Russia out of the war and the blockade gone. Germany would be able to supply herself in course of time with wheat, copper, tungsten, and other metals. Nevertheless, it was clear that Germany was not satisfied with the prospect of a continuation of war on that basis and was prepared to concede something to secure peace.

SIR EDWARD CARSON urged the importance of the economic weapon, and called attention to Herr Erzberger's speeches, and other evidence of Germany's apprehensions on this head. It was very important, he pointed out, to complete our organization in this respect.

He himself was opposed at this stage to telling any of our allies of the German advances—even M. Painlevé.

THE PRIME MINISTER considered that we must tell M. Painlevé particularly after he had been so frank with us.

MR. BALFOUR agreed, but wished to tell the American Ambassador (Mr. Page) also. President Wilson was particularly interested in all matters connected with terms of peace.

THE PRIME MINISTER did not consider this necessary. At present we wanted the U.S.A. to fight and there was no need to discuss questions of peace with them.

SIR EDWARD CARSON was in favour of telling all the allies or none.

Conclusion

The Prime Minister was authorized to inform M. Painlevé of the German proposal, and to tell him that the War Cabinet were disposed to receive a communication if sent.

It was generally agreed that we could not refuse to hear what the German proposals were, but all action in regard to the reply to be made, and as to any communication with our allies, other than France, was postponed until after the Prime Minister's conversation with M. Painlevé.

122. (*War Cabinet 239A, 27 September 1917, Cab/23/16*)

THE PRIME MINISTER said that he had ascertained from M. Painlevé during a conversation at Boulogne on the previous day that the German peace approach to France is serious. The suggestion was that M. Briand should meet in Switzerland either an ex-Chancellor, the present Chancellor, or some more exalted person. M. Painlevé had said that M. Briand had fluctuated somewhat in his reports of what terms the Germans were prepared to offer. At one moment he had said that they were willing to give up everything the allies desired in the west—e.g. Belgium and Alsace-Lorraine. Afterwards he had said that they were willing to *discuss* Alsace-Lorraine. One of the most serious considerations was that M. Briand was in favour of entering into this negotiation. M. Painlevé and M. Ribot however were both opposed to it. What M. Painlevé seemed to fear was not that the approach was NOT *bona fide* but that it was *bona fide*. He evidently doubted whether France would continue fighting if it was known that the Germans had offered both nine-tenths of Alsace-Lorraine and the whole of Belgium. The Prime Minister expressed similar doubts as to whether in the event of such an offer this country would continue the war [illegible insertion] and Sir Edward Carson expressed similar doubts. [illegible marginal insertion.]

MR. BALFOUR expressed the view that, if the British people thought that Germany would be left stronger as a result of the peace, they would be ready to fight on.

MR. BARNES shared this view and considered that the British people would continue the war in order to prevent Germany from gaining such accession of strength as would enable her to undertake a fresh war in a few years' time with better prospects of success. The public however would want to know what they were fighting for. They would not be prepared to continue the war in order to win certain islands in the Adriatic for Italy.

THE PRIME MINISTER agreed. France, he pointed out, is not fighting now, as he had ascertained in his visit to France. Originally an attack was to have been made by the French on September 1st. Then it was postponed until Sept. 25th or 26th. M. Painlevé had, at the beginning of his conversations, been under the impression that it was to take place on September 26th, but later on had told him it had been postponed until October 10th. He had added that this had been agreed between General Pétain and Field Marshal Sir Douglas Haig. The latter, however, whom the Prime Minister had seen later, had absolutely denied this. No doubt when Oct. 10th arrived some reason for a further postponement would be found, and so on until the end of the fighting season.

During his conversations M. Painlevé had seemed almost wholly pre-occupied with the question that M. Briand should not make peace, with the withdrawal of some 300,000 men from the French army for agriculture.

The Prime Minister then mentioned that another point he had ascertained in France was that it was very doubtful whether we could capture the Clercken Ridge.

Having regard to the circumstance discussed above and the general situation, the Prime Minister felt that it was very unwise to make any unconditional declaration, such as Mr. Asquith had just made in his speech for the War Aims Committee at Leeds, to the effect that we should not make peace until the Germans were prepared to surrender the territory they had occupied in Russia, which he had treated in precisely the same manner as the occupied territory in France. When we came to consider peace terms reference must be had to the question whether France was doing her share of the fighting.

MR. BALFOUR considered that there was no harm in this statement, made by one outside the Government. He pointed out that Mr. Asquith, if asked, would probably say that every speech has certain implied assumptions, and that the assumption in this one was that Russia would continue to fight.

SIR EDWARD CARSON pointed out that the War Aims Committee was one on which the Government was represented, and it would be generally assumed that Mr. Asquith could therefore not make this statement without authority.

THE PRIME MINISTER said that France would not be prepared to go on fighting for Russia, if the Russians would not fight for themselves. We might have to say to Russia, 'We will go on fighting for you, as long as you will fight for yourselves.'

LORD MILNER was doubtful whether it would be wise to say this.

GENERAL SMUTS considered that, though it was difficult, we ought somehow to find a means of defining our position.

THE PRIME MINISTER reminded the War Cabinet that M. Tereschenko had announced his intention of coming over for a conference. This might be a good opportunity for some plain speaking. Field Marshal Haig and General Robertson had on the previous day at Sir Douglas Haig's Headquarters expressed the view that we ought to talk very plainly to our allies about the necessity for fighting harder. General Robertson had said outright that, if Russia went out of the war, we could not inflict military defeat on Germany, and he had asked Field Marshal Haig to send his considered opinion on this subject. He had also arranged for the Field Marshal to see General Pétain in order to put pressure on him on the subject of his offensive.

LORD CURZON said that the question of the effect of Russia going out of the war had two aspects, one military, and the other blockade. On the former he could claim no special knowledge. With respect to the blockade it had to be borne in mind that Russia was in so serious a state of disorganisation that probably 6 or 8 months would be required before Germany could sufficiently restore the situation to obtain any considerable amount of supplies.

MR. BALFOUR agreed that it would be a most serious blow if Russia went out of the war. We should then have to consider in conjunction with France and the United States of America whether we could not still make Germany's economic position very difficult.

He wished to emphasise that the danger of Russia going out would be enormously increased if it got about that we are prepared to make peace at her expense.

THE PRIME MINISTER agreed, but pointed out that this ought not to prevent the Cabinet from discussing the question amongst themselves. At any rate the Government ought to be careful not to commit themselves unintentionally or hastily to continue the war until the enemy was prepared to surrender the territory he had occupied in Russia whether Russia fought for that territory or not.

GENERAL SMUTS considered it clear that the Germans intended to make peace, if they could, at Russia's expense.

THE PRIME MINISTER raised the question of what the attitude of the United States of America would be.

MR. BARNES suggested that no great importance need be attached to their attitude, as they were not as yet doing very much in the war outside of financial assistance to the allies.

MR. BALFOUR pointed out that the U.S.A. was making a very great effort both in shipbuilding and in raising military forces.

LORD MILNER said that Germany would gain a great accession of strength, if she secured the occupied Russian provinces.

THE PRIME MINISTER thought that the American people would not continue fighting merely to prevent Germany from obtaining peace at the expense of Russia, when she declined to fight herself for her own possessions. The same was probably true of the British public.

LORD CURZON pointed out that it was not merely a question of the additional territory that Germany would acquire. Russia would become the vassal of Germany.

SIR EDWARD CARSON asked whether our own soldiers would be prepared to go on fighting? In the course of his recent visit to the front he had learned that there was great dissatisfaction among wounded men who had been sent back to the front. An expert in the censors' department had told him that the War Cabinet ought to have a digest of what was contained in the letters of men at the front that were stopped.

THE PRIME MINISTER said that an officer at the front had told him that the men, who for the first two years had never discussed such matters, were beginning to talk among themselves of what we are fighting for. They would fight for Belgium, but not for conquest, nor for Russia, unless Russia herself fought.

LORD CURZON said that these reports were not confirmed by the results of the censorship of the 'trick envelopes', which had recently been communicated to the War Cabinet by the Secretary of State for War.

[At this point there was some discussion as to the desirability of a conference between the allies, at which there should be some plain speaking. It was generally agreed that a very small Conference of one representative of each of the larger nations would provide the best opportunity.]

SIR EDWARD CARSON suggested that an attempt should be made to stretch our war aims. A start could be made from the *status quo* before the war and the necessary additions and limitations could be inserted.

MR. BALFOUR said that his own views differed but little from those he had presented to his colleagues in a Memorandum written two years ago. He attached great importance to the deprivation to Germany of any colonies, unless we could obtain guarantees that she would not break the peace, of which at present there appeared to be no prospect.

SIR EDWARD CARSON also attached importance to an examination by the War Cabinet of the internal conditions in this country.

THE PRIME MINISTER said that M. Painlevé had been willing that Great Britain should act as a post office in regard to the German peace offer through Madrid, and had undertaken to send a telegram on the subject.

MR. BALFOUR said that no telegram had yet been received. He himself still held the view that the proper course was to express our readiness to hear what Germany had to say, and to inform our allies that we had done so.

THE FUTURE OF ENEMY COLONIES

123. (*Memo. by Curzon, 5 December 1917, G.T. 182, Cab/24/4*)

Extract

Another question that is sometimes raised, though as it seems to me with singularly slender justification, is that of the ethical right of Great Britain or any other victorious Power to retain the colonies which she has won by conquest in war. The answer is simple. The right is precisely the same as that by which Germany acquired them in the first place, or if victorious would recover them now. It has been generally conceded that the higher standards of civilisation which have been developed by the white man have conferred upon him a general right of entry into the darker places of the earth where superstition and barbarism prevail. But this mission does not give an exclusive right of entry to any one nation or group of nations. Our right is not superior to that of Germany. But it is certainly no whit inferior, and in so far as the sentiment of the native populations is concerned, in parts of the world where, as in Africa, the two methods of government can be compared with each other, there is no cant in declaring that the British right has the sanction of a far greater measure of popular approval. When, therefore, the question is raised of deciding at a Peace Conference the fate of this or that territorial spoil of war by the votes of its inhabitants, while it is obviously impossible to have a plebiscite of Hottentots or Bantus, the decision, on the hypothesis of equality of rights, must obviously be influenced by a broad consideration of the character and results of the two governing systems.

Again, I have seen it argued that it may be desirable to purchase the good will of Germany in the future by making concessions which prudence would otherwise condemn. I ask the simple questions: 'Did the late Lord Salisbury by ceding Heligoland to Germany in Europe, or by yielding to her Dar-es-Salaam and the hinterland opposite Zanzibar in Africa, and deflecting the frontier line at every point to her advantage and our own detriment, conciliate her good will?' This war supplies the answer. I might also ask: 'Is Germany, in the event of victory, at all likely to make things pleasant for us?'

But we shall be told that the retention of these colonies is only another illustration of the land-grabbing proclivities of Great Britain and of the imperialistic aims with which she entered the war. The facts are in themselves a sufficient refutation of the latter charge, since the first authorisation of the Dominions' offensive was confined to the seizure and immobilisation of enemy wireless stations and bases, and it was not till we found the German possessions in Africa were used as a base of intrigue and offence against our own territories or dominions that we were driven to clear them of the enemy. How comes it that not only has British imperialism left untouched the weak colonial possessions of Belgium, Portugal and Holland, but that they actually find in it the main guarantee for their continued existence? And if British imperialism is to be denounced, with what face can it be proposed to re-enthrone German imperialism in its place? If it be a question of the two forms of imperialism, let the world judge. The truth is that the epithet 'imperialism', like the epithet 'capitalistic', has become one of the cant formulas of the doctrinaires of revolution; and the rescue of a subject people from cruelty and oppression, which is a virtue if achieved by a small people, becomes a crime if accomplished by a great Empire.

In this context the catchword of 'No annexation', which to many is endowed with so much attraction, may be thought to have a bearing on the African situation. What, however, does this formula mean? Does it signify that whatever any belligerent country possessed before the war, whether rightly or wrongly, is to be restored to it? Does it signify, for instance, that Armenia and Palestine are to go back to Turkey; that Arabia is to lose its tardily won independence; and that the African bushmen are again to acknowledge a German master? If so, the war will have been waged in vain, and millions of lives will have been sacrificed to stereotype the most shocking injustice. Or does it mean that the larger ambitions with which some Powers entered upon the war, *e.g.*, the desire of Russia for Constantinople, or of Italy for Dalmatia, shall be modified or abandoned? Even if there were not a great deal to be said for this solution, the logic of events will in any case enforce it; but may we not remark to the Germans, 'Que messieurs les assassins commencent'? Even so, it should be remarked that it is a very different thing to renounce that which you have not got and have no hope of getting, to surrender that which you have won by force of arms and hold in trust for future security. Or does the phrase only signify, as M. Tereschenko, when Foreign Minister of Russia, explained to the British Ambassador, a repudiation of 'the forcible occupation of any territory against the wishes of its inhabitants'? If so, the resettlement of the map of Africa will assuredly not be on German lines. Or do the words mean that there should be no actual incorporation of conquered territory in the dominions of the conqueror, but that the absorption may be veiled by such constitutional fictions as a protectorate, a sphere of influence, a buffer State, and so on? In one sense this may provide a not unfair solution, since, as has been pointed out, the setting up of Arab and Syrian and Armenian independence under the protection of one or other European Powers is one of the avowed war aims of the Allied Powers. But does anyone seriously propose a Hottentot Republic at one extreme? Or if, at the other, Germany, under the plea of 'No annexation', erects Poland, Lithuania and Courland into protected States, does anyone pretend that the reality of absorption will not be there? It seems desirable, in this or in any subsequent discussion, to eschew as far as possible the use of phrases which are ambiguous and misleading. From one point of view the policy of 'No annexation' may be one to which not idealists alone, but practical men, can honestly subscribe. From another it may turn out to be a subterfuge, masking grave hidden dangers.

But, putting aside all verbal refinements and subtleties, there is yet another sense in which, as Mr. Asquith frankly admitted in the House of Commons (May 16, 1917) annexation may well be justified, namely:

'for the purpose of maintaining strategic positions which are shown to be necessary, not for aggression, but for the purpose of self-protection and defence against further attacks. You must be most scrupulous and careful in the application of that principle, but that there are and conceivably may be cases in which the transfer of territory would be justifiable for that purpose seems to me to stand for common sense.'

Even if there were no other case, as there is, for the annexation of the German colonies in Africa, enough has already been said to show that on the above ground it is imperative and unassailable.

But there is yet another plea that is urged by some who in the desire to escape the snare of one catchword, fall incontinently into the trap of another. Why, it is said, not avoid the odium of annexation, by internationalising the territories which Germany has forfeited and cannot be allowed to redeem? What does internationalisation mean? If it means that in different parts of Africa there is to be set up administration by an International Board, composed, it may be supposed, of representatives of Great Britain, France, Belgium, Portugal, America, possibly of Germany itself, I tremble at the contrast that will be presented between the areas that are ruled by a single Government, and the suggested muddle of conflicting interests and ambitions. Gone for ever is the possibility of establishing the polyglot tyranny known as the Congo régime, so much sighed for by European captains of industry forty years ago. The experience of the Anglo-French condominium in the New Hebrides, which has been a failure so conspicuous that both parties are looking eagerly to the arrangements that will follow upon the termination of the war for its total abolition, is no more encouraging than was that of the Dual Control in Egypt. Ask the native himself, and he will at once reply that he would sooner work out his own salvation under the aegis of any one of the Allied Powers whom he knows, than under a mixed Cabinet of nations. Further, let not the future be forgotten. Whether Germany were or were not admitted to such a Board at the start, she would soon be represented there, and the era of intrigue and fraud would recommence. Relieved of direct authority the weary statesmen and officials of the other Powers would disclaim any national responsibility for wrong-doing under an International Board, and in the end we might see a coalescence of all the coloured races against any white-man interference with Africa at all.

The objections to Internationalisation would be not diminished but greatly enhanced, if as has been innocently suggested in certain quarters, the belt of tropical Africa so treated were enlarged, with a view to giving to it a substantial geographical continuity and a more ample scope, into a new Central African State, to which large contributions should be made, as the result either of sale or of gratuitous generosity, by the various European Powers. At the mere breath of such a rumour a few months ago, Portuguese opinion, always sensitive about its colonies, went into paroxysms of agitation. Belgium is not in the least likely to make any surrender of her Congo Empire, which after passing through a stormy and bloodstained childhood, has emerged into a healthy and remunerative adolescence. The surrender of any British colony in Africa, where there are white settlers, to such a State would mean a rebellion in far wider areas. It may be possible, and would probably be desirable, to have much greater uniformity of European administration in Africa after the war, with a system, either of complete free trade or low preferential duties throughout the tropical belt as laid down by the Berlin or Brussels Acts, and with a more or less identical code of municipal and domestic regulations. It may be both desirable and possible to limit by agreement the military training of African natives to police purposes. But an international administration would, it is feared, only be a nursery of international quarrel, and the prelude to greater disaster.

Fear has been expressed that the views put forward in this memorandum may not commend themselves to American opinion. I do not share that view. As long as the retention of the German colonies is made to wear an imperialistic or monopolistic aspect, suspicion will be aroused. But when it is realised that this is a question of world safety, of the future development of the black races, and of peace instead of war in Africa, the thoughtful judgment, both of Allied and Neutral States will be in general accord. Already there are signs of a marked reaction in the United States. President Lowell, of Harvard University, has openly stated in September 1917, that 'the oppression of one race by another must as far as possible be removed, and for that reason we cannot consider the return to Germany of her former colonies, that their people may be exploited in the future as they have been in the past.' An American War Society has been formed, one of the planks in whose platform is the non-return of the German colonies. Articles have appeared in the American papers arguing on the ground, not of British but of colonial sentiment, that retrocession is impossible.

What should be the moment at which a statement of these views is made, if they are accepted as a part of the war intentions of Great Britain, and, as I hope, of the Allies—it is not necessary now to discuss. The important thing is that the arguments should be known, and should be judged upon their merits. It is in order to bring them to the notice of those concerned that I have written this paper.

WAR AIMS, JANUARY 1918

124. (*Cecil to Balfour, 28 December 1917, F.O. 800/207*)

Czernin's pronouncement raises difficult questions. The first thing to do must be to establish the factors of the problem—What is the military position? What are the real facts as to submarining? Will it mean a serious diminution of the daily food of ourselves &

our allies? How will it interfere with our munitions supply. Personally, I suspect the answer to all these questions is rather vague. But I believe it to be the safer opinion that taking them all together we cannot reasonably hope for a decisive *military* success next year. Next, as to morale. I believe our people will go on. But I do not believe that the Italians will & I think it very doubtful if the French will. Clemenceau cannot last for more than six months. When he goes he will be succeeded by a government—perhaps headed by Briand—in which the Socialists will be the predominant force.

I have said our people will stand. But they will require a clear & definite statement as to what we are fighting for. Indeed, whatever we say to Czernin we must as it seems to me define our war aims. In order to do this I think we should ask France, Italy, America & Japan what, each from their own point of view regards as essential. And we must be prepared to state our own irreducible needs. The latter I suppose would be the status quo in Europe. (Personally I do not regard an independent Poland, or Jugoslavia or even Bohemia as a *British* interest.) Autonomous Armenia, Mesopotamia, Palestine. Independent Arabia. Retention of German Colonies in Pacific & South West Africa. Internationalisation of East Africa. Restoration of Cameroons & Togoland. In addition we are bound to support the reasonable demands of our Allies when stated including Alsace Lorraine and some rearrangement of Trentino.

Now the difficulty that I see is that except in the matter of the German colonies these terms are so like Czernin's offer—at any rate, in appearance—that if the Germans reply to us by suggesting a conference it will be difficult to refuse. We ought therefore very carefully to consider whether we have more to lose than to gain by entering a conference on such a basis.

I am just jotting these things down as they occur to me as my contribution to the preliminary discussion which the Prime Minister desires. But after all the main thing is how are we to get that future security which we have all said is our chief aim? Hitherto we have believed that it was only obtainable by a definite German defeat or a German revolution & I confess I do not see any reason to modify that opinion. The League of Nations may be a buttress to security but it is far too uncertain a project to be relied on as its foundation. Disarmament is, I

believe, a fraud. Delbruck has recently written an article to shew
that disarmament is quite safe for Germany since she will always
be able to arm more quickly than her neighbours & this is true.
If a German military defeat is impossible should we go on on
the chance of an economic victory? Will not Germany be able to
revictual her self from Russia? Is there any real chance of a
German revolution?

On the whole my provisional conclusion is that we should
avoid if possible entering into negotiations now. But we should
make every possible effort not to lose control of South Russia as
a mere rejection of Czernin's terms would certainly do. We
should therefore point out that as stated the terms were hopelessly
vague and ask for further details especially about Belgium &
Poland & Serbia, intimating that we regarded the proposals as
at present stated, as a trap. And we must prepare for a counter-
statement of our aims.

125. (*War Cabinet 312, 3 January 1918, Cab/23/5*)

8. The Prime Minister said that the War Cabinet had had several
conversations on the subject of the action to be taken in regard to
the statement issued by the enemy on the 25th December of their
negotiations for peace with the Bolshevik Party in Russia. Although the Allies were not in diplomatic relations with the Bolsheviks, and did not recognise their authority to treat for peace on
behalf of Russia, these negotiations had resulted in an important
declaration of policy by the Central Powers. The War Cabinet had
felt that we ought not to pass this declaration by unnoticed. We
ought to take advantage of it to issue such a declaration of our
own war aims as would maintain our own public opinion, and, if
possible, lower that of the enemy. In fact, the view to which the
War Cabinet inclined was to issue a declaration of our war aims
which went to the extreme limit of concession and which would
show to our own people and to our Allies, as well as to the
peoples of Austria, Turkey and even Germany, that our object
was not to destroy the enemy nations. He thought that there was
a general agreement of the War Cabinet as to the kind of terms
which we could offer. They must include the restoration of Belgium, and reparation for all the damage inflicted on that country.
The same applied to Serbia and Roumania. Germany had as yet
not even offered complete restoration of Belgium, for there were

phrases in the enemy statement which suggested the possibility of the retention of garrisons and economic control. Much less had Germany made any suggestion of reparation. On this point we might hope even to secure the assent of the Russian Bolsheviks. The next point brought us on to much more disputable ground, namely, Alsace-Lorraine. Whatever might be the opinions held by individuals as to the probability that France could realise the whole of her war aims in this respect, it would be dangerous at this stage of the war to suggest the contrary. We should treat Alsace-Lorraine as a matter in which we would support the wishes of the French democracy, who were making very great sacrifices. In regard to Italy, we could indicate in general terms our support to the Italian claims to be united with the peoples of Italian nationality now under Austrian rule, without specific reference to the whole of the Italian war aims. Some reference ought to be made in our statement to such races as the Italians, Croats, Slovaks Czechs, &c., who are under Austrian rule, and who seek some form of autonomy. A statement should also be made in favour of an independent Poland.

The most difficult point, so far as we were concerned, related to the German colonies. We must remove the impression, sedulously spread about by German propaganda, that we were merely trying to annex more territory to an over-gorged Empire. He thought the War Cabinet were in general agreement that our proper course would be to express our willingness to accept the application of the principle of self-determination to the captured German colonies. Precisely how the principle was to be applied need not now be discussed, but there were chiefs and heads of tribes who could be consulted. The same principle might be applied in the case of Mesopotamia—which was occupied by Arabs and not by Turks—and in the case of Palestine, which had a very mixed population. Our attitude should be that we were not going to hand these territories back to the Germans or Turks unless their inhabitants expressed a preference for German or Turkish rule. The first step to be taken, therefore, was to draw up a statement of the case for the consideration of the War Cabinet, in accordance with the democratic principles enunciated by the Bolsheviks and to some extent accepted by the enemy.

The next question which arose was as to whether we were to discuss the question with all our Allies before publishing a statement. This would take some weeks, and it would be very difficult to draw up a document to which general assent would be given which did not lack virility and individuality. Hence, if an answer was to be given promptly, this course was unsuitable, and we ought to adopt President Wilson's plan of an independent statement.

If this was agreed on, the question arose as to the form which our answer should take. Should it be a note, and, if so, to whom should it be addressed? We could not send a note to M. Trotzki, since we were not in diplomatic relations with him; neither could we send it to Count Czernin, because that would involve opening negotiations with the enemy. An alternative was to issue an official statement. Our Allies might justly complain if we took this course.

A second alternative was to make a statement in the form of a speech. Speeches were constantly made by political leaders of all the Allies, and there was no obligation to consult them before making a speech.

The suggestion that had been made to him was that, in the course of the negotiations which Sir Auckland Geddes was conducting with the trades union leaders on the subject of man-power and the release from certain pledges entered into earlier in the war, it should be arranged that the Prime Minister should read a carefully weighed statement of the War Cabinet's policy. This was the more easy to provide for, since it was understood that the trade unionists would raise the question of war aims in the course of the discussions with Sir Auckland Geddes. If the War Cabinet agreed to such a statement, it should, in his opinion, be couched in terms which would provide a counter-offensive to Count Czernin's recent statement, and which would weaken the enemy. The Germans had got their blow in first in this peace offensive, but there were not lacking signs that it was beginning to expend its force. Personally, he did not believe that the enemy's statement was a *bona fide* peace offer. Its object was to sow dissension among the Allies and to rally the German people.

Sir Edward Carson drew attention to an article in the 'Cologne Gazette' which indicated alarm on the part of the Germans lest they should be taken at their word in regard to their statement of peace terms.

Mr. Barnes stated that he attached great importance to the

psychological effect which would be produced at home by the issue of a full and reasoned statement of our war aims.

Lord Robert Cecil said that he would like an opportunity to express his views at full length, both in regard to the form and substance of the statement to be issued. He warned the War Cabinet that the speeches of Ministers in this country, and particularly those of the Prime Minister, were very closely scrutinised by our Allies. He was opposed to any unnecessary delay, but he urged that the subject should be most carefully weighed before a decision was taken.

The Secretary of State for the Colonies urged that, before any statement were made, he should communicate the general lines of it to the Governments of the self-governing Dominions.

The Prime Minister agreed, and suggested that Mr. Walter Long should tell the Dominions the reasons for making the statement. He thought that the press should be warned that this was intended as a counter-offensive to Count Czernin's statement.

One point which he proposed to add, if the War Cabinet agreed, was that if the Russian democracy had not taken the responsibility of entering into negotiations with the enemy by themselves, we should have stood by them, as we intended to stand by the French democracy.

This was agreed to.

The War Cabinet decided that—

(1) The question should be adjourned until 5 p.m.
(2) Mr. Barnes, who was to take the chair at Sir Auckland Geddes' conference with trade unionists in the afternoon, should endeavour to secure an opportunity for the Prime Minister to make his statement on Saturday, if an earlier moment could not be arranged.
(3) Before the meeting at 5 o'clock, the Secretary should reproduce and circulate the three draft statements prepared respectively by Mr. Philip Kerr, under instructions from the Prime Minister, General Smuts, and Lord Robert Cecil.
(4) The Secretary of State for the Colonies should be authorised to telegraph to the self-governing Dominions informing them that a statement was to be made, and explaining the reasons for this course.

126. (*War Cabinet 313, 3 January 1918, Cab/23/5*)

[*War Aims: The Form of the Announcement*]

1. With reference to War Cabinet 312, Minute 8, the War Cabinet continued their discussion on war aims. The first question discussed was the form which the statement should take. It was generally agreed that, if the House of Commons had been sitting, that would be the proper place for the Prime Minister to make a statement. It was suggested, and generally admitted, that there would be some adverse criticism to a statement made to the trade unionists, as suggested at the morning meeting, on the ground that it would give undue importance to the trade unionists as compared with the other sections of the community who were equally affected. On the other hand, it was pointed out that no other convenient opportunity offered itself, and that it would be advisable to take advantage of it. On the whole, therefore, it was agreed that a statement to the trade unionists was desirable.

[*Communication with the Leader of the Opposition*]

2. The Prime Minister informed the War Cabinet that before making a public declaration of the nature proposed, he had thought it his duty to communicate with the Leader of the Opposition. He had seen Mr. Asquith that morning, and had explained the whole position to him, and had indicated the general lines that the Government's declaration was likely to take. Mr. Asquith had quite agreed that Count Czernin's declaration ought to be treated seriously, and be given a considered reply, and that a declaration should be made by the Government. He had seen the difficulties of issuing any sort of Note or statement, and though he had made some criticisms of the proposal to make a public statement to the trade unionists, as had been urged at the War Cabinet, he had not opposed this course. Mr. Asquith had also agreed in the general lines of the statement it was proposed to make, though he had laid stress on the importance of the exact phraseology.

The Prime Minister said that, in seeing Mr. Asquith, following on his conversation with the Labour Leaders on the previous Friday, he had aimed at securing national support in the action the War Cabinet proposed to take.[1]

[1] *Note by the Secretary.*—It will be observed that by the presence of the Secretary of State for the Colonies, General Smuts, and Sir Edward Kemp, Imperial participation in the decision was secured so far as this was possible in the urgent circumstances of the moment. See also the decision in War Cabinet 213, Minute 8, that the

[*The Proposed Statement*]

3. In regard to the text of the proposed statement, the War Cabinet had before them three drafts, namely:

(1) Lord Robert Cecil's draft (G.T.-3181).
(2) General Smuts' draft (G.T.-3180).
(3) Mr. Philip Kerr's draft summarising General Smuts' (G.T.-3182).

Lord Robert Cecil read his statement, which was discussed in some detail.

The Secretary of State for the Colonies uttered a *caveat* against laying too much stress on the principle of self-determination. It was not his province to say what the effect would be in India or Egypt; but there were some of the Crown Colonies which would certainly be affected; as one example, he mentioned Cyprus, where an agitation has long been carried out for union with Greece, and where the Greek section of the inhabitants are mainly adherents to King Constantine. It was suggested that this difficulty would be surmounted by confining the principle of self-determination to the territories actually affected by the belligerent operations.

The Prime Minister urged that the War Cabinet should not neglect to consider the drafts from the point of view of their value as a counter-offensive to the German peace move. He did not in the least underrate the suggestion made by some Members of the War Cabinet that the statement should be drawn up so as to be of real value in the ultimate peace negotiations. In his opinion, however, the terms which we were bound to set out in the document were not such as Germany could accept. He reminded the War Cabinet that, at the moment, Germany was in the hour of triumph, and this was the atmosphere of the German people. In these conditions, no German Government could concede all that we were bound to insist on. Hence, it was essential that this statement should be regarded rather as a war move than as a peace move. In this connection it was important to bear in mind its effects on Germany's Allies. There would be a great difference between an Austria that desired to fight and one that was lukewarm. In the former case Austria might send 300,000 men to the Western front.

Secretary of State for the Colonies should communicate with the self-governing Dominions in regard to this statement.

In the latter they would be a nominal army such as Russia had been for the last 18 months. Similar considerations applied to Turkey. The publication by the Bolsheviks of the Allied Treaties affecting Turkey had had a great effect in that country. What kept the Turks fighting was the fear of dismemberment and of losing Constantinople. If they knew that they would retain the Turkish part of their Empire they might be much less inclined to fight.

Lord Curzon suggested that it was undesirable to differentiate between the statement regarded as a peace or a war measure. In reality it was both. It was a genuine and sincere attempt to secure a reasonable peace, but he agreed that, in the present temper of the Germans, it was not likely to lead to much. Lord Robert Cecil expressed similar views.

The suggestion was made that both Lord Robert Cecil's and General Smuts' statements were too long.

Among the points of detail that were discussed, Lord Robert Cecil urged the importance of not using any phrases which would lead Roumania to think that we had in any way abandoned our obligations towards her. We had laid great stress on the sanctity of treaties, and we ought not to suggest in any statement that we would not carry out a treaty until we had been released from our obligations by the nation concerned. Moreover, at the moment, Roumania was a very important factor in the war, being, indeed, the only barrier between the Germans and the great resources of South Russia.

Lord Robert Cecil also uttered a warning against any suggestion that we would not carry out our treaties to Italy. Signor Giolitti and his adherents were sedulously propagating the rumour that the British Government would not keep its obligations in Italy, and it was important not to encourage this idea.

Another point of detail related to Montenegro, which it was generally agreed should be omitted from the statement, as the best solution of the Montenegrin question might be its incorporation in Serbia.

Mr. Barnes, entering towards the end of the Meeting, gave some account of the trade unionist meeting. After he himself had promised a statement on war aims by the Prime Minister, Mr. J. H. Thomas had intervened and urged all the arguments against the proposal raised at the Cabinet in the morning. In the result Mr. Barnes had thought it advisable not to carry a resolution asking for a statement on war aims by the Prime Minister, and the question had been left open.

Further consideration was adjourned until the following day.

127. (*War Cabinet 314, 4 January 1918, Cab/23/5*)

[*War Aims*]

1. With reference to War Cabinet 313, Minute 1, the War Cabinet resumed their discussion on war aims. The Prime Minister said that he had seen M. Albert Thomas that morning, and had shown him his rough draft of the statement he proposed to make on the morrow to the trade unionists. M. Thomas had said that this would suit France.

The Prime Minister said that he had arranged to show the draft, as approved by the War Cabinet, to Mr. Asquith and Lord Grey on the morrow. If the War Cabinet agreed he proposed to state in his speech that he had recently had the opportunity to consult the Leader of the Opposition and the Leaders of Labour, and that he had consulted such representatives of the Dominions as were available, and that what he said might be taken as representing the views of the nation.

This was agreed to.

[*The Statement*]

2. The Prime Minister then proceeded to read the statement which he proposed to make, which was based partly on Lord Robert Cecil's (G.T.-3181), and partly on General Smuts' draft (G.T.-3180).

Subject to certain amendments the new draft was approved, and is reproduced in the Appendix.[1]

[*The Principle of Self-Determination*]

3. With reference to War Cabinet 313, Minute 3, it was agreed that the passage dealing with the principle of self-determination of races should be modified so as to apply, not to all races indiscriminately, but merely to the settlement of the New Europe.

[*Russia*]

4. Some discussion took place as to a passage in which the Prime Minister proposed, as agreed by the War Cabinet (War Cabinet 312, Minute 8), to notify the Russian Bolsheviks that if they had not taken the responsibility of entering into negotiations with the

---

[1] Not printed.

enemy by themselves, we should have stood by the Russian democracy, as we intended to stand by the French democracy. The Prime Minister gave as his reasons for including this statement that it was necessary to give warning to the Bolsheviks that we did not any longer consider ourselves bound to fight on in Russian interests, so that there should be no misunderstanding on the subject in the future; also, that he wished to give a hint to the enemy in the same direction. Against this it was urged that the statement would be somewhat discouraging to our friends in Russia, who still wished to fight on in the interests of the Allies as a whole.

It was pointed out that the prevention of Courland and Lithuania falling into the hands of the Germans was an important Allied interest, since if this occurred the Baltic would become more than ever a German lake. For many years past one of the greatest dangers to peace had been the desire of Russia to reach open water. If the Baltic were entirely under German control, the Black Sea exits practically subject to Turkish control, and Vladivostock very possibly in the hands of the Japanese, Russia would have no outlet except in the Arctic Ocean. It was impossible to imagine that this vast amorphous nation, when it recovered from its present prostration, would be content with these conditions, and Russian lack of access to the ocean might prove a constant source of future wars. In fact, a settlement on these lines was not consistent with a just and durable peace.

The Prime Minister undertook to find a form of words which would meet both points of view.

[*Austria*]

5. There was some discussion as to the manner in which Austria should be alluded to in the statement. After referring to the legitimate claims of Italy, Serbia and Roumania, the Prime Minister had proposed to insert a phrase indicating that, subject to the fulfilment of our war aims in regard to these countries, we considered the existence of a strong Austria to be desirable. His main object was to give a clear indication to Austria that we did not wish to destroy her, and to make her people lukewarm in the war, thus deterring her from using her strength actively against us. Against this it was urged that our Allies on the borders of Austria-Hungary might be discouraged.

It was decided:

To include some milder phrase than that used in the original draft in the sense that, subject to the fulfilment of the legitimate claims of our Allies, we felt that Austria-Hungary should be in a position to exercise a powerful influence in South-East Europe.

[*Roumania*]

6. With reference to War Cabinet 313, Minute 3, there was some further discussion as to the manner in which Roumania should be alluded to in the statement. Eventually, it was decided that:

A suitable reference should be made to the Balkans as a whole, indicating that the boundaries of all Balkan States should be settled on an ethnographical basis, and full reparation made to Serbia and Roumania for damage done in Serbian and Roumanian territory.

NEGOTIATIONS WITH AUSTRIA-HUNGARY FOR A SEPARATE PEACE

128. (*Draft by Balfour of 28 December 1917 of telegram to President Wilson, F.O. 371/3133/2002*)

[It was despatched as amended on 2 January 1918.]

As Colonel House will have informed you, the Paris Conference authorised us to carry on informal conversations on Peace Terms with the Austrians, should a fitting occasion arise. In accordance with this policy a British and an Austrian representative met in Switzerland last week with every precaution of secrecy; and interviews of a friendly and unofficial character were held on two successive days. The British representative, acting on instructions, refused, on this occasion, to discuss the question of a general peace which should include Germany. The Austrian representative, acting also on instructions, held out no hopes whatever of Austria separating herself from Germany during the continuance of the War. In these circumstances no conclusions could be, even provisionally, arrived at sufficiently precise to lay before the Allied Governments. Nevertheless, our representative returned with some very definite impressions, and was able to come to some important suggestions. He gathered that Austria was exceedingly anxious for peace, and that, though she would not and could not abandon her Ally, she would be prepared to exert the strongest pressure to induce that Ally to accept a 'reasonable settlement'. He further gathered that, however closely Austria might be bound to Germany during the war, she had no desire to be Germany's vassal when the war was over. His statement that the destruction of Austria was no part of British War Aims was received by the Austrian representative with much satisfaction, and his expression of our strong desire to see the various nationalities of which the Empire is composed given an opportunity for autonomous development was received with much sympathy—a sympathy which was said to reflect opinions in the 'Highest Quarters'.

[Our representative came away with the impression that, if we had to deal with Austria alone, there were no insuperable difficulties in the way of a satisfactory arrangement, though these difficulties were much increased by the resentment felt at the conduct of Italy and Roumania.][1]

The Austrian representative expressed the earnest wish that these conversations should be renewed at an early date, a wish with which the British Government will probably comply.

Nothing has so far been said to any Allied Government about these conversations: and for obvious reasons it is most desirable that as few persons as possible should know of them until they issue in something definite and tangible.

129. (*War Cabinet 357A, 1 March 1918, Cab/23/16*)

THE PRIME MINISTER read a number of extracts from some of the most reliable intelligence agents concerning affairs in Austria. The general tenor of these reports was that economic conditions in Austria are very bad, the desire for peace is general, and seditious tendencies are manifesting themselves.

MR. BALFOUR gave a resumé of political events relating to the possibility of negotiations for a separate peace with Austria, which had occurred since the matter was last considered by the War Cabinet (Feb. 4, War Cabinet 338-A). On Feb. 13th we had received from Berne an account of an important conversation between Dr. Herron, an American, and Professor Lammasch, who alleged that he had been sent by the Austrian Emperor to Switzerland to get a message through to President Wilson. According to this information the Emperor's personal ideas favoured a Danube Monarchy composed of seven autonomous

---

[1] This passage was not sent.

states, and the complete restoration of Serbian independence uniting Montenegro and part of Albania with the Serbian Kingdom.

Subsequently a message had been received from Col. House asking for advice in regard to a message which the President had received from the Emperor of Austria through the King of Spain. The Emperor's message to the President, which had no doubt been prepared by Count Czernin, and which the Foreign Office had reason to believe was sent with the knowledge of the German Government, was much less favourable as a basis for discussion than the Lammasch–Herron conversation. (It practically amounted to the *status quo ante bellum* in Europe subject to an exception in the case of Bulgaria and such alterations as might be agreed to.) Mr. Balfour (after Lord Robert Cecil had read an account of the message sent through the King of Spain) read to the War Cabinet the telegram which he himself, with the assent of the Prime Minister, had sent to Colonel House. In this telegram he had pointed out the difference between the proposals made through the King of Spain and Herron–Lammasch conversations, the former proposals omitting Italy and the subject races of Austria, and being irreconcilable with the President's own declaration; he had pointed out that risks would be run in embarking on conversations of which Germany had knowledge, but he had not opposed them, if President Wilson cared to run the risk; Mr. Balfour, in his telegram also recalled his own action in acquainting the allies when Germany had made approaches to us through the King of Spain; and he had advised the President to take a similar course, if he decided to enter into conversations on the basis of the approaches made through the King of Spain, but if the Herron-Lammasch basis was to be followed up, he had advised him to carry the conversations out independently.

Mr. Balfour drew attention to two further telegrams which had been received from Berne, during the period covered by the interchange of telegrams with Colonel House. The first of these was No. 273, in which M. de Skrzynski, an Austrian political agent at Berne, was reputed to have stated that Count Czernin would be ready to give a formal declaration that Austria would only discuss her own affairs in any conversations she might have with England, America and Allies; who have indicated that now was the moment to act against Germany, particularly in view of

Kühlmann's public insults to Austria; to have laid stress on Austria's urgent need of financial help from America after the war; and to have offered to furnish a written declaration in the above sense. M. de Skrzynski was also stated to have made it fairly obvious that Austria desired a separate peace. The second telegram (No. 274 from Berne) referred to Poland and stated, again on the authority of M. de Skrzynski, that a good effect would be produced if England could state that she would have no objection to one of the Emperor of Austria's brothers, who is now fighting on our side in Flanders, becoming King of Poland, as this would enlist the support of the Empress of Austria, whose influence is very great. Finally Mr. Balfour drew attention to a telegram from Lord Reading, in which he laid stress on the danger of alienating Italy in any conversations.

THE PRIME MINISTER said he was somewhat apprehensive of President Wilson's intervention in this question. President Wilson was not making a success of his own administration. All accounts agreed that matters were very behindhand in regard to the raising of men, construction of aircraft, shipbuilding, the provision of railway material for France, and the organisation of the American railways. In these circumstances there was a real danger that the President might want to end the war, and might agree to conditions that we could not accept. It was plain from the proposals made through the King of Spain that President Wilson's four conditions could be interpreted in a sense hostile to us.

MR. BALFOUR pointed out that they were really platitudes, which could equally easily be interpreted in our favour.

THE PRIME MINISTER pointed out that, if Colonel House was to come over to Europe to discuss peace conditions with Austria, all the world would know about it, and it would be tantamount to a peace conference. He was inclined to think we ought to tell President Wilson that we considered any such conversations dangerous, and that, in the meantime, we ourselves, following up the message from Skrzynski, should probe about, and ascertain what was the real position. General Smuts might resume his conversations with Count Mensdorff, or someone higher.

GENERAL SMUTS asked that his name might not be introduced. He pointed out the risks which the British Empire had at stake in these transactions, and uttered a warning against entrusting our interests to the United States, particularly as we had obtained from our continental allies authority to act in this matter, which was equivalent to the diplomatic predominance in the alliance.

[N.B. Earlier in the afternoon General Smuts had described a conversation he had had with Baron Sonnino of Rome on the subject of his conversations with Count Mensdorff. Baron Sonnino had consented to a continuance of these discussions, without expressing any optimism as to the outcome.]

LORD ROBERT CECIL commenting on the Prime Minister's proposal, said that the real difficulty was that, if you once said you were going to hold conversations with Austria, President Wilson would insist that he was the man to do it.

LORD CURZON supported this view. President Wilson, he pointed out, aspires to become the great figure in the peace negotiations.

MR. BONAR LAW asked if we were not jeopardising the position we had so long desired to reach, namely that Austria should be willing to make a separate peace. Several of the recent telegrams indicated that we had reached this position. He suggested that Mr. Balfour should inform President Wilson of the message from M. de Skrzynski and should say we proposed to follow the matter up.

LORD ROBERT CECIL proposed that we should try to obtain a message in writing as proposed by de Skrzynski. The statement should come from Count Czernin, de Skrzynski was a person of no consequence. A written communication was the only chance of remaining undiscovered. If we sent anyone we must tell President Wilson. If we decided to do this, the best plan would be to tell the President that we had a mandate from our allies, and to suggest that we should be allowed to act for him also.

MR. BONAR LAW informed the War Cabinet of a conversation he had had with the American, Mr. Cravath. The latter, it appeared, had an understanding with Col. House, that he should write whenever he saw a change in the situation. He thought he had observed two such changes recently.

1. He thought opinion was weakening in this country, and appeared to have based his opinion partly on conversations with Liberal statesmen in this country. Mr. Bonar Law had rebutted this view, pointing out that in all the previous wars of our history there had been much stronger peace parties than exist here at present.

2. He was disturbed at our attitude about peace. Mr. Balfour's

speech had appeared to him to bang the door to a real advance on Hertling's pact. In reply to this Mr. Bonar Law had said that the Government did not believe that the Germans meant peace, and that their policy in these circumstances was to hold out no hopes to our own people. Mr. Cravath had agreed that this was an intelligible policy.

THE PRIME MINISTER said that this supported his view of the danger of allowing President Wilson to enter into peace conversations with Austria.

LORD CURZON agreed that our main object should be to prevent President Wilson from such conversations. Could we not advise him that this was dangerous.

GENERAL SMUTS suggested that the matter should be left where it was, viz., at Mr. Balfour's last telegram to Colonel House.

LORD MILNER asked if this meant that nothing would be done. He himself was in favour of continuing the conversations with Austria, but he was opposed to asking for a written communication from Austria, as it would lead to nothing.

THE SECRETARY drew attention to the serious delays that had occurred in dealing with this question. As long ago as January 12th de Skrzynski had stated that Count Czernin would be ready to come to Switzerland to meet Mr. Lloyd George, and no sort of reply had yet been sent.

It was true that on Jan. 18th the War Cabinet had authorised a reply in the sense that Gen. Smuts could meet Count Czernin (War Cabinet 325-A), subject to Mr. Balfour's consent, and the Secretary read from the Minutes the reasons on which this discussion was based. At Mr. Balfour's request however action had been postponed owing to the approaches to President Wilson.

MR. BALFOUR said he was certain that Austria would not accede to a peace such as we wanted.

THE PRIME MINISTER agreed, but pointed out that, by continuing conversations a very important secondary object might be achieved namely Austria might be deterred from making an attack and gradually induced to a state of inactivity similar to that which preceded the commencement of peace negotiations between Russia and the Central Powers.

(*Conclusion*)

The War Cabinet decided:

That the Secretary of State for Foreign Affairs should telegraph to Berne in the sense that we are awaiting further news as to the matter dealt with in Sir Harold Rumbold's telegram No. 273 of February 23, 1915.

130. (*Memo. by Smuts, 14 March 1918, Lloyd George Papers, F/45/9/10*)

The war is leading to very great and surprising developments, and the end of the war may yet see a very different Europe from that of 1914. While we are talking about Alsace-Lorraine and other comparatively small matters, Germany has broken the Russian Empire and has increased her potential strength far beyond what it was in 1914. Central Europe is no longer an ideal war aim, but a reality far greater and more dangerous than any we dreamt of, and besides new routes for its expansion to Central and Southern Asia are being opened up.

These great developments must be met by an equal change and re-adjustment of our plans. Diplomacy must now come in to reinforce our military strategy. If we cannot defeat Central Europe we must break it by far-sighted and daring diplomacy. The break-up of Russia has given us diplomatically a free hand in many important respects which we must be prepared to play as effectively as possible.

The principal feature of my idea is still, as foreshadowed to Mensdorff, to detach Austria from Germany either before or at the peace, by holding out to her the prospect of a large increase in territory and position. The future federal Austria may include not only Austria, Hungary and Poland, but now also the Ukraine. She will then have a larger territory and population than Germany. The conditions of this increase are that she detaches herself from Germany, that she agrees to Bosnia, Herzegovina and part of the Dalmatian coast going to Greater Serbia, and that she cedes to Italy the Trentino and some other minor rectifications and recognises Italian claims to Valona and a protectorate over Albania.

To this plan I would now add the following: I am afraid the Germans have bought the Turks with Armenia and the Caucasus, and our Turkish negotiations will drag on for ever without any result. I would reply by buying Bulgaria. If she will not be satisfied with less, we should offer her Constantinople if she will take it; and we should offer to move our Salonica army to the north to protect Bulgaria while the Bulgarians move to occupy Constantinople. This will finish Turkey and the war. It is awkward to negotiate with that fox Ferdinand, but Constantinople will probably fetch him, and that the Germans cannot give him. Indeed we have no other buying counter of any first class value. Bulgaria will then add to her territories European Thrace as well as the uncontested zone in Macedonia and the part of Bulgaria which was torn off by Roumania in 1912. All the rest of the territory occupied by her she must restore to Serbia, Roumania and Greece. Roumania will also get Bessarabia in lieu of Transylvania.

Besides solving the Balkan tangle on more or less national and satisfactory lines, this plan will break the chain of Central Europe at three points—(1) Austria, (2) Greater Serbia, and (3) Greater Bulgaria, the first and third of whom having deserted Germany will become independent of and antagonistic to her, and give a quite new orientation to the diplomacy of Europe.

Such an arrangement will compel Germany to come to reasonable terms with the Entente, and a favourable and durable peace could be concluded.

131. *(Rumbold to Balfour, 26 March 1918, no. 429, F.O.*
371/3133/2002)

Very secret.

My telegram No. 376 of March 17th.

Parodi reports Skrzynski sent for him on March 23rd saying he had a communication to make to Parodi on behalf of Austro-Hungarian Government.

Skrzynski stated that he had received a long memorandum from Czernin in reply to report he had made of conversation he had had with Mr. Kerr on March 14th. He was authorised to communicate to Parodi principal points of this memorandum which may be considered as exactly representing Czernin's views on the subject of peace.

Parodi took these points down in writing and then read them over to Skrzynski so as to avoid all possibility of a misunderstanding.

Following are points which Czernin wishes passed on to His Majesty's Government: [End of K.]

Le Comte Czernin a de la peine à croire que les déclarations de M. Kerr visent réellement à amener une paix générale basée sur la justice, puisqu'il a laissé de côté l'unique difficulté qui se présente pour la conclusion d'une paix juste et durable, qui est le désir d'annexions de la France et de l'Italie. Jamais les empires centraux ne reconnaîtront ces désirs de conquêtes qui leur paraissent injustifiés.

Tant que l'Italie voudra annexer des territoires Autrichiens et que la France déclarera qu'elle ne peut faire la paix sans acquérir l'Alsace Lorraine, une paix avec ces deux états est absolument impossible.

Si l'Italie et la France abandonnaient leurs buts de conquêtes le Comte Czernin ne voit rien qui puisse empêcher la conclusion d'une paix immédiate, juste et durable.

Tant que l'Angleterre doit soutenir ses Allies dans leurs projets d'annexions, il est difficile qu'il se trouve quelqu'un dans les Empires Centrales qui puisse penser qu'elle désire conclure une paix juste et durable.

Les Empires Centraux n'ont pas la moindre idée de s'occuper des affaires intérieures des Allies, pas plus qu'ils ne veulent que l'on s'immisce dans leurs affaires intérieures.

Le Comte Czernin croit que le reproche au sujet de la paix avec la Roumanie est injustifié et la preuve est que le peuple Roumain ne désire rien de plus que l'arrivée au pouvoir d'un Ministère Marghiloman qui lui permettra de se rapprocher des Empires Centraux d'une façon profitable. Le peuple Roumain pense que les profits qu'il retirera d'un rapprochement seront plus grands que les sacrifices que comporte la paix pour lui.

Quant à l'aprés guerre, le Comte Czernin déclare qu'il est absolument décidé à se tenir à un programme qui aura pour but d'empêcher, les guerres futures et qu'il ne démordra pas. Mais il faut d'abord finir la guerre actuelle, ce qui sera possible quand la France et l'Italie ne parleront plus de conquêtes, on pourra alors causer de l'avenir.

[K. recommences]

I think it is now clear from above that either that Skrzynski owing to his not being in close personal touch with his Government has throughout exaggerated what Czernin was prepared to do in order to obtain peace and resumed his conversations with Parodi under the impression of strikes and economic distress in Austria or that Czernin is a thorough opportunist and is waiting to see result of German offensive. In any event Czernin's reference to Alsace Lorraine question shows he has abandoned if he ever accepted formula of only discussing questions concerning Austria. I venture to think also that his remarks about attitude of Roumania towards Marghiloman Ministry are sufficient evidence of his bad faith. No useful purpose would seem to be served by allowing Parodi to see Skrzynski again for the present and I hope subject to your approval to tell Parodi that if Skrzynski seeks another interview he should reply that we are too far apart to make such an interview profitable. It is probable that quite apart from results of offensive situation in Austria will change in a couple of months when Austrians realise that they will not get much relief from Ukraine and if there is a recurrence of strikes in Austria. But I am convinced there is nothing to be done with Austria for the moment.

Minute: In present circumstances there is clearly nothing more to be done.

L. O[liphant]

Approved A. J. B[alfour]

132. (*War Cabinet 391A, 15 April 1918, Cab 23/16*)

Personal Note by the Secretary of a discussion with regard to the letter from the Austrian Emperor, published by authority of the French Government, April 1918

The Secretary of State for Foreign Affairs asked the War Cabinet what answer he should give to the following question which was to be put to him that afternoon by Mr. Outhwaite:

To ask the Secretary of State for Foreign Affairs whether at the time, a year ago, of the refusal of the British Government to consider peace negotiations, and in particular the proposals of the Kerensky Government, he was aware that President Poincaré was in possession of a letter from the Emperor Karl of Austria stating that he would support, by every means and use all his personal influence with his Allies, the French just claims regarding Alsace-Lorraine, and affirming that the sovereignty of Belgium should be restored, as also that of Serbia with an outlet to the sea provided.

In the discussion that ensued the Prime Minister related that he had met M. Ribot at Folkestone, and M. Ribot had shown him the letter now revealed by M. Clemenceau. The Prime Minister had made a copy of the letter in pencil which he was asked by M. Ribot to show to no one but the King. The two Prime Ministers had agreed that nothing could be done without consulting the Italians.

At St. Jean de Maurienne, on April 19th, the Prime Minister had met Baron Sonnino, who flatly declined to negotiate with Austria and regarded the letter as a trick. The letter, however, was not a trick, and the Prime Minister read a translation in which the words 'just claims' represented the French original 'justes revendications'. The copy of the original French document was then read by Mr. Bonar Law.

The War Cabinet then discussed the advisability of publishing in this country and in France a facsimile of the original document, with a view to sowing seeds of discord between Austria and Germany. They were, however, of opinion that it would be a mistake to insist too much on an occurrence revealing the Emperor Karl as a traitor to his Allies and a liar to us, as this would finally close any avenue to a separate understanding between the Allies and Austria.

The Secretary of State for Foreign Affairs said that he thought the best plan would be to return an answer in the House of Commons in the following sense:

> That His Majesty's Government, after giving careful thought to the matter, considered that it was not in the public interest to have any public discussion on the subject.

The Minister for Blockade pointed out that, while the answer would be sufficient for the moment, it must be anticipated that the question would be pressed further at a later date. The question might then be asked why, if His Majesty's Government had known of the offer, they had not pursued it.

To this it was pointed out the answer was that we had pursued it up to the point of Italian refusal to co-operate. Our reason, therefore, was loyalty to our Allies.

Another answer was that Emperor Karl had been offering what belonged not to him but to his Allies.

This second point was reinforced by a second letter, dated May

9th, from Emperor Karl to his brother-in-law, Prince Sixte of Bourbon, a translation of which, as well as of the first letter, made by Prince Sixte, had been left by him with the Prime Minister's Secretary.

The War Cabinet approved the answer proposed by Mr. Balfour.

IMPERIAL OBJECTIVES, AUGUST 1918

133. (*War Cabinet 457, 13 August 1918, Cab/23/7*)

[*War Aims Review by the Secretary of State for Foreign Affairs*]

7. The Secretary of State for Foreign Affairs gave the Imperial War Cabinet a general survey of our aims and obligations over the whole field of politics. Touching upon our obligations, by treaty or by declaration, to our Western Allies, France and Italy, he expressed the view that any suggestions of compromise with regard to those obligations would have to come from France and Italy, and not from ourselves.

With regard to the Central European question, which now included the whole field from the Arctic Ocean to the Ægean, he pointed out that an issue which had to be decided on the threshold of the whole question was that of the fate of Austria-Hungary, and gave his reasons for concluding that the breaking up of Austria-Hungary on national lines would be the best solution in the general interest. With regard to Poland, he suggested that the promise given both at Versailles and by President Wilson, to secure for Poland free access to the sea, opened a wider question which affected the position of all inland countries, and which might usefully be taken in hand by the League of Nations. His general conclusion with regard to Poland was that we should insist on free navigation of the Vistula, secure an ethnological frontier for Poland on the east, and leave the difficult question of the western frontier of Poland open to deal with when we knew to what extent we had beaten Germany. Continuing to describe the principles of mutual conflict and common dependence upon herself on which Germany was building up the ring of border states which she had carved out of Russia, he insisted that the breaking down of the Brest-Litovsk Treaty must be an essential object of our policy. That would be the most effective way of disposing of the dangers in the Middle East, with regard to which Lord Curzon had warned the Imperial War Cabinet (Imperial War

Cabinet No. 20, Minute 5). Briefly indicating the outlines of the position in the Balkans, he laid stress upon the great difficulty created by Greek and Serbian animosity against Bulgaria.

In the Near East our chief diplomatic difficulties were created by the Sykes–Picot Agreement, which, though still remaining as a diplomatic instrument, was historically out of date, and by the jealousy between France and Italy. He alluded to the great work of reconstruction already achieved in Palestine and Mesopotamia, and to the impossibility of letting those countries relapse under Turkish rule. There was also, in the case of Mesopotamia, the vital necessity for the British Empire to secure a settlement which would not endanger our facilities for obtaining oil from this region.

As regards the German Colonies, he mentioned that his own views and those of other members of the Imperial Cabinet, had already been stated in a series of papers (P.-25, G.-182, G.T.-4774, G.T.-1816, and G.T.-5132). He summed up his own views by saying that he was vehemently opposed to restoring to the Germans any opportunity of creating new submarine bases or levying armies of black troops; that he considered that Australia, New Zealand, and South Africa should retain the adjacent German Colonies which they had conquered; as regards the remaining German African Colonies, while he realised the objections to every plan which might be put forward, he thought it desirable that, after all our disinterested professions, we should try to avoid coming out of this war with accessions of territory compared with which those of other States would sink into insignificance.

Sir Robert Borden expressed his general agreement with Mr. Balfour's views as to the German Colonies. The people of Canada were not willing to fight for the mere sake of extending the territories of the Empire. If that Empire was to remain a world institution, it would have to rely not only on the British Dominions but also on the co-operation and support of the United States. The more it was possible to get the United States to undertake responsibility in world affairs, the better for the world as a whole and for the British Empire. For his own part, speaking of the German Colonies generally, and not dealing with the specific interests which other Dominions might have with respect to some of them he would be perfectly ready to let any of these Colonies pass under the direct protectorate or even the actual ownership and control of the United States. The real difficulty would be the reluctance of the Americans themselves to depart from their historic policy. As to the League of Peace its purpose commanded our best effort even if we were not convinced of its enduring practicability. The first attempt to assure international order might be through a 'Vigilance Committee' of respectable and powerful nations.

Mr. Massey asked if it was intended to go back on the reports of the Imperial War Cabinet Committees, more particularly that which had been presided over by Lord Curzon, which dealt very fully with these questions, and had submitted definite conclusions?

The Prime Minister considered that those conclusions were certainly still subject to discussion.

Lord Reading, dealing with the suggestion that the United States might be asked to act as a trustee for the Powers in Palestine, considered that such a suggestion would appeal very strongly to the United States both in view of their general idealism and of the political importance of the Jewish element in their population. Generally speaking, as long as President Wilson remained at the head of affairs, America would not stand at the Peace Conference for direct annexation either by herself or by others. As the war progressed she would, however, be increasingly against giving back territory to an unregenerate Germany. In this connection the arguments used by Mr. Hughes with regard to New Guinea and the Pacific, had had considerable effect. We should have to try wherever possible to secure our aims by methods which fell short of direct territorial acquisition.

Mr. Chamberlain pointed out that the United States had not said anything in this war against territorial acquisition stronger than the declarations made on the outbreak of the Spanish-American war, when it thanked God that, unlike any other people, America had entered into a war without any idea of gaining territory.

The Prime Minister suggested that if we approached the United States with a view to their undertaking the responsibilities of trusteeship, say for Palestine and one of the German African Colonies, they might be prepared to recognise our trusteeship elsewhere, as for instance in Mesopotamia.

The further discussion of the question of war aims was postponed to 3.30 p.m. on Wednesday, the 14th August.

[The League of Nations: Publication of the Phillimore Report]
8. Lord Robert Cecil raised the question whether the report of Lord Phillimore's Committee should not be published. In view of the danger of the whole subject being drowned in a welter of plausible faddist schemes, it would be desirable to set up a standard such as would be furnished by the conclusions of a body of men who had seriously faced the practical difficulties. It need not necessarily be published as expressing the views of the Cabinet.

Lord Reading pointed out that President Wilson was very anxious that nothing should be published here which might appear to commit the British Government until he had submitted his own views to them. For some time past, he had discountenanced public agitation on the subject of the League of Nations not because he had changed his views, but because he thought the moment inopportune. It was at his instance, in fact, that a great League of Nations meeting had been converted into a 'win the war' convention. He would, however, have his memorandum on the question completed in another two or three weeks, and would then submit it to the British Government. He did not think that the President was doing this merely for the sake of getting in first with the publication of his views.

Mr. Hughes suggested that it was desirable that the Imperial War Cabinet should come to a definite conclusion about its own policy in the matter before it committed itself to the publication of a document which dealt with the policy in detail. General statements such as that to which the Prime Minister had confined himself recently were quite harmless.

The Prime Minister considered that there were two chief objections to publication besides the personal objections of President Wilson. There was first of all the fact that if published the scheme would inevitably be regarded as inspired by the Government, and therefore it ought not to be published until it had received at least a second reading approval from the Imperial War Cabinet; secondly he was very afraid that the publication of any scheme at such a time would take away the people's mind from that victory which was the only sure basis of any League of Nations. The end of the war was still a long way off and Germany was nowhere near accepting tolerable terms.

134. (*War Cabinet 458, 14 August 1918, Cab/23/7*)

[*War Aims*]

7. Sir Rennell Rodd, resuming the discussion on War Aims, suggested that a good deal of what had been criticised as Imperialistic aims on the part of Italy were really defensive aims connected with her position in the Adriatic and in the Mediterranean generally. There had been in recent months a great change of view with regard to the Bohemian and South Slav questions. Baron Sonnino would either have to acquiesce in that change or resign. His attitude was based, firstly, on the idea that Italy should not be expected to renounce her claims unless there was a general renunciation all round, and, secondly, on the fear that a Jugo-Slav State, under whatever auspices it started, would eventually fall within the orbit of the Central Powers. Relations with Greece were much more satisfactory, and he believed Italy would agree to a settlement in connection with the Ægean Islands, providing she retained some one point, *e.g.*, Rhodes, for herself.

Mr. Massey, though disposed to regard the suggestion that Palestine should be entrusted to the United States as worthy of consideration, was not prepared to agree to the idea that America should be given any of the Pacific Islands, which we had conquered. These islands, and more especially Samoa, from its strategic position, would be of the greatest consequence to the great British population which was destined to inhabit the Southern Pacific in the future. He illustrated the strategic importance of these islands from the experiences of the first few months of the war, and concluded by expressing the hope that when our delegates went to the Peace Conference they would be definitely united on the policy of no restoration to Germany and no condominium. As far as Australia and New Zealand were concerned, nothing would be satisfactory to them except the retention by Britain of the German Pacific Islands.

Mr. Hughes said that as regards the Pacific Islands his attitude was that if anyone wanted to shift Australia from them they would have to come and do it! On the general question, he wished to have time for more careful consideration. What was essential was that there should be complete agreement in the Imperial War Cabinet as to what the attitude of the British delegates at the Peace Conference should be, and, as far as he could see, that complete agreement had not yet been established. From the point of view of Australia, it was vital that she should have a voice in the settlement before it was made, and he should like, if possible, to have these matters settled definitely before he returned to Australia.

General Smuts suggested that Mr. Balfour had stated our War Aims from the Foreign Office point of view and on the assumption of the complete defeat of the enemy. He could not see that the programme based on that assumption was justified by the present military situation. He did not suppose that anything would happen materially to affect that situation during the present year. Nor had he any expectation that the Allies would be able to force a decision in 1919 on the Western front, which, by the experience both of the enemy and ourselves, had always proved a fatal theatre to the attacking party. He doubted the possibility of a real restoration of the Russian front, and feared that the enemy, giving ground slowly on the West, would concentrate a considerable effort, mainly carried out by Turkish troops, in the East. The menace there was to ourselves and no one else, and what he feared was the campaign of 1919 ending inconclusively in the West and leaving our whole position in the East damaged and in danger. He was very loth to look forward to 1920. Undoubtedly Germany would be lost if the war continued long enough. But was that worth our while? Our Army would shrink progressively, and we might find ourselves reduced, before the war ended, to the position of a second-class Power compared with America and Japan. It was no use achieving the object of destroying Germany at the cost of the position of our own Empire. From this point of view he considered many of the items in the Foreign Secretary's programme not as war aims to be secured in the treaty of peace, but as things that would come of themselves in the revolution which would follow the war. His own suggestion was that we should concentrate on those theatres where our military and diplomatic effort could be most effectively brought to bear together, *i.e.*, against our weaker enemies: Austria, Bulgaria, and Turkey. A serious offensive from Italy against Austria, efforts to widen the breach between Bulgaria and Turkey, and hard blows struck at Turkey itself, were the objects we should concentrate upon. Beyond that, we should perfect our economic policy, not necessarily as a settled *post*-war policy, but as a sword to hang over Germany, and a safeguard in the event of incomplete victory.

With regard to the German Colonies, he pointed out that the Germans themselves now concentrated all their colonial ambition on the establishment of a great, solid block across Africa. This block, with its potentialities of a huge black army and of submarine bases threatening the whole of our world-traffic, could not be conceded. In this issue our principal trouble would be with the United States, and it would be essential to conciliate them by bringing them into the business. The suggestion which he had already made was that, while we should retain the German Colonies territorially, the whole of tropical Africa should be placed under a Development Board, the Presidency of which should be entrusted to the United States.

A certain amount of discussion followed as to the precise scope and powers of such a Development Board and of its relations to the actual territorial Sovereign. It was pointed out that the scheme was susceptible of immense modifications according as practically all the powers were given to the Board and territorial sovereignty limited to police duties, or the Board confined to the mere overseeing of the carrying out of certain treaty restrictions. It was also pointed out that the other colonial Powers affected might object to such a Board, most of all, perhaps, a Power like Portugal, in whose case external control was most desirable.

(The discussion was adjourned to 11.30 a.m. on Thursday, the 15th August, 1918.)

135. (*War Cabinet 459, 15 August 1918, Cab/23/7*)
[*War Aims*]

9. Lord Curzon, continuing the discussion on War Aims, expressed his dissent from the pessimistic view taken by General Smuts with regard to the military situation. That situation had greatly improved in the West, and, generally speaking, the *morale* of the Allied nations stood as high as ever, while that of the Germans and their Allies had been dashed by the failure of their expectations. In the East, too, he considered the danger of the position had been exaggerated by General Smuts. In Russia itself there were signs of reviving effort, while in the Middle East the position though serious, was not as yet menacing. He did not himself contemplate a great tide of invasion rolling against our Eastern Empire while our efforts were being sterilized in the West. Nor

did he agree with General Smuts that we should consider the next offers of peace made by Germany, even if superficially plausible until further military results had been obtained. Even more serious, to his mind, than the prospect of the War ending with the United States and Japan relatively unexhausted and predominant, was that of its ending with a predominant and unexhausted Germany. He was convinced that it was essential to go on hammering till Germany was definitely beaten and brought to a different frame of mind, so that we could secure a peace which Germany would keep and not have the strength to break. He thought General Smuts had hardly been quite fair to Mr. Balfour's statement as regards the European situation. That statement appeared to him not so much to lay down war aims, as to outline war aspirations which it did not rest with us to settle, though they might be settled, in so far as they were attainable, by a Conference with our Allies before we entered into any Peace Conference with the enemy. As regards war aims outside of Europe, these ranged from a small area of definite certainty to a wide region as to which there were differing degrees of doubt. The area of certainty comprised such matters as the Islands of the South Pacific and German South-West Africa, which could not in any circumstances be given back. In the middle sphere there was such a question as that of Mesopotamia. Mesopotamia obviously could not be handed back to Turkey except in the case of a complete German victory, and its development as part of the future Arab State could only take place under the guidance of ourselves, who were the initiators of the Arab idea, and had already taken the work in hand. As regards Palestine, he was prepared to accept the suggestion of the trusteeship being offered to America, though his own information led him to doubt whether America would be as willing to undertake it as Lord Reading had suggested, President Wilson's mind running in the direction rather of an international police than of American administration. At the other end of the scale came such a crucial and difficult case as that of German East Africa. The possibility of that territory ever going back to Germany ought to be resisted to the very last, in view of the dangers, arising not merely from black armies, but from enemy harbours, docks, submarine stations, wireless stations, and aerodromes, which it would involve to our whole position, and more particularly to our naval position in that part of the world. Speaking for himself, with a life's experience of seeing the work done by England in the development of backward countries, he saw no reason why we should be so urgent in handing over such a region to anybody else. While entirely in favour of the idea of the United States extending its responsibilities where it could properly do so, he was not otherwise anxious to set up a series of American colonies everywhere in proximity to ours, and he deprecated the idea of our going to the Peace Conference with the notion of only receiving as much as President Wilson chose to offer us.

Mr. Barnes expressed surprise at General Smuts' pessimistic forecast of the military situation, and pointed out that it disagreed with the forecast given by the Chief of the Imperial General Staff in his Memorandum. He agreed, however, that our statement of War Aims had been too ambitious in the past. Our people would not fight indefinitely for all these aims, and both in this country and in France there was a growing movement in a pacifist direction. The most effective way, in his opinion, of torpedoing that movement was to summon an Inter-Allied Conference for the revision of our War Aims, so as to bring them more into line with the views of the respective peoples. As regards the German colonies, he agreed with General Smuts' conception that the Tropical African colonies should be retained by the Powers now in possession, but subject to the oversight of an International Board, or of the League of Nations itself. With regard to the islands in the South Pacific, he heartily supported the view expressed by Mr. Hughes and Mr. Massey. If those islands were handed back to the Germans the South Pacific would no longer be safe to live in. As regards Mesopotamia, he considered it should be an Arab State under British guardianship, and believed the same also to be the destiny of Palestine. He did not consider that the British people, after all the efforts and sacrifices they had made, would be at all in favour of handing over Palestine to any other guardianship even that of America.

Mr. Chamberlain thought that the pessimistic tone of General Smuts' survey was due to the fact that he had purposely confined his review to the purely military situation, and had not taken account of the increasing effect upon the enemy of internal exhaustion. The extent of that exhaustion would depend, above all things, on our success in denying Russia to Germany. As regards Europe, he agreed with Lord Curzon that all we could do was to indicate ideal solutions, and he agreed that it might be necessary to revise some of the provisional undertakings given, which were contingent on the assumption of complete victory. But he was quite clear that the demand for revision should come from our Allies and not from us. After all, they would recognise sooner than anyone else whether the situation would allow of the fulfilment of their full war aims. It would be fatal for our future in Europe if we created the impression that we should extend our responsibilities, or invite the jealousy involved in great extensions of British territory. But he was clear that, whatever happened, we could not surrender to anyone either the South Pacific Islands or German South-West Africa. With regard to Mesopotamia, Palestine, and East Africa, the question resolved itself into one of the security of the British Empire and of its Allies. No one conversant with the position of the Indian Empire could contemplate the possibility of allowing a revival of the threat implied in the old Baghdad Railway scheme. It was equally essential that German East Africa should not revert to the Germans, and he suggested it might be desirable that a reasoned statement of the case with regard to German East Africa, from the point of view of our security, should be informally communicated to our Allies, and more particularly to President Wilson. As regards Tropical Africa generally, he was willing, in the last resort, to contemplate some such solution as General Smuts had advocated, though he did not consider it desirable in itself, in view of the difficulty of clearly defining the functions of the International Board. In any case he was absolutely opposed to any form of condominium. He was entirely in favour of the United States taking an increased responsibility in oversea affairs, and thought the idea of an American protectorate of Palestine probably the only one which would be well viewed by any of our Allies. It was interesting, however, to find in that connection how strongly Mr. Barnes had expressed himself against our abandoning it.

Mr. Hughes hoped that the British Government would not commit itself to what General Smuts had said with regard to the acceptance of German offers of peace. He agreed with Lord Curzon that it was essential to bring Germany to a right frame of mind. He was also opposed to the suggested Allied Conference on War Aims. To discuss these matters with President Wilson at this stage would only create serious embarrassment.

War Aims and Peace Terms

The Prime Minister expressed the conviction that an Inter-Allied Conference on War Aims, so far from leading to a general moderating of claims, would lead to each Ally accentuating its claims with a view to subsequent bargaining. His experience of past Conferences convinced him that such moderate statements of War Aims as those which he and President Wilson had put forward at the beginning of the year would never have been accepted at a Conference. On the question of Peace Terms he considered it essential that Germany should first be beaten. That was more important than the actual terms themselves. Germany had committed a great crime, and it was necessary to make it impossible that anyone should be tempted to repeat that offence. The Terms of Peace must be tantamount to some penalty for the offence. It was from this point of view, as well as for other reasons, that he thought it essential that Germany should be deprived of her colonies. When it came to the question of what was to be done with those colonies, the thing that really mattered was that they should be properly developed in the interests of their inhabitants. It did not seem to him, in view of the immense territories already in our possession which called for development, that the fullest development would be secured if we took them over. But he considered that America, with her immense wealth and enterprise, would do far more for the development of such a region as East Africa than we could, and therefore, from the point of view of development, in the interests both of the inhabitants and of the civilised world generally, as well as to commit her to oversea responsibilities, he was all in favour of inviting America to take in hand the trusteeship of that colony. He agreed, however, in answer to an interjection from Mr. Hughes, that, if America declined, the responsibility would have to fall back on ourselves. As regards the military situation, he quite admitted the possibility of our not breaking through and definitely beating the Germans in 1919. But he was confident that we should achieve such progress, both actually and from the point of view of the progressive deterioration of internal conditions among the enemy, that we could hope in 1920 to inflict upon Germany a defeat which she herself would recognise to be a defeat. He was not alarmed by the evidences of pacifism to which Mr. Barnes had referred. The temper of the French public was better than it had been at any period during the war, and our own workmen were not going to give in until we had beaten the

Germans. He was convinced that we ought to go on until we could dictate terms which would definitely mark the view taken by humanity of the heinousness of Germany's offence, and which would be the effective starting-point of a League of Nations.

In a brief discussion which followed, Mr. Massey and Mr. Montagu both drew attention to the effect upon the Moslem population of the British Empire of handing over Palestine, which was mainly a Moslem country, to the United States, which had no experience of administering the Moslems, and whose ideas as to the future of Palestine might be thoroughly unsympathetic to them.

Lord Reading expressed the view that America would not accept any proposal to make herself responsible for East Africa.

The Secretary of State for Foreign Affairs pointed out that, even if the whole of the War Aims he had indicated in Europe were fulfilled, Germany would still remain the biggest military Power in Europe, and that those War Aims were, therefore, such as Germany could, in the last resort, accept if beaten.

Chapter 4

The Far East

ESSENTIAL TO RENEW THE JAPANESE ALLIANCE
136. (*Grey's speech to the Imperial Conference of 26 May 1911, Cab/
38/18/40, printed in* P. Lowe, Great Britain and Japan, *p. 247*)

Extract

A paper has been circulated explaining what the strategical situation would be if the Japanese Alliance came to an end. If it came to an end owing to our giving notice to terminate the alliance, it cannot be doubted that not only would the strategical situation be altered immediately by our having to count the Japanese fleet as it now exists as possible enemies, but Japan would at once set to work to build a fleet more powerful than she would have if the alliance did not exist. We, on the other hand, instead of keeping the modest squadron in Chinese waters which we do at the present time, would have to keep—if we are to secure the sea communications between the Far East and Europe, and also between the Far East and Australia and New Zealand—a separate fleet in Chinese waters which would be at least equal to a two-Power standard in those waters, including in that two-Power standard counted possibly against us not only the Japanese fleet as it is at the present time, but the fleet which Japan would certainly build if we put an end to the alliance. I think the paper I have referred to shows what a tremendous and undesirable change that would be in the strategical situation; and I am convinced that in the interests of strategy, in the interests of naval expenditure, and in the interests of stability, it is essential that the Japanese Alliance should be extended. I mean extended in time—not extended in scope. I do not mean it should be made a bigger thing than it is, but that it should be prolonged in its present form. There is one thing that occurs to me as a possible objection which might be brought against that, and it is this: most parts of the British Empire are not only very averse to admitting Japanese immigrants but they are perfectly determined that never under any circumstances will they admit Japanese immigrants in a sense which would include numbers of Japanese in the population, and introduce Japanese competition into their own countries. I think people may say: 'Is it possible that you should continue an alliance with Japan, and that Japan should not sooner or later raise the question—what she would call her claim, I suppose—to have her people admitted into the territories of her ally?' She has never raised that point yet. She has never mentioned it in connection with the alliance at all. So long as she is willing to extend the alliance, and has no word to say about immigration, and so long as she leaves our hands, and the hands of every Dominion Government as free as they are now with regard to their immigration problems, I can conceive no objection whatever to extending the alliance... I do not think there is the least chance of a quarrel with Japan, because I am quite convinced that the Japanese policy—her whole arrangements with Canada show it, and I find it in every way—is to concentrate her people in Korea and Manchuria and the parts neighbouring to herself in the Far East, and she does not want to encourage them to go abroad, though she has some difficulty in preventing them.

BRITISH INTERESTS IN CHINA—THE TWENTY-ONE DEMANDS

137. (*Memo. by Alston, 1 February 1915, F.O. 371/2326/15089*)

Extract

We are in the anomalous position in China of working entirely at political cross-purposes with our allies, the Japanese. In the purely industrial sphere we are actively in conflict with them. Our avowed policy is the maintenance, so far as possible, of a strong China—as opposed to the known desire of Japan for a weak China; and in the forefront of this problem is the conflicting attitude of the two Governments with regard to Yuan Shih-kai himself. We have made up our minds that the preservation of Yuan is a guarantee for the continued integrity of China, and, for good or evil, we have staked our money on him and given him to understand that we are prepared to back him as the one force in China calculated to keep the country in order. Yuan, in return, acknowledges our good intentions, and recognises that he owes his position in part to our support. But he also knows that behind his back we have made, or tried to make, a bargain with

Russia over one considerable portion of the old Chinese Empire; and a bargain with Japan over another considerable portion. This knowledge goes far to invalidate our position in his counsels, and to foster a suspicion in his mind that our support of him is not bound, under all circumstances, to be whole-hearted, and might even be withdrawn.

The Japanese, on the other hand, have made no secret of their enmity to him and of their intention to keep China in leading strings. In fact, it is common knowledge that they are trying feverishly to discredit him, and using every means within their power to bring about his downfall. A subsidised Japanese daily paper in Peking attacks him in and out of season, and the efforts of the Japanese Legation are unceasingly directed to undermining his power and influence. The Japanese Government have, it is true maintained a correct attitude on the surface, but there can be little doubt that they have been secretly encouraging every movement of hostility to him that has taken place in the last two years.

Yuan Shih-kai declines, not unnaturally, to be misled by official assurances of friendship from the Japanese Government, and he is entirely convinced that the whole future of China depends on warding off the danger to her integrity which the Japanese advance entails. He quite realises that the European Powers have their own problems and troubles in the West. Their centre of gravity is not in the Far East. But Japan has nothing else to think about, and China is, and must be, the objective of all her foreign policy. Accordingly, Yuan's main preoccupation is to find a set-off to her activity and a barrier to her further advance, and in our consolidation in the Yang-tsze Valley lies, or ought to lie, his salvation. With a friendly Power predominant in this area, he can in an emergency become master of the situation by having the control of the whole railway system that radiates from Hankow in unresisting British hands. With the same region entirely overrun by hostile Japanese, he will be obstructed at every point and reduced to impotence.

The anti-Yuan policy of the Japanese is therefore at the same time anti-British. It may be that it is not primarily intended to be so, but there are indications that the Japanese are up against us specifically in every direction where our policy lies. There was not the least apparent reason, from an industrial point of view, why the Japanese should make such a strenuous effort to get the concession for the enormous Yang-tsze railway from Nanking to Hsiangtan. Industrially they were admittedly unable to see it through, and their object must have been a purely political one. That has failed and they are determined to get an equivalent in an almost equally considerable railway from Nanchang to Hankow to connect, it is true, with a line of theirs from Foochow through Fukien. For this they can with some plausibility show an industrial motive. They point to their Hanyang ironworks at Hankow, and the Pingshsiang mines in the neighbourhood of Changsha. They are avowedly bent on invading the Yang-tsze, at least industrially, to a greater extent than they have done up to the present, and in proportion as their interests accumulate there the predominance of British interests tends to become undermined. But at the bottom of it all must be a political motive of some sort.

Reference should not be omitted to the overtures made to us by the Japanese for an economic alliance in China in addition to our political alliance. We have nothing to gain, but, on the contrary, much to lose by such an association. Nor should we, from the point of view of China, stand to gain by the proposal for a Russo-Anglo-Japanese alliance in the Far East, whereby we should be sandwiched between China's two deadliest enemies. The future of China has been said to lie in the hands of Japan and Great Britain—and there is no reason why this view should not be correct. It is based on the fact that while Japan is China's most powerful neighbour and has larger interests at stake than anyone else, she can never, while the Yuan régime lasts, gain confidence of the Chinese Government. Their ear and confidence is possessed by Great Britain, if by anybody; and therefore a mutual understanding between the allies might be followed by joint control of China's destiny, which is now suggested as our terms for the rendition of Kiaochow to China. As it is, no such understanding exists: our policies are often diametrically opposed, and although the President was told officially at the outbreak of the revolution in 1911 that we should act together in our policy towards China, he has repeatedly during 1913 pointed out to His Majesty's Minister and to me the obvious divergence of our policies, and it has been impossible to answer his arguments.

Has the moment arrived when, without recriminations of any kind, we can ask the Japanese Government in the friendliest fashion to state frankly what it is they are aiming at, and endeavour, on the strength of the alliance, to create a solidarity between them and ourselves which will at least remove the increasing risk of general political friction?

138. (*Grey to Greene, 20 February 1915, no. 47, F.O. 371/2322/9499*)
Your telegram No. 64 of 10th February: Japanese demands on China.

In view of the last sentence of the communication made to me by the Japanese Ambassador on 1st October, 1913 (see Confidential print), I was, I think, justified in supposing that the memorandum respecting the demands had been communicated to me for my observations. As, however, Baron Kato says that he has not invited my views, I shall of course not offer any remarks in regard to the details of the demands.

I wish, however, to make two general observations:

1. If any of the demands or wishes presented by the Japanese Government should be found to conflict with British commercial interests, such as concessions already held by or promised to British subjects, I am confident that the Japanese Government will be ready to discuss them with us as freely as we discussed with them concessions in Manchuria granted to British subjects which they held to be in conflict with Japanese interests, such as South Manchurian Railway.

2. I am also most anxious that Japan should not put forward any demands which could fairly be held to impair the independence or integrity of China, as His Majesty's Government would be in a difficult position if called upon to explain how such demands could be reconciled with the terms of the Anglo-Japanese Alliance.

I want to maintain the solidarity of that alliance by taking the side of Japan whenever any question about Japanese demands in China is raised by any other Power, but to do this I must be able to show that any demand questioned is not in conflict with the avowed object of the alliance.

Please speak to Baron Kato in the above sense.

139. (*Jordan to Grey, 1 March 1915, no. 40,*
F.O. *371/2322/9499*)

The general effect of Japanese demands would be to place China largely under tutelage of Japan and to give Japan a privileged position in South Manchuria, Eastern Inner Mongolia, Shantung and Fukien. The demands, if examined with aid of a map, will be seen to be admirably conceived for the purpose of obtaining strategical and political advantages of highest importance.

In north they supply political formula and all the machinery necessary to consolidate Japanese position in Manchuria and to leave the way for its eventual absorption, while extension of the same procedure to Eastern Inner Mongolia draws a circle of the Japanese domination land round Peking.

Similarly, possession of Port Arthur and Kiaochow at opposite ends of the Gulf of Chihli, with Japanese-owned railways controlling means of communication far into the interior, will give Japan complete command of approaches by sea and will place Government at Peking at her mercy.

In south, extension of Japanese influence is much less advanced, but policy is the same. Here Formosa serves as base of advance. Japan's position there gives her control of coast line of two provinces of Fukien and Chekiang, and a network of railways has been designed to link up ports on the coast line with great commercial centres on Yang-tsze. The region comprised within a line drawn from Chaochow-fu (in Canton province) to Wuchang and from Nanchang to Hangchow, and bounded on the east by sea between Chaochow and Hangchow, is a measure clearly covered by Japanese programme. Permeated by Japanese national railways and subjected to peaceful means of penetration which invariably accompany all such undertakings, and which during the past fifteen years have transformed Corea and Manchuria into Japanese provinces, it could only be question of time until all this vast region became sphere of Japanese influence in which British trade would struggle for a bare existence as it now does in Manchuria.

But if Japan obtains consolidation of her position in Manchuria and Inner Mongolia and reversion of German rights in Shantung, she can easily afford to make good her promise to restore Kiaochow to China and to forgo her ambitious railway projects in South Yang-tsze, or at least confine them to her original claim for a railway from Nanchang to Fuchow.

(Repeated to Tokyo.)

140. (*Grey to Jordan, 7 May 1915, no. 78, F.O. 371/2324/9499*)

Chinese Minister has informed me of the serious state of things between Japan and China, and has asked me, by instruction, what our attitude would have to be, as an ally of Japan, if there was a breach between Japan and China. He had observed from statements made by me in Parliament that we had received confidential information from Japan.

I said that I understood that Japan had also given information as to her demands to some other Powers. We had received some information from Japan about her demands after they had been presented to China, but we had not been consulted about them, nor been a party to them, and we therefore had no responsibility with regard to them. I had, however, recently expressed the earnest hope to Japan that a peaceful settlement might be arrived at. I understood from the Japanese Government that the Chinese reply had put forward new demands, and went back upon some things that had been regarded as settled, and I heard to-day that Japan had sent an ultimatum to China in consequence. Japanese Minister for Foreign Affairs, however, had said that, notwithstanding this, in order to arrive at a peaceful settlement, even at the eleventh hour, Japanese Government were willing to withdraw all the articles of group 5 still outstanding, and to reserve them for consideration at some later date.

I told the Chinese Minister that I understood the difficulty of yielding to an ultimatum that contained no concession; but, as the outstanding articles of group 5 were withdrawn from the scope of the ultimatum, this was a concession, and it appeared to me that China should take advantage of this to come to an agreement.

I observed to the Chinese Minister that the nations of the world were now so engaged that I saw no prospect of any interference in the dispute between China and Japan. The dispute would have to be settled by these two countries alone, and I earnestly hoped that, now the outstanding articles of group 5 were withdrawn, an agreement would be reached.

You should use your influence to get China to accept the last

Japanese demands if the outstanding claims under group 5 are excluded from the ultimatum.

EXPULSION OF GERMANS IN CHINA

141. (*Grey to Jordan, 11 February 1916, no. 30K, F.O. 371/2647/50*)

The general situation with regard to the war and more especially with regard to the supply of munitions to Russia and Japanese naval co-operation which we are again asking them to consider make it essential that the Allies should obtain the whole-hearted support of the Japanese Government. I am not sanguine of doing so unless the Allies are prepared to give in return some concrete example of their goodwill in the form of some definite material concession to Japanese aspirations. Such a concession can, I fear, be found only in China. But I would make it clear from the onset that it is not proposed to take any action which could be described as satisfying Japan at the expense of China, without the consent of the latter and without providing compensation for her acquiescence. The following is a brief outline of a proposal which suggests itself to us:

China to be asked to break with Germany in the sense not only of expelling all Germans including the Minister and Consular Officers from German concessions and elsewhere, but also of repudiating all financial and industrial agreements made with Germany prior to the war. This would have the effect of depriving Germans of all loan and indemnity payments and would be a severe blow to her. The mere prospect of it would do much to bring home to Germany how much she has to lose by continuing the war. It would also set free the German concessions at Tientsin and Hankow, the northern section of the Tientsin–Pukow Railway, and the Hankow–Ichang section of the Hukuang Railways. His Majesty's Government would make no claim to any of the above assets and it is hoped that a similar disclaimer would be made by the Russian and French Governments. The assets, to which we might possibly be prepared to add the retrocession of Wei Hai Wei to China, would be the inducement to obtain the acquiescence of the Chinese in the general expulsion scheme and the co-operation of the Japanese both in that scheme and in the general conduct of the war. Neither China nor Japan can be expected to co-operate heartily in a European quarrel unless their own interests are assured. I fully realise, above proposal cannot but be disappointing to you since it entails renunciation of much for which you have fought so successfully during recent years. Compensation to Japan however will, in any case, have to be found for the part which she has played so far and under this proposal, we shall merely be helping her, in return for her co-operation which is sorely needed, to obtain now certain advantages most of which she will certainly claim at the end of the war when I should not feel justified in opposing her acquisition of them.

I should be glad to receive your frank observations on the proposal.

On receiving your observations I will consult with French and Russian Governments. You should in the meantime say nothing to your French and Russian colleagues.

142. (*Jordan to Grey, 15 February 1916, no. 68*K, *F.O. 371/2647/50*)

Minutes

We are well aware that every Chinese individual and every intelligent British businessman in the Far East would infinitely prefer that the Germans should remain in China than that they should be expelled and their present possessions given to the Japanese. If the war had not broken out, the Legation policy of opposing any Japanese move likely to prejudice our position might have been continued indefinitely. But the present state of affairs has shown that it is quite impossible to maintain this attitude. In talking of the future of the German Concessions, the Secretary of State has, for example, found it necessary to state that H.M.G., speaking for themselves, would have no objection to their acquisition by Japan. We have thereby tacitly concurred in the acquisition by Japan of assets which will enable her to improve her position at the expense of our own future commercial development and of our good name among the Chinese.

We are in fact, by the policy which circumstances have forced upon us, undermining our future position in China without gaining either the material support of the Japanese government or the good will of the Japanese people. It is now for the Admiralty and War Office to decide in how far it is necessary for us to obtain the whole-hearted co-operation of Japan in carrying on the war. If such co-operation is really essential, we must buy it at the expense both of our prestige and of our commercial future in China. If it is unnecessary, let us concentrate our efforts on saving as much as possible from the troubled waters in which the Japanese are now able to fish with impunity—we shall thereby preserve also the good will of the Chinese which will be a useful asset in the future.

T.H.L[yons]

(Minutes by Alston, Langley and Nicolson substantially as above)

I agree with Sir A. Nicolson's view, which I think is also that of the other minutes. I do not wish to make offers to Japan at the expense of China, but in my opinion if we had not made it clear that we should not bar Japan's expansion of interests in the Far East it would have been clearly to Japan's advantage to throw in her lot with Germany. Japan is barred from every other part of the world except the Far East and the Anglo-Japanese Alliance cannot be maintained if she is to be barred from expansion there also and if we are to claim the German Concessions in China as well as taking German colonies in Africa and elsewhere.

E.G[rey]

RECOGNITION OF JAPANESE CLAIMS

143. (*Colonial Office to Foreign Office, 2 February 1917,*
    F.O. 371/2950/9266)

Following message received from Japanese Government:

Having regard to possibility of peace conference at some future date, it is considered by the Japanese Government that the time has come to approach His Majesty's Government with a view to obtaining from them an assurance of their willingness to support Japan's claims in regard to disposal of Germany's rights in Shantung and possessions in islands north of the Equator on the occasion of such a conference. His Excellency said that an announcement had lately been published that eventual occupation of Constantinople by Russia had been assented to by the Allies, and a special agreement had been signed in connection with the entry of Italy into the war. These and other possible international arrangements in the future had been discussed between Viscount Grey and Japanese Ambassador in London from time to time. Japanese Government hoped that in these circumstances they might now receive an assurance from His Majesty's Government in the sense desired. Imperial Government would, on receiving such an assurance, next approach French and Russian Governments with a similar request.

His Majesty's Government had intended to address a full despatch to you on the subject of the disposal of the German colonies in the Pacific, and, if possible, to discuss matters with your Prime Minister, and they much regret that the urgency of the matter compels them to raise the question in this form.

His Majesty's Government are very unwilling to give any pledge to Japan before peace negotiations, and doubt, indeed, whether they are justified in so doing without consent of their Allies; but Admiralty are very anxious to secure some additional light cruisers in South Atlantic to deal with enemy raiders and additional destroyers to cope with submarines in Mediterranean.

Japan was very recently asked by His Majesty's Government for naval assistance in this direction, and for this reason they desire to be in a position to give some undertaking, if necessary, showing that they are willing to meet wishes of Japan as regards islands north of Equator. The question of Shantung is one of great difficulty and complexity, but the islands are in Japanese possession, and to induce her to surrender them would be practically impossible. We should not, therefore, in fact be giving up anything if we recognise Japan's claim to the islands, and I should be glad to learn that, should His Majesty's Government find themselves unable before the conference meets to avoid giving some pledge on the subject, your Ministers are prepared to acquiesce. In any case, no assurance would be given without a corresponding assurance from Japan that they will support us in our general policy and in our retention of German Pacific colonies south of Equator. Desired assurance not to be made public without consent of His Majesty's Government.

INCOMPATIBILITY OF JAPAN AND THE U.S.A.

144. (*War Cabinet 142, 22 May 1917, Cab/23/2*)

12. The War Cabinet discussed a telegram received from Mr. Balfour (Appendix II) conveying a suggestion that if the United States were to build more destroyers in the place of some of the capital ships on their present programme, we should guarantee to replace those capital ships in the case of any attack upon the United States by a third party, and that this guarantee might eventually be developed into a general defensive Naval Alliance

between the two Powers. As the Power which the United States feared most was Japan, the proposed guarantee or the Alliance would raise the whole question of our relations with Japan.

Lord Robert Cecil explained that it might be possible to gain Japanese assent to our alliance with the United States either by adopting Lord Grey's policy of giving Japan a free hand over the whole of China (which he personally strongly deprecated as involving serious dangers in future to India and to our position generally), or by giving her a free hand in a definite sphere in a portion of China, *i.e.*, Manchuria and Shantung. It might also be possible to induce Japan to come into a Triple Alliance with ourselves and the United States, on the basis of American assent to the suggested Japanese sphere of influence in China. Personally he was inclined, at the moment, not to go further than explaining to the Japanese that we were giving this guarantee in order to secure the necessary destroyers, and reassuring them that we would certainly not lend them to the United States for the purpose of an attack upon Japan. But he was informed that the Japanese would not be content with such an explanation, and would regard the agreement as involving in fact a general Anglo-American Alliance affecting the situation in the Far East, and interfering with Japan's ambitions in China.

In the course of a general discussion it was urged that it would be very inadvisable to do anything at the present stage of the war that could give the Japanese any justifiable ground for alarm or suspicion, and so upset the present position in the Pacific. This view was endorsed by the Secretary of State for the Colonies, who pointed out that Australia and New Zealand, which had originally assented with some reluctance to the Japanese request for our support in the matter of the Pacific islands north of the Equator, were now satisfied both with the arrangement and with the general attitude of Japan, and would no doubt be seriously disturbed by anything that would endanger the safety of the Pacific.

It was also urged that it by no means followed, from the suggestion confidentially made to Mr. Balfour, that the American Senate would endorse anything in the nature of an Anglo-American Naval Alliance, and that consequently there was a danger of our upsetting existing relations with Japan without securing anything tangible from the United States.

The First Sea Lord further suggested that the proposed

guarantee might, as a matter of fact, not really be necessary, as he was by no means certain that, for the purposes of a war with Japan, the United States were not really more in need of additional destroyers than of further capital ships.

The War Cabinet approved the telegram already sent in reply to that from Mr. Balfour, and directed a further telegram in the same sense to be sent.

The First Sea Lord was also instructed to furnish a detailed examination of the probable requirements of the United States in the matter of capital ships or destroyers in the contingency of a war with Japan, for communication to Mr. Balfour, in order to convince the United States Government that destroyers would be of more use to them than capital ships in any war with Japan.

JAPANESE INTERVENTION IN SIBERIA

145. (*War Cabinet 417, May 1918, Cab/23/6 Appendix*)

I. Note of a Conversation between Lord R. Cecil and the Japanese Ambassador.
II. Copy of a Telegram from Baron Goto to the Japanese Ambassador in London.

I.

Note of a Conversation between Lord R. Cecil and the Japanese Ambassador, in the form of a Draft Telegram to Sir C. Greene, Tokyo

The Japanese Ambassador called on me to-day and left with me a copy of a telegram which he had received from Baron Goto.

He read it to me, and I told him that the questions raised in it were so important that I could not give him a final answer without further consideration; but if he would allow me to express my private opinions on the subject, for what they were worth, I should be glad to do so.

He assented, and I then told him that, in my view, the situation in Russia rendered the question of intervention extremely urgent. As far as I was concerned, I should be quite willing that Semenoff should be supported, if that was the wish of the Japanese military authorities. In the same way, the Government had been anxious to make use of the Czecho-Slovaks now collecting at Vladivostock, and we had approached the French Government on the subject. I recognised that these forces could be effective only if they were strongly supported by Japan, and if that happened I should be quite willing that Japan should take the direction of the whole expedition, provided of course that the Japanese made it clear that they were going into Siberia, not for the purpose of obtaining any territorial advantage, but in order to assist Russia and the Allied cause generally: and provided that the Japanese were prepared to push their expedition as far west as Chiliabinsk, or somewhere in that neighbourhood.

With respect to the particular questions in the telegram that he had read to me, I told him that Mr. Lockhart believed that joint action in Moscow with the Soviet Government would be successful, but that he had now arrived at the conclusion that intervention was so urgent that we ought to act whether we obtained the invitation of the Bolshevist Government or not. I did not deal specifically with the second and third questions, nor did I express a definite opinion as to whether we should leave Semenoff in the lurch, but I promised to consider that.

The Ambassador asked me what was the state of affairs in Washington.

I avoided giving him a direct reply, but I read him a passage from your telegram No. 535, in which Baron Goto is reported to have said that the President showed some signs of reconsidering his objections, and I told the Ambassador that we would spare no effort to obtain American approval for intervention.

I then asked him whether he thought that his Government, with American approval, would be prepared to intervene to the extent of sending a force to Chiliabinsk or thereabouts for the purpose of making a diversion which might oblige the Germans to diminish their forces on the Western front.

The Ambassador professed that this was an entirely new idea, and said that his Government had so far considered only the necessity of intervening to prevent German penetration to the Pacific coast. The proposal that they should intervene in general assistance of the Allied cause had not, as far as he knew, been fully considered by them.

I then said that the matter was of the utmost importance; that the whole course of the war might be determined by an effective intervention in Siberia; and that I ventured to appeal to the Japanese, as our Allies, to do their utmost to come to our assistance. I added that if we knew that they were ready to intervene on this scale our hands would be greatly strengthened in any negotiations we might have in Washington.

He again said that, from his own point of view, he would be glad to give a favourable reply, but that he felt he could not do so without consulting his Government, as the matter was undoubtedly a new one to them.

I did not tell him that this appeared to be inconsistent with the tenor of Baron Goto's observations to your Excellency and with the various communications which have been made to us by the Japanese General Staff.

The Ambassador left me, saying that he would report to his Government the observations I had made as coming from myself, and that he would hope to have in the course of a few days an official reply to the telegram which he had left with me.

(Initialled)   R.C.

Foreign Office, May 22, 1918.

II.

Copy of Telegram, dated May 19, from Baron Goto to the Japanese Ambassador in London

Some time ago the British Government made a proposal to the Imperial Government looking to an intervention in Siberia, which they deemed necessary in order to check the penetration of German influence. Subsequently, however, having regard to the attitude of the American Government in the matter, the British Government are understood to have found it advisable to induce, if possible, the Soviet Government to invite the Allied intervention, and instructed Mr. Lockhart to enter upon the negotiations with the Soviet Government on these lines. The recent course of these negotiations is unknown to the Imperial Government, but it is presumed that no concrete result has yet been obtained. On the other hand, the British Government, fearing that the continued support on the part of the Allies to the Semenoff detachment, whose avowed object is to crush the Bolsheviks might hinder the progress of the negotiations above referred to, requested the Japanese Government to give also an advice to

Semenoff, with a view to restraining for the time being the advance of his detachment. The desired advice was given to Semenoff through a Japanese in touch with him, but it is found impossible to dissuade him from his determination. On the contrary, he is continuing his advance encouraged by the success he has so far achieved over the Bolsheviks, and, thanks to the continuous enlistment of the Cossacks in his detachment, its strength has already reached 5,000 and is growing stronger every day. He is now menacing Kalimuskaya.

You are hereby requested to seek an interview with the Secretary of State for Foreign Affairs, and in calling his attention to the above circumstances you will express to him the deep concern felt by the Imperial Government in regard to the situation thus created for them as well as for the Allies, and ask for the frank expression of his views on the following points:

1. Is there any positive prospect of Mr. Lockhart's efforts in inducing the Soviet Government to invite the Allied intervention being crowned with the desired success in an immediate future?

2. In the event of an invitation for the Allied intervention being extended by the Soviet Government, the immediate object aimed at by the latter would presumably be either the suppression of the recalcitrant elements in the country or the defence of Russia against the German invasion. In the opinion of the Imperial Government, it appears that in the first case there would be no reason for the Allies to accept the invitation, while in the second case, so long as the German military operations do not extend to Siberia, the scheme of despatching troops there, as originally proposed by the British Government, would not be compatible with the object as held in view by the Soviet Government. What would be the views of the British Government on this point?

3. It is true that the Soviet Government are now exercising the actual power in various parts in Russia, but they can hardly be said to represent the will of Russians in general. It is a patent fact that there exist a great many elements totally incompatible with the said Government owing to the profound animosity felt against them. In these circumstances, it is feared that the Allied intervention undertaken as the result

of an understanding with the Soviet Government, even though with the object of resisting the German aggression would be liable to provoke the ill-feelings of these elements against the Allies, as having the effect of strengthening the position of the Soviet Government. What would be the opinion of the British Government on this point?

4. Semenoff launched forth the present enterprise in entire reliance upon the moral and material support of the British, French and Japanese Governments, and it is not without reason that he should be counting upon the continuous assistance of the Allies. If the Allies were to stop their help suddenly at the present moment and leave him in the lurch, would it not bring about the loss of their prestige in the eyes of Semenoff's friends, and give the false impression to the general populace in Russia that the Allies are unreliable, with the result of driving them into the arms of Germany?

RENEWAL OF THE ANGLO-JAPANESE ALLIANCE

146. (*Report of the Anglo-Japanese Alliance Committee, 21 January 1921, D.B.F.P. 1st series, XIV, no. 212*)

Extract

In accordance with the terms of reference, your Lordship's Committee have examined the two following questions:

(1) Whether the Anglo-Japanese Alliance should be renewed, and, if so, on what terms; and

(2) The policy which His Majesty's Government should in future pursue in the Far East.

26. We now come to an aspect of the matter which, in our judgment, outweighs in importance all other considerations, and to which we wish to call the most serious attention of His Majesty's Government. If the cardinal feature of our foreign policy in the future is to cultivate the closest relations with the United States and to secure their whole-hearted co-operation in the maintenance of peace in every part of the world, the renewal of the Alliance in anything like its present shape may prove a formidable obstacle to the realisation of that aim.

27. We now pass on to the consideration of the second point of the terms of reference, viz.: 'The policy which His Majesty's Government should in future pursue in the Far East.'

28. We have no fault to find with the principles which have hither-to determined our policy in the Far East, nor do we recommend any departure from them, but we do hold strongly that a purely passive attitude, even with physical force behind it, is not best calculated to uphold them. In the last analysis the independence and integrity of China, which is among our foremost aims, depends upon the reality or otherwise of the open door policy. That is the crux of the whole situation. All forms of economic penetration are opposed to that principle, for they ultimately lead to the closing of the door and the usurpation of political control. Experience has shown us that neither military or naval force, nor any treaty formula can, in themselves, be regarded as a sufficient safeguard against that insidious method of political encroachment. Salvation must, therefore, be sought elsewhere. In our opinion, the best safeguard against a danger which lies as much in the weakness of China as in the aggressive tendencies of Japan, is to be found in a constructive policy for the rehabilitation of China. It would carry us too far to enter into the details of such a policy, but suffice it to say that it has already been outlined in its main features and remains on record. Its beginnings may already be perceived in the formation of the Four Powers' Consortium. We would, however, repeat that in our opinion it would be hopeless to embark upon such a policy singlehanded, or without adequate naval support. Japan could thwart us at every turn. The war has left us too exhausted to cope with so great a problem. To succeed in such an effort we believe the co-operation of the United States to be indispensable. American ideals in China are identical with our own. Neither Power seeks territorial aggrandisement or privileged position. Both are actuated by a feeling of goodwill towards China and a genuine desire for peace in the Far East as elsewhere.

Recommendations

29. A careful consideration of all the arguments, both for and against renewal of the Alliance, has resulted in the unanimous con-clusion that it should be dropped, and that in its stead should, if possible, be substituted a Tripartite *Entente* between the United States, Japan and Great Britain, consisting in a declaration of general principles which can be subscribed to by all parties with-out the risk of embarrassing commitments.

. . . .

For the effective support and the ultimate success of those principles we must rely on the closest co-operation with the United States rather than with Japan.

30. In submitting these recommendations to your Lordship we desire to add that we have approached the question not solely as a matter affecting the Far East, but from the broader standpoint of world politics, which are dominated by our relations with the United States as constituting the prime factor in the maintenance of order and peace throughout the world.

31. In the regrettable event of America finding it impossible to enter into any sort of arrangement with us such as indicated above, we would suggest as an alternative the conclusion of an agreement with Japan, brought up to date and in harmony with the spirit of the League of Nations, and so framed as not to exclude the eventual participation of the United States.

147. (*Cabinet, 30 May 1921, Cab/23/25/43*)

Extract

Lord Curzon then said that he proposed to summarise the arguments which had been advanced for and against the renewal of the Alliance. He would then explain the view held by those who were in close touch with the matter, and would give to the Cabinet the proposals of his Department as to how the question should be dealt with. Against the renewal of the Alliance it was said, in the first place, that the reasons which had led originally to His Majesty's Government entering into the Alliance had now ceased to exist. It had been first formed as a counterpoise to an aggressive Russia in the Far East, and the identity of our own and Japanese interests had brought us together against that Power. It was true that Russia was now disintegrated and that Germany, who had later in the day appeared as a dangerous rival in the Far East, had ceased to exist as a Great Power. There was, consequently, force in the argument brought forward to the effect that the main reasons for the Alliance had ceased to exist. He would, however, later on, when he came to give the arguments on the other side, call the attention of the Cabinet to how the political situation might again change in the future. The second argument used against the renewal of the Alliance was that its existence was not only a source of suspicion and irritation but of actual embarrassment in the United States. It was only right to say, however, that the cause for such a feeling had been largely removed by the insertion of Article IV and by the subsequent understanding with the Japanese Government, to whom it had been made quite clear that Great Britain would not go to war in order to support her in a conflict with the United States. Even so, it could not be denied that there was considerable suspicion of the Alliance in America, and it might almost be said that the United States authorities were tempted to make it an excuse for adding to their naval armaments. The third argument against the renewal of the Alliance was that it was alienating from us the sympathy of China and rendering our tasks there more difficult. Our policy in China had always been that of the 'open door'. Lord Curzon then proceeded to explain what an unwieldy and helpless country China had become, and pointed out how it must naturally be the desire of His Majesty's Government to see China built up again and some sort of cohesion arrived at in that country. Almost at the door of this great, helpless body there existed Japan, whose national temperament was fiercely imperialistic and where the German spirit of disciplined aggression had been imbibed to a great extent. Japan herself was incapable of maintaining more than her present population, and it was natural that she should look to China. This was the great factor in the Far Eastern world, and he would like to remind his colleagues of the degree to which, by her action in Korea, Formosa, the Pescadores, Manchuria and Shantung, Japan was already forming a ring round China. It would naturally be said by the opponents of the Alliance that its renewal would give strength to this aggressive Power, and that Great Britain was encouraging Japan's policy, which she really ought to resist. Those were the arguments which had been used against a continuance of the Alliance, and he would now explain what, in his opinion, were the reasons that might be advanced in favour of its renewal, and which, he thought, on the whole made out the stronger case.

Firstly, he did not think that anyone could doubt that the Alliance had proved a great and substantial success. It had, at different times during its existence, helped both the contracting parties. It had undoubtedly been of assistance to Japan in her war with Russia, and, similarly, no one could deny that it had benefited us considerably in the late War. People at home, indeed, hardly realised what the Alliance had meant to Great Britain in the Pacific, to say nothing of what the Japanese had done in the Indian Ocean and the Mediterranean.

The Prime Minister, interposing at this stage, said that he would like the Admiralty and the War Office to prepare Papers showing the extent to which the Japanese Alliance had respectively assisted in the naval operations during the War and also in supplying the Russians with war material.

The Secretary of State for Foreign Affairs, continuing, said there could be no question that the Alliance had been a success, and that this must be regarded as one argument in favour of its renewal. The second argument in favour of its renewal was that, although Russia and Germany had for the moment ceased to be Great Powers which had to be taken into account, there was no certainty that in a few years' time we should not have a regenerated Russia; and, whatever the form of the Russian Government might then be, the dangers of the past would again be revived. Moreover, with a resuscitated Russia and a revived Germany, it might well be that in ten years' time we might be faced with a combination of these Powers in the Far East, and to meet such a situation an Alliance with Japan would be the natural guarantee. Again, granting the aggressive character of Japan, should it not be remembered that the Alliance had given us the means of putting a check on Japan's ambitions: for example, the Japanese Government had been negotiating railway agreements with China, which had aroused suspicion on all sides; but since he (Lord Curzon) had entered the Foreign Office in succession to Mr. Balfour, the 'consortium' of Powers had been arranged, which Japan, sooner than be left in isolation, had been compelled to join. This included China, Great Britain, the United States, and France, and Belgium as a prospective member. Once such agreement was arrived at it was possible to tell Japan that she must fall into line with these arrangements or else the Powers concerned would fight her commercially. The result was that Japan had agreed to co-operate, and we were now in a position to exert pressure on her. There was another point, from the naval and military point of view, and that was that so long as the Alliance remained in force we were absolved from maintaining large naval and military forces in the Far East. There was yet another argument in favour of a continuance of the Alliance, and that was that it was looked on with considerable favour by our Allies. He ventured to think that France, on account of her Possessions in the Far East, would regard with dismay any proposal on our part not to renew the Alliance. Holland would unquestionably take the same view, on account of her Possessions in the East Indies, since it would be a great temptation to an unfriendly Japan to pounce on and seize these possessions. Lastly, the feeling in Japan itself had to be considered, and there was no question that the Japanese as a whole were in favour of the renewal of the Alliance. Our general experience had been that the Japanese were scrupulous and faithful in carrying out their obligations. No doubt, as was often said, the Japanese were not above intrigue, but he would like to ask if they were the only people who did this? He personally could not think of a single instance when the Japanese had not carried out their word.

148. (*Cabinet, 30 June 1921, Cab/23/26/56*)

Extract

(2) With reference to Cabinet 43 (21), Conclusion 2, the Cabinet met to consider the attitude to be taken up by the Prime Minister and his colleagues of the British Government at the Imperial meetings at which the question of the renewal of the Anglo-Japanese Alliance was being discussed.

The Secretary of State for Foreign Affairs gave to the Cabinet a summary of the changes which had taken place in the situation since the question was last discussed some three weeks previously, and also explained the attitude which had been taken up by the Prime Ministers of the various Dominions (*see Stenographic Notes of the 8th, 9th and 10th Meetings, which have been circulated to the Cabinet*). Briefly, Mr. Meighen, the Prime Minister of the Dominion of Canada, had opposed the renewal of the Treaty even more strongly than had been anticipated. He had emphasized the very strong opposition in America to the renewal of the Alliance, and had given the impression that the Canadian Government would be unable to agree to any form of exclusive Agreement with Japan, and that Canada would have to dissociate herself from a decision to enter into any such Agreement. Mr. Hughes and Mr. Massey, on the other hand, had rebutted Mr. Meighen's arguments and had supported the renewal of the Alliance. They had pointed out that by throwing over a friend who had stood by them in the late War the British Empire would earn the contempt of the world at large, and that such action instead of raising would probably lower the British people in the estimation of the American public. General Smuts had made a thoughtful speech, but had adopted a somewhat balancing attitude which was half helpful and half embarrassing. The general points made by General Smuts had been that we must do nothing to antagonise Japan, the Prussia of the East, while maintaining good relations with the United States of America. General Smuts seemed, on the whole, inclined to favour a discussion with Japan and the United States of America, leading to an exchange of identic notes.

The Secretary of State for Foreign Affairs then called attention to a new factor which had arisen since the Cabinet last considered the question, and that was that the British Ambassador in Washington (Sir Auckland Geddes), who had originally advised a renewal of the Alliance, had, on the 6th of June of this year, advised the substitution of a tripartite arrangement, and, again, on June 24th had reported a conversation with the American Secretary of State, when it had been made clear that the renewal of the Alliance would have very serious effects on American opinion; further, that it was unlikely that the American Senate would ratify a Treaty between the United States, and Japan and Great Britain. At the conversation in question a proposal had emerged for the substitution for the Treaty of a declaration of policy embodied in identic notes to be exchanged by the American, British and Japanese Governments (*Telegram No. 436 D., dated June 24, 1921, from the British Ambassador at Washington*). In addition, the Secretary of State for Foreign Affairs informed the Cabinet that he had had an important conversation with the American Ambassador in London, which had shown that the United States Government were quite willing to discuss the matter if His Majesty's Government took the initiative. Lord Curzon then referred to the various alternative proposals which had been made as a solution of the question, during which he expressed some doubt as to whether the Japanese Government would be likely to agree to the proposal for the issue of identic notes by the three Powers, and he called attention to the fact that the greatest difficulty at the moment was that His Majesty's Government did not know exactly what views were held by the

American and Japanese Governments. In the circumstances, Lord Curzon suggested that he should be allowed to approach the Japanese and United States Ambassadors, and, while explaining to them frankly the difficulties with which His Majesty's Government were faced, ask them to ascertain the views of their respective Governments. If this were done, he (Lord Curzon) would like to suspend for a short time the discussion of the question with the Dominion Prime Ministers.

During the discussion which followed, it was pointed out that, looking at the question from a strategic point of view, there could be no war between America and Japan in the next few years, as, for want of naval bases, neither Power could operate against the shores of the other, so that Great Britain was really the only Power which Japan could attack. It was true that she could occupy the Philippines, but this would be almost more to the disadvantage of Great Britain than to that of the United States. Looking at the diplomatic aspect of the question, it was suggested that the matter might be regarded from two points of view; firstly, from that of Australia and New Zealand and the other islands in that part of the Pacific, and, secondly, the Far East, including China. As regards the latter it might be possible to enter into a defensive Alliance with Japan against any European Power or combination of European Powers. Regarding the other part of the question, there might be a tripartite arrangement which would include the whole of the Pacific, following the British point of view regarding the 'open door'.

After some further discussion, during which attention was called to the importance of bearing in mind that Japan might resent being thrown over, the Prime Minister summed up the question, pointing out that there were certain fundamental points which had to be adhered to, viz.:

   (i) Great Britain could not quarrel with the United States of America:

  (ii) It was essential not to insult Japan by doing anything which would be tantamount to casting her aside after the loyal way in which she had observed the Treaty in the past:

 (iii) China must be carried with us and be a party to any conversation.

The Prime Minister then called attention to the remarks made by Sir Edward Grey at the Imperial Conference in 1911, when the latter had pointed out the effect the termination of the Alliance would have upon Anglo-Japanese relations; and emphasized the fact that since then Japan had rendered enormous services to the British Empire during the War, when, without her assistance, the Allies would have been deprived of the use of something like 1,600,000 men in the main theatres of operation. Further, the Prime Minister emphasized the fact that Japan had come into the War not because she was an enemy of Germany, nor because of her friendship with France, but because she was Britain's Ally; and even in this capacity it was very doubtful if she was under any obligation to do what she had done. To cast off, in the manner suggested, a Power which had stood by us like Japan was to his mind an inconceivable action, and he regarded it as fundamental that Japan should not be insulted. Again, as regards America, in his opinion they were even more concerned about the future of Yap than about the Anglo-Japanese Alliance, and if the British Government could do anything in assisting to find a solution to that problem it certainly ought to be done. Referring to China, the Prime Minister called attention to the fact that this country was just awaking, and that whereas the amount of trade in China was only £1 per head of the population, in Japan it was something like £10 per head, and there were possibilities that trade in China might eventually total £4,000,000,000. It was essential, therefore, that we should not leave China to be walked over by America and for the latter country to get the whole benefit of China's trade. Regarding the question of the renewal of the Alliance, although it had been assumed that the communication which had been sent to the League of Nations was tantamount to denouncing that Alliance, he wondered whether it would not be possible now to get out of the difficulty by saying to Japan either that we would withdraw that notification or treat it as not being a denunciation of the Alliance. If this were done it would modify the situation considerably, and Mr. Meighen, instead of pleading for the non-renewal of the Alliance, would have to plead for the issue of a notice denouncing it. His point was that if the British Government and Japan agreed that the Treaty still held good, it would then be a question as to whether we should give notice of its determination or not, and this would depend on the result of the

Conference which it was suggested should be held between the Powers concerned.

After some further discussion with the Lord Chancellor as to the legal position in connection with the notice given to the League of Nations, the Cabinet agreed:

(a) That the representatives of the United Kingdom at the Imperial Meetings should have authority to propose or assent to the initiation of full and frank conversations with the Governments of both the United States of America and Japan with a view to some arrangement satisfactory to all parties;

(b) That in order, if possible, to gain time for these conversations without the necessity of taking the overt step of a temporary renewal of the Treaty, to which the Canadian Government objected, the Lord Chancellor should be asked to give an opinion as to whether the notice given to the League of Nations in regard to the Anglo-Japanese Alliance must inevitably be held as equivalent to a denunciation of the Treaty of 1911;

(c) That the Foreign Office should be asked to transmit all the necessary papers, with the least possible delay to the Lord Chancellor, who should, if possible, attend the Meeting of the Representatives of the United Kingdom, the Dominions and India, that afternoon, and be ready to give his opinion.

WASHINGTON CONFERENCE

149. (*Balfour to Lloyd George, 11 November 1921, D.B.F.P. XIV, no. 415*)

Extract

4. From the discussions which took place at the Cabinet before my departure I formed the clear impression that the ultimate aim of the British Empire Delegation at the Washington Conference is to secure the largest possible limitation of armaments consistent with the safety of the British Empire. It is clear, however, that if satisfactory and durable results are to be achieved in regard to naval disarmament, which mainly affects the British Empire, the United States of America and Japan, an agreement must also be reached in regard to certain political problems which have arisen in China and the Pacific.

5. First and foremost among these latter problems is that of the Anglo-Japanese Alliance. Evidence continues to reach me, from those Delegates and officials who arrived in Washington before us, in confirmation of previous reports to the effect that adherence to the Alliance in its present form will be very unpopular in the United States of America, and will render the conclusion of a satisfactory and enduring arrangement for the limitation of armaments extremely difficult to negotiate. Further, it is undeniable that, with the collapse of the Russian Empire and the elimination of Germany from the Pacific, the conditions which brought the Anglo-Japanese Alliance into existence have disappeared for the time being, though it would perhaps not be prudent to assume that they will never be re-created. On the other hand, we are bound to give the utmost consideration to the feelings of an ally who has loyally stood by his engagements and rendered us valuable support in the late War, and we cannot contemplate any action calculated to alienate, much less to outrage, Japanese sentiment. Finally, the utmost weight must be given to the strong views expressed at the recent Imperial Meetings in regard to the importance which Australia and New Zealand attach to the maintenance of the Anglo-Japanese Alliance in some shape or form.

6. In order to harmonise these partially conflicting elements in the problem, I have devised a formula in the shape of a draft tripartite agreement between the British Empire, the United States of America, and Japan, dealing with the preservation of peace and the maintenance of the *status quo* (*Enclosure I*)[1]. The object of this scheme is:

(a) To enable the Americans to be parties to a tripartite arrangement without committing themselves to military operations:

(b) To bring the existing Anglo-Japanese Alliance to an end without hurting the feelings of our Ally:

(c) To leave it open to us to renew a defensive alliance with Japan if she should again be threatened by Germany or Russia:

(d) To frame a Treaty which will reassure our Australasian Dominions:

(e) To make it impossible for American critics to suggest that our Treaty with Japan would require us to stand aside in the case of a quarrel between them and Japan, whatever the cause of that quarrel might be.

[1] Not printed.

Chapter 5

Britain and the Russian Revolution

150. (*War Cabinet 304, 21 December 1917, Cab/23/4*)

10. Lord Robert Cecil drew attention to Foreign Office telegram No. 2054 from Sir George Buchanan, and No. 1502 from Sir George Barclay at Jassy. He added that the French Ambassador in London had been to see him, in regard to the subjects dealt with in both telegrams, on the previous day, and reported to him that the French Government had suggested a delimitation of South Russia into British and French spheres of activity. As the French had a large Military Mission in Roumania, and had facilities both military and financial in this quarter, the Ukraine and adjacent districts would naturally fall into the French sphere, whereas the Caucasus and Don Cossack regions, being nearer to Persia, might form the British sphere. General Berthelot had been placed in charge of relations with the Ukrainian Government by the French Government, and the French Government suggested that instructions should be given to General Barter not to interfere with General Berthelot. He gathered from the reports in the morning newspapers that the Cossacks had succeeded in capturing Rostoff, killing 800 of the Red Guards, and that the Bolsheviks admitted their defeat. The policy advocated by Sir George Buchanan and by the Allied representatives at Jassy raised an important and deep question of principle. It would be impossible any longer to go on running two horses; we must decide definitely whether we are to support the Bolsheviks in their claim to be the supreme Government throughout Russia, or whether we are to recognise and assist the other *de facto* Governments in Russia. We must either support the Ukrainians, Cossacks, Georgians, and Armenians, or the Bolsheviks; we could not do both. In his opinion, the forces in Southern Russia had a fair fighting chance of success in the event of our supporting them. If we did not support them, the blockade of Germany would be at an end and the terms of the armistice in-

volved the despatch of grain and other raw materials of Southern
Russia to Germany via the Danube. Nearly all the supplies in
Russia that were of value to the enemy were in Southern Russia,
and now in the hands of the people who were opposing the Bolshevik Government. The Separatist sentiment in the Ukraine was
an old story, and it appeared that the Bolshevik Government were
prepared to recognise the principle of self-determination in regard
to the Ukrainian peoples, and to recognise the Rada. The Ukranians had been fighting with the Bolsheviks in Odessa, and here
they appeared to have the support of the Jews against the Bolsheviks. We could hope for nothing from Trotzki, who was a Jew
of the international type and was solely out to smash Russia and
to revenge himself, not only on the governing classes, but upon
the peasants of Russia. Money was now being spent by the French
and ourselves in the Ukraine, and it was a question for the Cabinet
to decide whether this should continue.

General Macdonogh stated that the Roumanian army of fifteen
good fighting divisions, with 300 French officers attached to it,
would form a valuable support to the Ukranians, provided
Ukranian supplies were made available for the Roumanian army.
Between Roumania and Ukrania lay Bessarabia, which was
mainly Roumanian in population. Bessarabia had appointed a local
Government of its own. With regard to the Cossacks, he estimated their strength at approximately 250,000, and read a telegram, received through General Bertholot, from a French officer
who had seen General Alexeieff on the 17th December, which
gave a very hopeful account of the Cossack situation. He then read
a telegram from General Marshall, stating that the Russian
General Bicharakhoff, who had 3,000 men with him at Khanikin,
on the Diala, had burnt his boats and was prepared to continue
the war in co-operation with the Allies, irrespective of any orders
from the Bolsheviks.

It was pointed out that the information available regarding the
situation was somewhat scanty and insufficient to justify the Cabinet in coming to so momentous a decision as that raised by Lord
Robert Cecil. There was a danger that, by backing a losing horse in
Southern Russia, we were destroying any hope of preventing the
Germans appearing in Petrograd as the friends and helpers of an
all-powerful Bolshevik Government. In this matter it was necessary to take a long view, as that Power which assisted the future

Russian Government in the reconstruction of the country would have the whole of Russia's resources at her command. It was further pointed out that much turned upon the military resources and military value of the Southern Russian nationalities, and that it appeared, on the face of it, that the French Government had more information than we had regarding their prospects.

Sir Edward Carson stated that he and Lord Milner had held an important and interesting conference on the previous day with certain officers and others familiar with Russia, and that among the evidence submitted to them was a statement to the effect that the present German policy in Russia was designed to produce as much anarchy and chaos as possible, with a view to Russia being compelled to make a separate peace that would include the repudiation of Russia's financial debts to her Allies, and that, after this had happened, they would use the German prisoners and officers now in Russia to restore the autocracy under the Germanophil Grand Duke Paul Michaelovitch.

Lord Curzon pointed out that if we continued to back the Ukrainians, a sharp rupture with the Bolsheviks would follow inevitably. He was prepared to take the risk of backing the Ukrainians, but was definitely of the opinion that, whatever decision was come to as a result of further conferences with the French, the decision should be taken by the whole War Cabinet.

The War Cabinet decided that:

(*a*) A Special Mission, consisting of
> Lord Milner,
> Lord Robert Cecil,
> General Macdonogh,

should proceed at once to Paris to confer with M. Clemenceau, with a view to the submission of recommendations to the War Cabinet.

(*b*) The Secretary to the War Cabinet should inform the British Military Adviser of the Supreme War Council at Versailles that the War Cabinet wished the Military Adviser forthwith to examine and report on the military question as to whether reliance could be placed on the Provisional Governments of South Russia to resist a Bolshevik Army under German control.

(*c*) Meanwhile, the Director of Military Intelligence should provide the British Military Adviser at Versailles with all possible information bearing upon this subject.

(*d*) The question of the recognition of General Bicharakoff at Khanikin should be left to the unfettered discretion of General Marshall.

151. (*Cecil to Buchanan, 3 December 1917, no. 2407, F.O. 371/3018/ 224839*)

The War Cabinet considered the Russian situation this morning and they are of opinion that all our efforts should be concentrated on trying to prevent Russia from making a separate peace with Germany. They believe that the only hope of doing this is to strengthen by every means in our power those elements who are genuinely friendly to the Entente of whom the chief are Kaledin, Alexeieff and their group. They do not believe that the constitution of coalition between Bolsheviks, Social Revolutionaries and even Mensheviks would be any real improvement. Such a combination would be under Bolshevik influence and would besides consist of talkers and theorists. If on the other hand a southern block could be formed consisting of the Caucasus, the Cossacks, the Ukraine and the Roumanians, it would probably be able to set up a reasonably stable Government and would in any case through its command of oil, coal and corn control the whole of Russia. You are therefore authorised to take whatever steps you regard as possible with a view to carrying out this policy either directly or through such agents as you select. No regard should be had to expense and you should furnish to Cossacks or Ukrainians any funds necessary by any means you think desirable. I am sending instructions on similar lines to Jassy and Teheran.

152. (*War Cabinet 306, 26 December 1917, Appendix, Cab/23/4*)
Memorandum prepared by Lord Milner and Lord R. Cecil on Suggested Policy in Russia, and accepted by M. Clemenceau and M. Pichon on December 23, 1917

At Petrograd we should at once get into relations with the Bolsheviki through unofficial agents, each country as seems best to it.

We propose to send Sir George Buchanan on leave for reasons of health, but we shall keep a Chargé d'Affaires there. We do not suggest that our Allies should follow our example. Sir George

Buchanan's long residence in Petrograd has indelibly associated him, in the minds of the Bolsheviki, with the policy of the Cadets, and he stands to them for much the same, as say, M. Miliukoff.

We should represent to the Bolsheviki that we have no desire to take part in any way in the internal politics of Russia, and that any idea that we favour a counter-revolution is a profound mistake. Such a policy might be attractive to the autocratic Governments of Germany and Austria, but not to the Western democracies or America. But we feel it necessary to keep in touch as far as we can with the Ukraine, the Cossacks, Finland, Siberia, the Caucasus, &c., because these various semi-autonomous provinces represent a very large proportion of the strength of Russia. In particular, we feel bound to befriend the Ukraine, since upon the Ukraine depends the feeding of the Roumanians, to whom we are bound by every obligation of honour.

As for the war, we should carefully refrain from any word or act condoning the treachery of the Russians in opening peace negotiations with our enemies. But we should continually repeat our readiness to accept the principles of self-determination, and, subject to that, of no annexation or indemnities. We should press on the Bolsheviki the importance of not being satisfied with empty phrases from the Germans, and point out that unless they get specific undertakings from them as to such questions as Poland, Bohemia, the Roumanian parts of Transylvania, not to speak of Alsace-Lorraine and the Trentino, they will get nothing. Meanwhile their powers of resistance are melting away, and they will soon be, if they are not now, at the mercy of the German Kaiser, who will then snap his fingers at all their fine phrases and impose on them any terms he pleases. They should be told that it is now probably too late to do anything to save the personnel of the army. But the material of the artillery can still be preserved, and at the very least it should not be transferred to our enemies to be used against the Western democracies. Most important of all, the Bolsheviki should prevent, if they can, the wheat districts of Russia, such as the Ukraine, falling into the control of or being made available for the Central Powers. This makes another reason why we are anxious to support and strengthen the Ukraine, and why we urge on the Bolsheviki that, so far from trying to coerce the Ukrainians, they should enter into close co-operation with them.

In Southern Russia our principal object must be, if we can, to save Roumania. Next we must aim at preventing Russian supplies from reaching Germany.

Finally, we are bound to protect, if possible, the remnant of the Armenians, not only in order to safeguard the flank of our Mesopotamian forces in Persia and the Caucasus, but also because unless an Armenian, united, if possible, with a Georgian, autonomous, or independent State, is the only barrier against the development of a Turanian movement that will extend from Constantinople to China, and will provide Germany with a weapon of even greater danger to the peace of the world than the control of the Bagdad Railway.

If we could induce the Southern Russian armies to resume the fight, that would be very desirable, but it is probably impossible. To secure these objects the first thing is money to reorganise the Ukraine, to pay the Cossacks and Caucasian forces, and to bribe the Persians. The sums required are not, as things go, very enormous, but the exchange presents great difficulties. If the French could undertake the finance of the Ukraine, we might find the money for the others. It is understood that the United States will assist.

Besides finance it is important to have agents and officers to advise and support the provincial Governments and their armies. It is essential that this should be done as quietly as possible so as to avoid the imputation—as far as we can—that we are preparing to make war on the Bolsheviki.

We would suggest that the Ukraine should be again, in this matter, dealt with by the French, while we would take the other south-east provinces. A general officer from each country would be appointed to take charge of our respective activities, but they would of course keep in the closest touch with one another through carefully selected liaison officers in order to ensure the utmost unity of action.

It is for consideration whether we should facilitate the return to Southern Russia of the numerous Russian officers at present in France and England.

BALFOUR PREPARED TO WORK WITH THE BOLSHEVIKS

153. (*War Cabinet 295, 10 December 1917, Cab/23/4*)

[*Russia: General Policy*]

15. The War Cabinet considered their general policy in regard to Russia, and in this connection had before them a Memorandum by the Secretary of State for Foreign Affairs (Paper G.T.-2932), dated 9th December, 1917 (Appendix).

It was suggested that His Majesty's Government was not primarily or specially concerned with the composition of the Russian Government, or with the local aspirations of the Bolsheviks or other political parties, except in so far as they bore on their attitude to our conflict with the Central Powers. This was the line we had taken during the Czar's reign, and there was no reason to depart from it. Our dominant purpose throughout the revolution should be:

(*a*) If possible, to keep Russia in the war until our joint war aims were realised; or

(*b*) If this could not be secured, then to ensure that Russia was as helpful to us and as harmful to the enemy as possible. For this purpose we should seek to influence Russia to give to any terms of peace that might be concluded with the enemy a bias in our favour.

It was difficult to foretell how strong the Bolsheviks might become, or how long their power might endure; but if, as seemed likely, they maintained an ascendancy for the next few months only, these months were critical, and to antagonise them needlessly would be to throw them into the arms of Germany. There were at the moment signs that within a few days, when the elections for the Constituent Assembly had been completed, the Bolsheviks would be installed in power not only in a *de facto*, but also in a constitutional sense.

In this connection reference was made to recent messages which had been received from the British Embassy at Petrograd. In a telegram dated the 8th December, 1917 (Foreign Office No. 1984), the terms were given of a six months' armistice proposed by the Bolsheviks, and it was stated that there was a remarkable change in the official press, the Allies not being attacked, for the first time for several weeks.

In *The Times* of that day there appeared a report that the Germans were making the following conditions:

(*a*) Germany to obtain, for fifteen years, a control of the Russian wheat market.

(*b*) Importation into Russia of all German goods duty free.

(*c*) No territory now occupied by German troops to be surrendered.

Attention was also drawn to a telegram to the Chief of the Imperial General Staff, dated the 5th December, 1917 (No. 1404), recounting a private and unofficial interview with Krikenko, the Bolshevik Commander-in-Chief of the Russian Army, during which he said that he had issued an order that all armistice agreements should contain a clause forbidding transfer of troops from one front to another. He appeared most anxious to make a favourable impression on Allied officers, and had carried out all suggestions made to him for safeguarding the lives of officers and their families. In a telegram dated the 6th December, 1917 (Foreign Office No. 1971), Sir George Buchanan reported an interview between Captain Smith and Trotzki, at which the prohibition of British subjects leaving Russia was discussed in connection with the detention in this country of Messrs. Tritchirine and Petroff. Trotzki denied that the prohibition was intended as a threat. His object had been to emphasise the difference between the treatment accorded to Russian subjects in the United Kingdom and British subjects in Russia. On publication in the local press of a communiqué to the effect that the British Government would reconsider the cases of all Russian subjects interned in Great Britain and would give facilities for return to their country of all Russians innocent of any offence punishable by the laws of Great Britain, he (Trotzki) would the same day restore full liberty of movement to all British subjects in Russia. Sir George Buchanan urged His Majesty's Government to agree to accept the compromise proposed by Trotzki, otherwise he feared that British subjects would be held up indefinitely.

The War Cabinet were impressed with the fact that, by continuing to intern Tritchirine and Petroff the lives of thousands of British subjects were being endangered, and that the case for their internment was not a very strong one. On the other hand, the dangers of any traffic with the Bolsheviks were very real. The strength of the Bolshevik Government lay in the fact that it supported peace, and that if it abandoned its efforts for peace it would probably be overthrown. Further, to take any action on the lines suggested above—action for which the Bolshevik Government had pressed—could hardly be regarded as consistent with the support which was being proffered to General Kaledin in the South. Was it desirable to treat with both Trotzki and Kaledin at one and the same time? Our policy towards Kaledin had been decided upon. Would it not be wise to wait and see whether the Bolshevik Government was going to last?

To this it was replied that our assistance to Kaledin was directed against the Germans and not against the Bolsheviks, and was specially intended to help the Roumanians.

The War Cabinet, without making any change in their recent policy towards Russia, authorised

> The Secretary of State for Foreign Affairs to inform Sir George Buchanan that the policy proposed in his telegram No. 1971 was accepted.
>
> The Secretary of State for Foreign Affairs also undertook to deal with Tritchirine and Petroff in the best way he could, in consultation with Sir George Buchanan and the Home Secretary, and to deal with three other Russians who were reported as having been interned here.

APPENDIX

G.T.–2932

NOTES ON THE PRESENT RUSSIAN SITUATION

As I may not be able to be present at Cabinet to-morrow, I desire to make these notes.

The following points have to be specially kept in view:—

1. The safety of our Embassy in Petrograd and of British subjects in Russia.
2. The interests of Roumania and her army.
3. The best course to adopt in order to diminish as much as possible the advantage which Germany will be able to extract from the dissolution of the Russian army as a fighting force.

These subjects are all interconnected, though so far as possible I will deal with them separately.

Britain and the Russian Revolution

1. The greatest danger to Sir George Buchanan and the British colony arises probably out of the possibility of mob-violence, excited by the anti-British propaganda fomented by German money in Petrograd and elsewhere. The only real security against this is to be found either by the establishment of a strong and order-loving Government in Russia, or by the removal of the British, official and unofficial, to some safer country.

The first we can do nothing to secure. The second cannot be obtained unless we are able (*a*) to provide the necessary transport either through Sweden or through some northern port of Russia, and (*b*) to win the goodwill (in however qualified a form) of the present rulers of Petrograd.

The question of transport is hardly a Foreign Office matter, but the policy of avoiding the active malevolence of the Bolshevik party raises most important diplomatic issues.

It was suggested at Cabinet on Friday that, after their recent proclamations, the Bolsheviks could only be regarded as avowed enemies, and to treat them as anything else showed a lamentable incapacity to see facts as they are, and to handle them with decision.

I entirely dissent from this view and believe it to be founded on a misconception. If, for the moment, the Bolsheviks show peculiar virulence in dealing with the British Empire, it is probably because they think that the British Empire is the great obstacle to immediate peace; but they are fanatics to whom the constitution of every State, whether monarchical or republican, is equally odious. Their appeal is to every revolutionary force, economic, social, racial or religious, which can be used to upset the existing political organisations of mankind. If they summon the Moham-medans of India to revolt, they are still more desirous of engin-eering a revolution in Germany. They are dangerous dreamers, whose power, be it great or small, transitory or permanent, depends partly on German gold, partly on the determination of the Russian army to fight no more; but who would genuinely like to put into practice the wild theories which have so long been germinating in the shadow of the Russian autocracy.

Now, contrary to the opinion of some of my colleagues, I am clearly of opinion that it is to our advantage to avoid, as long as possible, an open breach with this crazy system. If this be drifting, then I am a drifter by deliberate policy. On the broader reasons for my view, I will say a word directly, but its bearing on the narrower issue of the safety of Sir George Buchanan and the British colony is evident. I am personally of opinion that the Cabinet should reverse the decision it came to some little time ago, and should deport to Russia the two interned Russian subjects in whose fate the Russian rulers appear to be so greatly interested. I was not in England when the decision to retain them was come to, and I am imperfectly acquainted with the reasons for it. Doubtless they were sufficient. But I certainly think that we may now with advantage send these two Russians back to their own country, where, judged by local standards, their opinions will probably appear sane and moderate.

I have already instructed Sir George Buchanan to abstain completely from any action which can be interpreted as an undue interference with the internal affairs of the country to which he is accredited, and I am unable to think of any other step which would help to secure his safety.

2. As regards the Roumanian army, events have marched rapidly. Everything that could be done, even as a forlorn hope, has been done to enable the army to join with other forces in Russia prepared to continue the struggle, but for the moment no such forces appear to exist, and the Roumanian army is under the strictest military necessity of acquiescing in the armistice, or rather the cessation of hostilities, on its part of the line.

Very difficult and important questions, such as those raised by General Bertholot in a memorandum I have ordered to be circulated, still remain to be decided, but these call for no immediate action. I hope that General Berthelot's memorandum will be carefully considered by the Headquarters Staff.

3. I have already indicated my view that we ought if possible not to come to an open breach with the Bolsheviks or drive them into the enemy's camp. But there are wider reasons for this policy than the safety of the British colony in Russia. These wider reasons are as follows:—

It is certain, I take it, that, for the remainder of this war, the Bolsheviks are going to fight neither Germany nor anyone else. But, if we can prevent their aiding Germany we do a great deal, and to this we should devote our efforts.

There are two possible advantages which Germany may extract

from Russia's going out of the war: (i) She may increase her man-power in other theatres of operation by moving troops from Russian front, or by getting back German prisoners. There is little hope of stopping this, and I say no more about it. (ii) She may obtain the power of using the large potential resources of Russia to break the Allied Blockade. I am not sure that this is not the more important of the two advantages, and it has so far been very imperfectly examined. As regards oil, we want to know what means of transport there is in the Black Sea available to the Germans, and how far the anti-Bolshevik elements in the Caucasian regions can be utilised to interfere with the supply on land. As regards cereals, the difficulties the Germans are likely to have arises mainly, I suppose, from the chaotic condition of the country, the disorganisation of all means of transport, and the determination of the Russians to use their own produce for their own purposes.

If we drive Russia into the hands of Germany, we shall hasten the organisation of the country by German officials on German lines. Nothing could be more fatal, it seems to me, both to the immediate conduct of the war and to our post-war relations.

Russia, however incapable of fighting, is not easily overrun. Except with the active goodwill of the Russians themselves, German troops (even if there were German troops to spare) are not going to penetrate many hundreds of miles into that vast country. A mere armistice between Russia and Germany may not for very many months promote in any important fashion the supply of German needs from Russian sources. It must be our business to make that period as long as possible by every means in our power, and no policy would be more fatal than to give the Russians a motive for welcoming into their midst German officials and German soldiers as friends and deliverers.

154. (*Balfour to Lindley (Petrograd), 24 January 1918, no. 129 F.O. 371/3283/2*)

You are apparently under the impression that our informal relations with the Bolshevists commit us to some measure of approval of their proceedings and are necessarily inconsistent with any attempt that may be made in other parts of Russia to foster efforts favourable to the Allied cause.

We do not take this view. Wherever any 'de facto' administration is set up, we have the right to establish informal relations with it, without prejudice to the informal relations we may choose to cultivate with organisations beyond its effective jurisdiction.

That in these circumstances events may at any moment occur which would render impossible the continuance of even the formal relations is plain enough. The question to be considered from day to day is whether it is wise to wait for these events, or whether we should anticipate them by a polite but immediate rupture. The principal argument for the latter course is our anxiety for the safety of the Embassy and British subjects, which might be better secured by this procedure than would be possible if the breach occurred as the result of a heated controversy. The principal argument against it is the fact that, so far as we can judge, the Bolshevists are the party who at this moment are doing most to hamper the conclusion of a separate peace. It is true that they neither can fight nor will fight. But this is apparently true of every party in Russia, while no other party in Russia seems as capable of insisting, in the face of irresistible military superiority, on terms which the Germans are reluctant to grant, but which it is extremely inconvenient to them to have to obtain by sheer force.

Of course we should abandon this policy of informal relations the moment it hampered our efforts to secure such objects as the support of the Roumanian Army, aid to the Armenians, security to the flank of our Mesopotamian Army, the denial of supplies to the enemy, and similar objects. But delay seems desirable, if only because it will give time for the situation to develop in South Russia and elsewhere.

155. (*Balfour to Lockhart (Petrograd), 6 March 1918, no. 4, F.O. 371/3285/6*)

This was written before you received my telegrams No. 1 and No. 3, which partly answers it. But your earnest appeal deserves a further reply and I therefore bring the following considerations to your notice.

There are, it seems, three courses open to Monsieur Trotsky and the Moscow Congress. (1) They may possibly accept German domination and all that it involves. In this case they can surely not complain of the Allies in sheer self-defence taking independent action, provided that this action does not threaten the integrity and independence of Russia: a danger against which ample precaution will be taken.

(2) A 'Holy War' against Germany may be proclaimed. But in the face of recent experience, can we seriously believe that this will end in anything but a new surrender and a new partition of Russia? Fine phrases may shatter an army; but they will never create one. The Bolshevists have striven by words and deeds to destroy the fighting spirit of the country: they have reason to be proud of their success.

(3) The Government and Moscow Congress may call to their aid in their resistance to the common enemy all the organised forces which are still available. These are, first the Roumanian Army. Secondly, if this is still in being such small assistance as Allied ships can render to threatened points in the White Sea and at Vladivostock. Third, the Japanese.

You regard this last expedient as disastrous. But Russia, during three years of war, has gladly employed Japanese guns and gunners: and the Japanese, if they consent to intervene would come as friends and allies; not, like the Germans, as enemies and conquerors. Monsieur Trotsky you tell me repudiates 'friendly relations' with us but desires 'a working agreement'. I sympathise with his point of view. But why will he not also try a working agreement with the Japanese?

In the common interests of Russia and of those who still deem themselves Russia's Allies, I press this policy on his consideration.

Your observation about the 'suppression of Bolshevism' is not understood. I have repeatedly and clearly explained that His Majesty's Government have no desire to interfere with the internal affairs of Russia, but are only concerned in the vigorous prosecution of the war.

THE GROWTH OF DISILLUSION

156. (*Balfour to Lockhart (Petrograd), 13 March 1918, no. 12, F.O. 371/3285/6*)

Extract

You say that the 'most fundamental mistake in our policy' is the supposition that Lenin and Trotski are German agents. On this point I am quite ready to accept the views of those who have a personal knowledge of the Bolshevist Leaders which I do not possess. If they say that Lenin and Trotsky are fanatics but not traitors I accept the statement without reserve. I should however have expected that in that case a diligent search would have detected some aspect of Russian policy which was favourable to the Allies and unfavourable to Germany. I cannot find it. The Bolshevists have destroyed every force which was capable of resisting the enemy: the Russian Army, the Roumanian Army, and the Trans-Caucasian Levies. The equipment with which the Allies supplied them has not even been destroyed: it has been surrendered without a blow. According to our reports, Bolshevists have aided the Turks in blocking Dunsterville's way to assist the Armenians and the Georgians. German officers are said to swarm in Petrograd. Only one Bank in Moscow is permitted to carry on business: we are informed that it is a German Bank. The Press, which is completely under Bolshevist control, has been systematically anti-British. Though of all the Allies we are the ones who without the least hope of material gain have made the greatest sacrifices for Russia, and without the smallest wish to interfere in its internal affairs, have shown most desire to work with its revolutionary Governments we are, under Bolshevist inspiration, systematically described as selfish and imperialistic.

What is there to be put on the other side of the account?

I am aware of only one transaction which has even the appearance of being anti-German, and that is the refusal to conclude the peace negotiations at Brest. Whatever the intention of this procedure may have been, its only effect has been to strip Russia of great provinces on the West and on the South; to hasten the defeat of Roumania; and to hand over Armenia to the Turks.

I am not aware of one single example of Bolshevist action which can be quoted on the other side. The Bolshevists have done nothing to help themselves; they make it as difficult as possible for us to help them. There are only two approaches through which Allied aid can reach Russia. One is on the North, the other on the East. We have received no invitation to use the first, and the very suggestion that Japan should use the second, under whatever safeguards for the integrity and security of Russia, is seemingly regarded as an intolerable wrong.

You ask us to 'play with the Bolshevists', and to 'adopt a more elastic attitude towards them, even to the extent of promising more than we can perform'. At present, however, they refuse to accept even what we can perform: and you give no hint or suggestion as to the kind of promise they would like us to make.

Everything that we do, or hope to do, in Russia, we should wish to do at Russia's request; and if you could induce those who at the present moment control her destiny to see facts as they are, and to co-operate heartily with the Powers which alone desire to see Russia independent and secure, you will perform the greatest possible service, both to Russia and to her Allies. But to allow Germany a free hand from the Vistula to Vladivostock while Russia unarmed and unaided is painfully endeavouring to re-create her nationality, seems the sure way of bringing into existence a reactionary Government wholly dependent on Germany both economically and politically.

THE NECESSITY OF JAPANESE INTERVENTION

157. (*Balfour to Reading, 29 March 1918, no. 1816, F.O. 371/3319/37087*)

Following views of General Staff may assist you in bringing home to Mr. Wilson the urgent military necessity of Japanese action in Siberia.

Germany has been enabled to produce in the West a critical situation through having her liberty of action entirely unfettered in all other theatres. Though there is every hope that Franco-British armies may, for the present, stem the tide in the West, Germany is capable of still further effort, as she may continue to bring away from the Eastern theatre German divisions to France and Austrian divisions to Italy.

The American Army cannot exercise its influence or weight for many months yet. The Japanese Army can be used at once. It has not yet been brought into play, but can be used, if used quickly, to great advantage and indeed it is possible that instant action, though at first producing only a moral effect, may prove the turning factor in the war.

The moral effect of a Japanese Army embarking for Siberia and occupying the Trans-Siberian Railway may well cause Germany to discontinue the withdrawal of troops from the East and it is there that she is now adopting measures to circumvent the blockade, jeopardize the security of British possessions in India, and carry the war into Persia and Afghanistan, allowing Turkey incidentally to swallow up Armenia.

History points to the egregious folly of supposing that armies called into being by proclamations or patriotic appeals can ever resist a disciplined and determined foe unless and until grafted on to a stable and thoroughly trained nucleus. Contrary opinions have been expressed only by civilians without military knowledge and when deceived by the wild promises of ignorant enthusiasts. The General Staff point to the Japanese Army as the only sound nucleus around which the loyal elements of Russia can gather and fight against Prussian domination of their own country. The Japanese are willing and eager to step into the breach and to accept the services of Allied officers and material assistance. Time is a vital factor of success. If the Japanese begin at once the embarkation of a force of 8 or 10 divisions they should, with the help of material assistance from America, be able to gain control of the Trans-Siberian Railway to the Tomsk area before the Austrian and German prisoners in Siberia are all armed and organised under efficient leaders and the railway bridges and tunnels have been destroyed.

The German engineered propaganda that Japan will keep what she occupies or join hands with Germany in dividing the spoil must be defeated by giving the expeditionary force an international character. On the grounds of efficiency, however, the control should be solely Japanese.

158. (*Balfour to Jordan (Peking), 30 April 1918, no. 238, F.O. 371/3291/383*)

It is important that you should be acquainted with the policy which is being pursued by His Majesty's Government with regard to Russia, and the following brief summary will give you the broad outlines.

The intervention of an Allied army from Vladivostock is an essential part of this policy. Its main object is the liberation of Russia from foreign control and exploitation, and we hope it will result in a rapid national revival leading among other things to the re-creation of the Russian Army and the resumption of effective military action against the Central Powers. Whatever may be the truth as regards the honesty of the Bolshevists, they represent at this moment the de facto Government of Russia with whom it is impossible not to reckon, and intervention undertaken in defiance of them might involve the risk of throwing them directly into the arms of Germany. Accordingly, our efforts have been directed to obtaining from them an invitation to the Allies to come to the military assistance of Russia. To achieve this end it is necessary for the Allies to avoid taking sides with Russian political parties or giving any pretext for the charge that their intervention will aim at supporting a counter-revolution. On the other hand it is equally important not to alienate the non-Bolshevist elements who may ultimately regain power, and we therefore do not propose to give formal recognition to the present régime.

His Majesty's Government have received a certain encouragement lately in their dealings with Trotsky who has shown signs that he desires co-operation with the Allies and has definitely requested from them a statement of the help they could furnish and the guarantees they would give, with a view to coming to an agreement.

We hope shortly to be in a position to comply with his request and to offer him allied intervention in order to fight the Germans and so enable the Russian people to recover their independence: and to accompany the offer by a declaration of complete disinterestedness in Russian internal politics and guarantees as to the evacuation of Russian territory by the Allies as soon as the war is over.

But, on the one hand, the consent of the United States Government, which has not yet been given, is essential; and, on the other hand, the only form of intervention which the Bolshevist Government and the United States Government would accept is one in which, while Japan provides most of the military strength and the supreme command, the Allies must effectively participate, and to this the formal assent of the Japanese Government has also still to be obtained.

We are at present awaiting a definite reply from the United States Government, and, if it is favourable, we shall at once approach the Japanese. We are even not without hope that America and Japan will succeed in arriving at an agreement of their own accord. But immediately we have obtained both American and Japanese consent, we hope that intervention will be pushed forward with the least possible delay.

Intervention to support Russia against Germany

159. (*War Cabinet 409A, 11 May 1918, Cab/23/14*)

The Prime Minister said that he would like to put a question to the Chief of the Imperial General Staff, and to ask him whether, in the event of the Germans failing in the next attack on the Western Front, it would be possible to transfer some of the Allied troops to help M. Trotzki, in order not only to prevent more German troops being moved from the Russian Front, but possibly, and even probably, to make the Germans transfer some Divisions from West to East. He asked whether it would not be possible for the Allied Governments to say to M. Trotzki that, if he was prepared to offer resistance, the French and British Governments would give him a certain number of troops, and that he could also have the use of the 70,000 Czech-Slovak troops now in Russia and Siberia. In that event it would be very difficult for the Japanese to refuse to join the Allied Forces in Russia. With regard to the landing of any Allied troops, he said that General Poole had suggested that the best place would be Archangel, as the situation at Murmansk was not clear and the condition of the railway from there in summer-time was always very bad. It was impossible to treat the latest telegrams from Mr Lockhart, with regard to M. Trotzki's attitude, as of no account. There was no doubt that up to a certain point M. Trotzki had played into German hands, but that his view had considerably changed, and that it could be assumed that it did not suit M. Trotzki now to be under German domination. He therefore would like to know whether some action such as he proposed was not possible, and suggested that some American troops might be diverted and landed at Vladivostock, pointing out that it would not be necessary to make use of highly-trained troops, but that it was very desirable that a nucleus of Allied troops should be sent to Russia so that M. Trotzki might feel that he had some force behind him.

In reply to Lord Milner, who said that he considered immediate action was necessary and that time was all-important, the Prime Minister said that he was not so sure of this, in view of the reports, which undoubtedly showed how the Germans were using brutal methods in Russia, particularly in the Ukraine, which methods were causing a fierce anti-German feeling to arise. He did not suggest that there would be long delay, as he assumed that in the next fortnight or three weeks it would be definitely known as to whether the German onslaught in France had been stopped.

The Chief of the Imperial General Staff said that, before answering this question, he would like to have some time for consideration. At any rate, it would not be possible to divert any troops at present, and probably it would not be known for some time—at any rate for many weeks—as to who was to be the master in the Western theatre of operations.

General Poole suggested that if even 5,000 troops could be sent now, it would make a start. These troops could be sent to Archangel and Vologda, and, if attacked at the latter place, the bridge at Vologda could be blown up, and they could remain at Archangel until further reinforcements were sent. The presence of 5,000 Allied troops would ensure the accumulation of 100,000 Russian troops behind them.

Mr Balfour said that, in connection with this proposal, he felt bound to draw attention to the arrangements which were being made by the French to transport the 50,000 Czech-Slovaks referred to in War Cabinet 405, Minute 8(i) from Vladivostock to France. Yesterday he had an interview with the three representatives of the Czech-Slovaks in London, and he had pointed out to them what seemed to him the impossibility of sufficient transport being procurable to send these troops to France, and had asked whether they would not be prepared to fight in Russia. He had understood the answer to be that the Czechs were afraid that they would only be used in Russia as gendarmes; that they were very anxious to fight the Germans; and that if they were to be used as troops under British and French officers they would not object. Mr Balfour pointed out that these troops would be invaluable in Russia, particularly as they were Slavs.

Mr. Chamberlain called attention to the last report from the Allied Maritime Council, which showed so serious a deficiency in tonnage that it called for review of all Army supplies and imports.

The opinion was generally expressed that there was no possibility, at any rate at the present, of transport being available to ship the Czech Divisions to France.

The question arose as to what M. Trotzki's attitude would be if he were informed that some 50,000 Czech troops and some 20,000 American, British and French troops, fully equipped, were ready to support him. In this connection Mr Balfour called attention to telegram No. 2871, which he had sent to Lord Reading, with reference to the gradual but most important change in M. Trotzki's attitude as reported by Mr Lockhart. In this telegram he had pointed out that M. Trotzki's present embarrassment arose from his belief, only too well-founded, that, while the Germans were in a position to attack them at once, the Allies, even if invited, would not for a long time be ready to come to his assistance.

The Prime Minister was of opinion that M. Trotzki could go no further than he had done. It was obvious that M. Trotzki could not trust M. Lenin, who was a disciple of Tolstoi, and that if he were to make open overtures to the Allies the Germans would know of this at once. Mr Lloyd George suggested that a Conference should be held to consider the best methods of organising some means for assistance to M. Trotzki. He also suggested that it would be advisable that a Mission should be sent to Russia, the importance of which M. Trotzki must recognise, in order that some definite policy might be agreed upon. It was obvious that the Allied Governments must be prepared to act without waiting for an invitation from M. Trotzki.

Lord Curzon expressed the opinion that this Conference should also enquire into the question of the proposed destruction of the Baltic Fleet, and said that he was afraid that, while we were discussing plans, the Fleet would be taken over by the Germans.

Sir Eric Geddes said that, in his opinion, the way to deal with the question of the Fleet was to instruct the Naval Attaché at Petrograd to continue his preparations. If someone could then go to M. Trotzki, he could be made to understand that we intended to destroy the Fleet with or without his acquiescence, rather than run the risk of letting the Fleet fall into German hands, as had happened to the Black Sea Fleet.

Mr Balfour suggested that he should telegraph to Mr Lockhart pointing out what had happened in the case of the Black Sea Fleet, and saying that, as it was vital that the Germans should not obtain possession of the Baltic Fleet, and as M. Trotzki had acquiesced in the principle of its destruction, we considered that we were entitled to destroy it. He proposed to ask him, if he had any objection, to wire at once, but not to speak to M. Trotzki on the question. Mr Balfour pointed out that if he sent such a telegram it would give Mr Lockhart an opening to say either that he considered we were going to do something with which he could not possibly agree, or that he was of opinion that the Russians would not view our action so seriously as to antagonise them.

Mr Chamberlain pointed out that the telegram received from the Naval Attaché said that some ships were ready for destruction, and that if this meant the means of destruction were already on board, it would be very dangerous to send such a telegram, which might lead to an examination of the ships.

Sir Eric Geddes said that, to his mind, this pointed to the necessity of someone who knew the mind of the Cabinet seeing M. Trotzki, but that in the meantime preparations should be continued for the destruction of the Fleet. All that Captain Cromie, the Naval Attaché at Petrograd, wanted was authority to spend money in order to complete his arrangements.

It was pointed out that the Germans were now only 150 kilometres, or three or four days' march, from Petrograd, and that it would be necessary for Captain Cromie to take immediate action if they advanced any further.

The War Cabinet decided that:

(a) The Secretary of State for War should convene a Conference consisting of: General Smuts, the First Sea Lord, the Chief of the Imperial General Staff, and himself, to consider the best method of organising some means of assistance for M. Trotzki, and to put a definite proposal on this question before the War Cabinet:

(b) The First Lord of the Admiralty should instruct the Naval Attaché at Petrograd to continue his preparations for the destruction of the Baltic Fleet; and that, if he had reason to believe that the Germans were advancing on Petrograd and that the Russian Fleet was in imminent danger, he was to take action. Captain Cromie was also to be informed that he was authorised to initiate any expenditure to carry out the above, but care should be taken not to alienate unnecessarily the Russian Government.

INTERVENTION IN RUSSIA

(Note by General Smuts with reference to War Cabinet 409 A)

The War Cabinet this morning appointed Lord Milner and myself, together with the First Sea Lord and the C.I.G.S., as a Committee to consider the question of the steps which could immediately be taken to organise military resistance to the enemy in Russia while the correspondence with America and Japan in reference to intervention was proceeding. We met this afternoon and arrived at the following conclusions:

1. A great deal of confusion and cross-correspondence was at present arising from the absence of any definition and apportionment of military responsibility in Russia among the Allies. It seemed to us, therefore, advisable to divide the responsibility for certain localities among the Allies as hereunder stated. It seemed also anomalous that, while great efforts were being made to secure the intervention of Japan in Russia, the Czecho-Slovak troops should be removed from that country to the Western front. The Shipping Controller reported that any transport of Czecho-Slovak troops would simply divert tonnage from the transport of equivalent numbers of American troops, and it appeared inadvisable to ask for Japanese tonnage for the purpose at the very time when we were pressing Japan to undertake intervention in Russia, which would absorb all her tonnage. We therefore came to the conclusion that the Czecho-Slovak troops now at Vladivostock or on their way to it should be taken charge of there and be organised into efficient units by the French Government, to whom the above difficulties in the way of their transport to France should be pointed out, and who should be asked that, pending their eventual transport to France, they might be used to stiffen the Japanese as part of an Allied force of intervention in Russia. Similarly the rest of the Czecho-Slovak force in Russia should be collected at Murmansk and Archangel, preferably the latter, and should be taken charge of there and organised by the British Government, and pending their transport across the sea should be used to hold those places and to take part in any Allied intervention in Russia. The Secretary of State for War undertook

to send a telegram in the above sense to M. Clemenceau, who had addressed a question to him about the transport of the Czecho-Slovaks from Vladivostock in execution of the Supreme War Council resolution on the subject. It was felt that the collection and organisation of large bodies of troops at the above ports would in itself be a warning to Germany against the removal of further divisions to the Western front.

2. It was decided that General Poole should proceed as soon as possible to Russia as our military representative in order to take charge of military affairs so far as the British Government was concerned, and to advise the War Office as to all steps to be taken in regard to our intervention in Russia. Meantime his London Office would collect the necessary officers and N.C.O.'s, more or less on the lines of the Dunsterville mission, to assist him in the task of organising the Czecho-Slovaks and other forces of intervention from Archangel and Murmansk. The First Sea Lord undertook to send some 200 marines for the defence of Archangel, and the War office to send such munitions and supplies as General Poole might deem necessary for the purpose of his mission. General Poole was to consider, while holding and safeguarding the positions at Murmansk and Archangel, how far he could work up from Archangel towards Vologeda with the forces at his disposal.

3. It was not considered advisable at the present juncture to move either American or other Allied troops from the West to Russia, though the matter should be reconsidered at a later stage of the present enemy offensive on the Western front.

4. After the discussion this morning at the War Cabinet, at which the Prime Minister pointed out how difficult and indeed impossible it was for M. Trotsky to invite Allied intervention in Russia, however much he might desire it, before an Allied force was on the spot to protect him against the enemy, it was felt by the Committee that an undue weight had been placed, in our recent correspondence, on the desirability of an invitation for intervention from the Bolshevik Government. It was therefore decided to recommend to the Foreign Office that the difficulties against such an invitation should be pointed out to the American and Japanese Governments, and that they should be pressed to be satisfied with the very strong expressions which had already fallen from M. Trotsky and the Bolshevik Foreign Minister without

waiting for a formal invitation which the Bolshevik Government could not be expected to make in their present helpless situation.

(Signed) J. C. SMUTS

2, *Whitehall Gardens, S.W.*

160. (*War Cabinet 413, 17 May 1918, Cab/23/6*)

[*Russia—Allied Intervention in Siberia: The Czecho-Slovak Forces*]

12. The War Cabinet discussed at some length the question of using Czecho-Slovak troops, now at Vladivostock, as a nucleus of a force on which to base Allied intervention.

Lord Milner explained that General Poole was leaving that day with a Military Mission for Archangel and Murmansk with a view to organising such Czecho-Slovak forces as might be sent to North Russia, as well as any others that might volunteer for the defence of that district.

The Prime Minister stated that, if we were unable to obtain the assent of the United States of America and Japan to intervention, the question arose as to whether we should not proceed without them. In his opinion, the matter should be reviewed from a military point of view. The Germans were withdrawing troops from the Russian front, our army was bearing the brunt, and no material American contribution had yet arrived to assist us. He therefore was of opinion that we had every justification for not allowing the Americans and the Japanese to block any attempts on our part to stultify these German withdrawals. If the Czecho-Slovak force possessed such good fighting qualities as had been reported, and if it was properly officered, there was the possibility, subject to military considerations, that they could be used in Siberia. The force, of course, could not be used alone, and it would be necessary to add Allied contingents. These contingents, however, including railwaymen from Canada, need not be of great numerical strength.

The Secretary of State for Foreign Affairs said that he thought that the Japanese would not consent to an enterprise into Siberia being undertaken without their taking a leading part. He thought that if we proposed to act without them, it would force their hand and they would immediately wish to join; and, once the Japanese joined the Expedition, he did not think American co-operation would be long withheld.

Lord Curzon stated that, on the previous day, he had seen the Japanese Ambassador, who had told him that public opinion in Japan was very much divided on this question, and in any case it was necessary to obtain the consent of the United States of America, in view of the financial and material considerations involved.

Mr. Balfour suggested that a telegram should be sent to Lord Reading on the subject, saying that we had a large force of 70,000 Czecho-Slovaks who would fight well if properly officered, and asking whether the United States Government saw any objection to these troops being used against the Germans, with the assistance of the Japanese.

Lord Milner said that he doubted whether the scheme would work. In the first place, the French were very keen that the Czecho-Slovak force should be transported to France, and he had had a telegram from M. Clemenceau on the subject that morning. In the second place, all our information tended to show that the Czecho-Slovaks themselves were unwilling to be involved in the internal strife of Russia. Their desire was to fight Germans, and not Bolsheviks.

Mr. Bonar Law pointed out, in this connection, that if the Czecho-Slovak force formed part of the Allied force, thus making it clear to them that they were not fighting the Russians, but the Germans, it was likely that they would not object to co-operate on Russian soil.

It was pointed out that it was difficult to find the necessary tonnage to bring the Czecho-Slovak troops to France. We had told the French that we could not get sufficient ships at the moment for this purpose, and had suggested that it would be better to use these troops in an Allied Expedition into Siberia. The remainder of the Czecho-Slovak force, which had not yet arrived at Vladivostock, which, it now appeared, amounted approximately to 50,000 out of a total of 70,000, might go to Archangel, and such numbers as were not required for the protection of that port and of Murmansk, could be shipped to France.

Lord Milner said that M. Clemenceau had demurred to this suggestion, as only very reduced numbers could be shipped from Archangel.

Lord Robert Cecil said that he was much impressed by the Prime Minister's suggestion. He thought that once we had taken definite steps in regard to intervention in Siberia, the rest of the Allies would soon conform. The French Government had always been pressing for intervention in Siberia, and he thought that if they realised we meant business they would consent to the Czecho-Slovaks being used for the purpose.

Lord Milner pointed out that as the Czecho-Slovak force was entirely the creation of the French, it was imperative that we should obtain their co-operation before employing such force, and added that, as far as American feeling was concerned, and its effect on reinforcements for the Western front, he would prefer to have 10,000 Americans in Siberia than in France.

The War Cabinet decided that:

(*a*) The General Staff should ascertain whether anything effective could be done in Siberia without the co-operation of the United States of America, using as a nucleus the Czecho-Slovak force, reinforced, perhaps, with Canadian railway elements, British troops from Hong Kong, and a French contingent, and with or without Japanese co-operation.

(*b*) Lord Robert Cecil should see M. Benish, and ascertain definitely whether the Czecho-Slovaks were willing to be used for this purpose, if it was explained to them that the object of the expedition was to fight Germans.

(*c*) If, after the above action has been taken, there was any promise of a scheme being put into operation, the Foreign Office should take such diplomatic action as might be expedient with the United States of America, Japan, and France.

161. (*War Cabinet 427, 6 June 1918, Cab/23/6*)

Extract

Lord Robert Cecil expressed the opinion very strongly that it was most unfortunate that the Supreme War Council had not been asked to deal with this question, principally in view of the fact that it was essential, in his opinion, that a strong recommendation in favour of intervention, passed by the Supreme War Council, should be received by President Wilson.

The Prime Minister pointed out that the Supreme War Council had had the matter under consideration, and referred to the agreement reached by the Foreign Ministers of France, Great Britain, and Italy, of which the Supreme War Council had taken note (War Cabinet 426, Minute 5 (iv)).

Lord Robert Cecil pointed out that the Supreme War Council had only taken note of an agreement between the three Foreign Ministers, and had not expressed any military opinion, nor had the Council recommended any approach to President Wilson until the assent of the Japanese to the proposal has been received. He said that he considered the manner in which this whole question had been dealt with was most unsatisfactory.

The Prime Minister explained the difficulties with which President Wilson was faced, and pointed out that the main opposition to any intervention in Siberia by the Japanese came from the Western Coast of America, where President Wilson had strong political interests. It was firmly believed by those in America who opposed Japanese intervention that, if once the Japanese sent forces into Russia, Siberia would become very largely, at any rate from an economic point of view, a Japanese province.

Lord Robert Cecil said that he saw no prospect of a successful conclusion to the war unless something were done in this matter. In the course of the next year it was certain that the Germans would be able, unless something were done, to get the Russians not only to work for them but perhaps to fight for them, thus adding very seriously to the sources of man-power in Germany and to the sources of supply to that country. With regard to the suggestion of operating from Archangel or Murmansk, Lord Robert Cecil said that he did not consider any force operating from those areas would produce a serious effect unless it was backed up by a large expedition from Vladivostock. He did not think that the War Cabinet had ever been quite certain of what it really wanted; that it had never been sure that intervention was right; and that, consequently, this feeling of uncertainty had also been felt by our agents abroad. In his opinion, opportunities had been lost in the past, for though at first President Wilson was not unfavourable, later, political interests began to operate. Since then we have been told that there has been a great change in public feeling in America, and he considered that, if strong pressure of a military character supported by a decision from the Supreme War Council, could be brought to the notice of President Wilson, President Wilson might agree, although perhaps reluctantly.

The First Lord of the Admiralty agreed that it was difficult to obtain a considered view of the War Cabinet on this question, but said that, in his opinion, in view of the grave difficulties of transport and communication which must result from an expedition from Vladivostock, the efficacy of an effort from Murmansk should be compared to the efficacy of an effort even with Japanese help west of Cheliabinsk. Sir Eric Geddes was strongly of opinion that to develop a railway from Vladivostock, capable of carrying stores and supplies, under modern conditions, was too colossal an undertaking for the Japanese to consider. He had never seen a considered and exhaustive study or report on the two possible efforts, and he thought the indefinite policy which Lord Robert Cecil complained of, and of which he was also very conscious, was due to the absence of such a report.

The Prime Minister agreed that the resuscitation of the Trans-Siberian Railway could not possibly be done without the whole-hearted co-operation of America, and pointed out the difficulties of transport which already existed in Siberia. Mr. Lloyd George also said that it was necessary to take into consideration the demand which had been made by M. Clemenceau that priority of claim to Japanese shipping should be given to the transport of Czecho-Slovak troops from Vladivostock to France.

The Secretary of State for Foreign Affairs said that no considered statement had been made by the Military Authorities as to the possibilities of intervention, or as to the strength of force which would be required. On this point he had sent a telegram some time ago to Lord Reading, giving the reasons why the British Government considered intervention necessary, and saying that this telegram would be followed by a detailed military argument. The telegram had been sent over to the War Office, but the War Office had declined to write any memorandum on the subject, giving as a reason that this question was not entirely a military one. Mr. Balfour agreed that the principal factor to be taken into consideration was the reception which any force would receive from the inhabitants of the country.

Sir Eric Geddes said that he thought the possibility of intervention should be considered by the Military Authorities from three points of view:

(*a*) With the inhabitants of Siberia friendly,

(*b*) Actively friendly, or

(*c*) Inert.

Before this question could be properly reasoned out there must be some considered opinion as to the force which would be necessary to produce useful results, and it was essential that the prospect of such results should be put before President Wilson. Sir Eric Geddes was of opinion that it should be considered on the most favourable footing of passive inertia from the local inhabitants, and also that a decision should be come to as to what force could be maintained at Cheliabinsk, or beyond. He was still of opinion, however, that a much smaller effort via Murmansk would give better results in diverting German forces from the Western front, but, in the absence of the exhaustive study of the possibilities of intervention in Siberia and Murmansk, he did not see how the Cabinet or President Wilson could adopt the definite policy which Lord Robert Cecil asked for.

Mr. Balfour pointed out that the objections to any operations from Murmansk were tonnage and men, and that the merit of intervention via Vladivostock was that 500,000 first-class fighting troops could be utilised, while operations from Murmansk would entail taking away troops already fighting in other theatres of war.

The Prime Minister suggested that, in view of the possibility of Lord Reading's return from America for a visit to this country, Lord Robert Cecil should himself go to America in order to lay his views on this question personally before President Wilson, and he said that the War Cabinet would equip Lord Robert Cecil with all the necessary military arguments, and also obtain the views of General Foch on the question.

162. (*Balfour to Young (Archangel)*, *2 July 1918, no. 88, F.O. 371/3305/4072*)

By this time you will, I hope, have seen Mr Lindley, who will have explained to you the policy of His Majesty's Government with regard to Archangel and Russia generally.

Briefly stated, our present object at Archangel is (i) to protect the Allied stores and, if possible, to prevent the removal of any more southwards; (ii) to prepare the ground for the possible intervention of a more active character.

The prospects of this will depend on the strength of the forces which we can ourselves spare and the number of Russians and non-Russians in Russia who rally to our support.

Any action that may be taken by the Allies in the nature of

intervention whether at Archangel or elsewhere will be directed not against Russia or any Russian party, but solely to strengthen Russia and helping her resist the enemy.

Any eventual landing of armed forces would have for its immediate object to protect the Allied stores and prevent their destruction by the agents of the Bolshevist Government with the probable result of the devastation of the town, and to strengthen the hands of the Local Authorities who appear at present to be prevented by the Central Government from concluding with the Allies a bargain which is manifestly both just and in their own interests.

Confidential

Forces which we have immediately available are not strong enough to occupy Archangel under present conditions there, and for the time being we shall probably follow line indicated in your telegram under reply.

HELPING OUR FRIENDS

163. (*Balfour to Barclay (Washington), 2 October 1918, no. 6001(D), F.O. 371/3339/18*)

We fully appreciate the attitude of the United States Government and their desire to act in such a matter in accordance with the advice of their Military Authorities. Our position is however a little different from theirs. In the first place our Military Authorities do not take the same view. As far as they are able to judge the Czechs if given full support by the Allies might still be able in conjunction with the forces under General Alexieff to hold the line of the Volga against any force that is likely to be brought there by our enemies. The position is very obscure and possibly further information might modify their judgment but that is the present view taken by our soldiers. Apart from this we feel the very greatest reluctance to abandon the elements in Russia loyal to the Allies. General Alexieff for instance has fought throughout the war against our enemies and in the early part of it he and his troops rendered essential and heroic services to the Allied Cause. Since the Revolution he has never wavered and we know that he has resisted many approaches from the German side backed though they were by old associates of his such as Miliukoff. We feel therefore honourably bound to do our very utmost even at some risk to our own interests to come to his assistance. If we were now to ask the Czechs to withdraw to the East of the Urals that would be to cut off from Alexieff and those with him their last hope of Allied assistance. We therefore propose subject to any observation that the United States Government may have to make to present this view of the situation to our French and Japanese Allies and to appeal to them to continue their efforts to stand by our friends in European Russia. We quite recognise that the above considerations do not apply to the United States in the same way as they do to those who fought side by side with the Russians in the early part of the war and the British Government will quite understand it if the American Government feel unable to take a more active line than that indicated in the telegram under reply. We venture however to express the hope that the American Government will appreciate our position in the matter and will not think it amiss if we endeavour to carry out the task that seems to be imposed upon us by obligations of honour. In short if they feel unable to assist us beyond the point indicated we hope that they will not discourage our other Allies from helping us.

164. (*War Cabinet 502, 14 November 1918, Cab/23/8*)

Extract

The Prime Minister said that it was important that the public in England should realise more fully what Bolshevism meant in practice. France was more secure against Bolshevism, owing to the existence of a large population of peasant proprietors. Here we had a great, inflammable, industrial population, and it was very desirable that our industrial population should know how industrial workers had suffered equally with the rest of the population of Russia at the hands of the Bolsheviks.

Mr. Chamberlain thought that the time had come when full publication should be given to the evidence which had been collected by Mr. Lockhart in regard to the behaviour of the Bolsheviks.

Mr. Balfour stated that the Bolshevik Government in Russia had used their control of food supplies to starve to death their political opponents. The people they had treated worst were people whom we should regard in this country as 'blood-red Socialists'.

The Chancellor of the Exchequer thought that it was most

important that we should get the press of the country to take up the question of Bolshevik excesses more fully.

Lord Robert Cecil stated that the Foreign Office had a good deal of information on the subject which could be made available.

Mr. Chamberlain added that the War Aims Committee also had a certain amount of material.

The War Cabinet decided:

(*a*) That the Foreign Office should collect as much material as possible in regard to the behaviour of the Bolshevik Government, and should confer with Sir George Riddell and Lord Burnham, with a view to its full and speedy publication.

(*b*) To approve the decisions of the Foreign Office Conference, with the exception of No. 9, which was left for decision by the Secretary of State for War, in consultation with the Secretary of State for India.

APPENDIX

Minute of the Proceedings of a Conference held at the Foreign Office on November 13, 1918, at 3.30 p.m.

Present:

The Right Hon. A. J. Balfour, O.M., M.P.
(*Chairman*)
The Right Hon. Lord Milner, G.C.B.
The Right Hon. Lord Robert Cecil, K.C., M.P.
The Right Hon. Lord Hardinge of Penshurst,
K.G., P.C.
Sir George Clerk, K.C.M.G., C.B.
Director of Naval Intelligence.
Director of Military Intelligence.
Director of Military Operations.

Lieutenant-Colonel F. H. Kisch.
Major Farmer.

At the Chairman's request, Lord Robert Cecil read a memorandum received from the General Staff with regard to present and future British military policy in Russia.

The Chairman observed that the memorandum raised most of the points which it was necessary to consider. He did not think it would be possible to adhere literally to the conclusion arrived at in the memorandum, that our troops should be withdrawn from Russia not later than the signature of peace:

Regarding the question broadly, the Chairman enunciated the following principles as a basis for discussion:

1. The British Government cannot embark on an anti-Bolshevik crusade in Russia. It was natural that our advisers on the spot should take a contrary line, as they were obsessed with the external and visible violence of Bolshevism. On the other hand, the people of this country would not consent to such a crusade.
2. It is necessary that support should be afforded to the border States of Western Russia from the Baltic to the Black Sea. These States should be recognised, and support should follow on recognition.

The Chairman observed that the General Staff paper took the view that the existence of these small States on the western border of Russia would inevitably prove the object of military ambition on the part of the latter country when Russia should again become a Power. He thought, however, that the League of Nations, if it were to be of any value at all, should be able to protect them. It had been suggested that Bolshevism was already in existence in these States, but he thought that what was really referred to was a form of agrarian revolution due to the existing systems of land tenure. Lord Milner mentioned that the clause in the armistice providing for the policing of these States by German troops might prove a danger in view of the break-up of *morale* in the German army.

The Chairman, continuing, proposed action on the following lines:

1. To support the Omsk Government.
2. To ensure the Czech troops in Siberia should be extricated.
3. To help Denikin in South-East Russia.
4. To help the small nationalities of the Caucasus.

Lord Milner expressed himself in general agreement with the Chairman's remarks. He agreed entirely that we could not crusade

against the Bolsheviks in countries where Bolshevism already pre-
vailed, but he thought we should do our best to protect other
countries from Bolshevik attack, particularly when invited to do
so. Anything which could be done to protect the Baltic States
should be done, but British troops could not be despatched to
these regions. On the other hand, considerations both of honour
and of interest demanded that we should keep Bolshevism from
the regions East of the Black Sea, *i.e.*, the Caucasus, the Don
country, and Turkestan. It was necessary that our military
objectives should be limited. Finally, Lord Milner invited reference to the Convention concluded in Paris on the 23rd December, 1917, defining the spheres of the British and French activity
in Russia, and urged that a similar convention was required to
meet the present situation.

Lord Robert Cecil was in substantial agreement with what had
been said by the Chairman and Lord Milner, but was not prepared
to go quite so far as to say that we should protect Border States
against Bolshevik attack. Our object should be to help the
Russians to stand by themselves, and we should therefore do
everything possible to support and strengthen existing organisations. His Lordship proposed:

(*a*) As regards Siberia:
    (1) To recognise the Omsk Government.
    (2) To encourage the Czechs to remain in Western Siberia.
    (3) To send military equipment and a staff of officers to
        Siberia.
    (4) To send the Canadian brigade as originally proposed, if
        this can be arranged.

(*b*) As regards the Caucasus:
We should, as was suggested by the D.M.O., establish ourselves on the whole line from Baku to Batum.

(*c*) As regards Denikin:
We should help him with arms and munitions, but not
troops.

(*d*) As regards Poland:
Nothing more can be done than (as proposed in the General
Staff memorandum) to furnish arms and equipment for the
existing Polish formations, and to transport to Poland as
early as possible the Polish troops in France.

(*e*) As regards the Baltic States:

> Lord Robert Cecil still adhered to his opinion in favour of the creation of a Baltic Block, failing which, he thought we should supply arms to any local authorities which might prove themselves capable of exercising control.

The D.N.I. urged that the maximum possible use should be made of our power of controlling food supplies, and mentioned that Captain Cromie in his last letter had said of Russia, 'the hand that feeds this country will rule it'. Admiral Hall drew a comparison between European Russia of to-day and Belgium during the German occupation, and mentioned that the power which kept Belgium solidly pro-Ally was the Belgian Relief.

The Chairman agreed in principle, but pointed out that in Belgium, the distribution and control of food supplies had been possible only owing to the presence of neutral diplomatic machinery.

After a short general discussion, instructions were given that the following decisions should be recorded:

1. To remain in occupation of Murmansk and Archangel.
2. To recognise the Omsk Directorate as a *de facto* Government.
3. To maintain our present Siberian expedition, and to encourage the Canadians to adhere to the arrangements contemplated prior to the armistice.
4. To endeavour to induce the Czechs to remain in Western Siberia, and to send out selected officers to that region.
5. To approve the proposal outlined by the D.M.O., for a *modus vivendi* with the French authorities on the subject of the relations between General Janin and General Knox.
6. To proceed with the occupation of the Baku-Batum railway.
7. To establish touch with Denikin at Novo Rossisk, and afford him all possible assistance in military material.
8. To supply the Baltic States with military material, if, and when, they have Governments ready to receive and utilise such material.
9. To authorise General Marshall to take over Krasnovodsk, subject to the concurrence of the India Office.
10. To adhere to the Convention of December 1917, if possible, extending the British sphere so as to include the country between the Don and the Volga.

165. (*War Cabinet 511, 10 December 1918, Appendix, Cab/23/8*)
Notes on our Policy in Russia by the Secretary of State for Foreign Affairs
November 1, 1918

The general tenor of the telegrams which reach me, not merely from Russian sources, but from our own officials who have to deal with Russian questions, seems to indicate a very insufficient apprehension of what His Majesty's Government aim at doing to meet the present Russian situation. This is not, perhaps, surprising, seeing that the whole problem has been profoundly altered by the defeat of the enemy and the terms of armistice which have been successively imposed upon our various enemies.

One result of this has been to modify the principal motive which prompted our expeditions to Murmansk, Archangel, Vladivostock, and the Caspian. So long as a life-and-death struggle was proceeding on the Western front between us and the Central Powers, it was of the first importance to prevent, as far as possible, the withdrawal of German forces from Russia to France; but with the conclusion of a German armistice this motive has no further force.

For what then are we still maintaining troops in various parts of what was once the Russian Empire? To judge by the character of the appeals made to us from many quarters, it seems commonly supposed that these military expeditions are partial and imperfect efforts to carry out a campaign against Bolshevism, and to secure, by foreign intervention, the restoration of decent order and a stable Government. We are constantly urged to send larger bodies of troops to carry out these great objects, and it is frequently suggested—sometimes asserted—that by our delay in sending them invaluable opportunities for carrying out an effective policy have been lost for ever.

This view, however, indicates a complete misapprehension of what His Majesty's Government are able to do, or desire to do. This country would certainly refuse to see its forces, after more than four years of strenuous fighting, dissipated over the huge expanse of Russia in order to carry out political reforms in a State which is no longer a belligerent Ally.

We have constantly asserted that it is for the Russians to choose their own form of government; that we have no desire to intervene in their domestic affairs; and that if, in the course of opera-

694

tions essentially directed against the Central Powers, we have to act with such Russian political and military organisations as are favourable to the *Entente*, this does not imply that we deem ourselves to have any mission to establish, or disestablish, any particular political system among the Russian people.

To these views His Majesty's Government still adhere; and their military policy in Russia is still governed by them. But it does not follow that we can disinterest ourselves wholly from Russian affairs. Recent events have created obligations which last beyond the occasions which gave them birth. The Czecho-Slovaks are our Allies, and we must do what we can to help them. In the south-east corner of Russia in Europe, in Siberia, in Trans-Caucasia and Trans-Caspia, in the territories adjacent to the White Sea and the Arctic Ocean, new anti-Bolshevist administrations have grown up under the shelter of Allied forces. We are responsible for their existence and must endeavour to support them. How far we can do this, and how such a policy will ultimately develop, we cannot yet say. It must largely depend on the course taken by the Associated Powers, who have far larger resources at their disposal than ourselves. For us, no alternative is open at present than to use such troops as we possess to the best advantage; where we have no troops, to supply arms and money; and in the case of the Baltic provinces to protect, as far as we can, the nascent nationalities by the help of our fleet. Such a policy must necessarily seem halting and imperfect to those who on the spot, are resisting the invasion of militant Bolshevism. But it is all that we can accomplish in existing circumstances, or ought to attempt.

WITHDRAWAL FROM RUSSIA

166. (*Lloyd George to Churchill, 16 February 1919, Lloyd George Papers, F/8/3/19*)

Am very alarmed at your second telegram about planning war against the Bolshevists. The Cabinet have never authorised such a proposal. They have never contemplated anything beyond supplying armies in anti-Bolshevik areas in Russia with necessary equipment to enable them to hold their own, and that only in the event of every effort at peaceable solution failing. A military enquiry as to the best methods of giving material assistance to these Russian armies is all to the good, but do not forget that it is an essential part of the enquiry to ascertain the cost. And I also want you to bear in mind that the W.O. reported to the Cabinet that according to their information intervention was driving the anti-Bolshevists parties in Russia into the ranks of the Bolsheviks.

I had already drafted a reply to be sent to Philip Kerr about your first telegram. I am sending that reply along with this. I adhere to it in its entirety. If Russia is really anti-Bolshevik, then a supply of equipment would enable it to redeem itself. If Russia is pro-Bolshevik, not merely is it none of our business to interfere with its internal affairs, it would be positively mischievous: it would strengthen and consolidate Bolshevik opinion. An expensive war of aggression against Russia is a way to strengthen Bolshevism in Russia and create it at home. We cannot afford the burden. Chamberlain says we can hardly make both ends meet on a peace basis, even at the present crushing rate of taxation; and if we are committed to a war against a continent like Russia, it is the road to bankruptcy and Bolshevism in these islands.

The French are not safe guides in this matter. Their opinion is largely biassed by the enormous number of small investors who put their money into Russian loans and who now see no prospect of ever recovering it. I urge you therefore not to pay too much heed to their incitements. There is nothing they would like better than to see us pulling the chestnuts out of the fire for them.

I also want you to bear in mind the very grave labour position in this country. Were it known that you had gone over to Paris to propose a plan of war against the Bolsheviks, it would do more to incense organised labour than anything I can think of; and what is still worse, it would throw into the ranks of the extremists a very large number of thinking people who now abhor their methods.

I sincerely hope you will stand by your first proposals, subject to the comment which I have passed upon them.

Please show these messages to Foreign Secretary.

167. (*Churchill to Lloyd George, 8 March 1919, Lloyd George Papers, F/8/3/29*)

I send you the following notes on our conversation this morning.

(1) It is your decision and the decision of the War Cabinet that **we are to evacuate** Murmansk and Archangel as soon as the ice

melts in the White Sea. Russians (including women and children) who have compromised themselves through working with us are to be transported, if they desire it, to a place of refuge.

If reinforcements are required to cover the extrication of our forces and the withdrawal of the aforesaid Russians, they may be taken for this purpose from the volunteers now re-engaging for service in the army. It will be made clear to these men that they are only going to extricate their comrades and not for a long occupation of Northern Russia.

Subject to the above, I am to make whatever military arrangements are necessary to carry out your policy.

(2) It is also decided by you and the War Cabinet that we are to withdraw our army from the Caucasus as quickly as possible. This will certainly take 3 or 4 months, as the detachments which have been thrown out as far as Kars to the Southward and the troops on the other side of the Caspian have also to be withdrawn, and our lines of communication from Hamadan to Enzeli have to be wound up.

Denikin will be compensated for the loss of the support of this army (a) by arms and munitions and (b) by a military mission, which may if necessary amount to 2,000 in all of technical assistants and instructors. This military mission is to be formed of officers and men who volunteer specially for service in Russia and not by men of the regular volunteer army ordered to proceed there. In return for this support, we should secure from Denikin undertakings not to attack the Georgians and others South of a certain line which the Foreign Office are tracing; and later instalments of arms and munitions will be dealt out to him as he conforms to this agreement. If he fails to conform to this agreement, it will be open to us to withdraw our mission. The limits of our assistance to Denikin will be clearly stated to him, and it will be open to him to accept or reject our conditions and our help.

(3) You have also decided that Colonel John Ward and the two British battalions at Omsk are to be withdrawn (less any who volunteer to stay) as soon as they can be replaced by a military mission, similar to that to Denikin, composed of men who volunteer specifically for service in Russia.

(4) On these lines and within these limits, I should be prepared to be responsible for carrying out the policy on which you and the War Cabinet have decided. It will be necessary to inform the

allies of our intention, and this I presume will be done by yourself or Mr Balfour.

If, however, I have wrongly interpreted your decisions in any respect, I hope you will let me know what you really wish, in order that I may see whether it can be done.

CHURCHILL v. LLOYD GEORGE

168. (*Churchill to Lloyd George, 26 April 1919, Lloyd George Papers, F/8/3/43*)

I do hope that amid your many anxieties and preoccupations you have not lost sight of the very considerable change which has come over the military situation in Siberia.

Koltchak has been steadily making his way through innumerable difficulties and is achieving at the present time a very remarkable measure of success. It is thought that he now has a very good chance of reaching the line of the Volga in the near future, and there are possibilities that he may be able to advance further towards Moscow. At the same time his advance enables him to stretch out his right hand in the direction of the Archangel force, and communication by patrol has actually been established between them in the neighbourhood of Vyatka. The Russian forces in the Archangel area, which now number 15,000, have been fighting extremely well, and if the dangers of the next month are passed through satisfactorily in that quarter, this Russian force may well increase in numbers to 25,000 men.

It seems to me that this development would be important for you because if fostered and seconded with real good will it would enable you to withdraw from North Russia without either having to carry away many thousands of the local inhabitants who have compromised themselves with us or leaving them to be massacred by the Bolsheviks.

The Government of Monsieur Tchaykovsky which we have called into being in North Russia is the most democratic of the three Russian National Governments, and it would have been an unpleasant thing to have had to leave them in the lurch. There is, however, now a fresh chance of avoiding this and the reproach inseparable from it and at the same time carrying out your policy of evacuation.

Everything is, of course, very changeable in these Russian

situations, but the changes which have taken place and appear still to be taking place in Siberia seem to offer us the prospect of escaping from our difficult position without discredit.

It seems to me, therefore, that we should do everything in our power to help and encourage Koltchak and to build up these Russian forces in North Russia which may conceivably, in the improving circumstances, be able to defend themselves when we are gone.

The advance of Koltchak's armies is the more remarkable in view of the fact that it is being conducted exclusively with Russian troops. The Czechos, who were formerly the only other troops on this front, are now employed simply on guarding the railway a long way back. The whole credit of regaining this really enormous stretch of country rests with a purely Russian army of about 100,000 men. There is, however, as you know, another Russian army of 100,000 in an advanced state of formation in Siberia, and five divisions from this army are expected to reach Admiral Koltchak during the course of the next three months. As the front has advanced Westward, districts containing large numbers of men have been recovered, and these men are already being used to fill up the divisions at the front. Apparently wherever Bolshevism has been tried it is loathed. It is only popular where it has not been felt, and Koltchak's armies have been well received by the population on their onward march.

We can, I think, claim to have given more effective support to Koltchak than any of the other great Powers, as we have supplied him with nearly 12 million pounds' worth of our surplus munitions, and by the labours of our officers and agents this great mass of stuff has been filtered along the Siberian railway. In fact, the Russian forces in which we are interested, whether in North Russia, Siberia or those of Denikin, have received from us assistance which has already been substantial and may shortly prove effective.

You will have seen papers circulated by the Foreign Office and the General Staff advocating the recognition of Admiral Koltchak's Government. This is the advice given by Elliot as well as by the military men, and I most earnestly press it upon you at this juncture. Its influence on the military situation would be most favourable. It would give the greatest possible satisfaction to the overwhelming mass of your Parliamentary supporters. It would consolidate our Russian policy and strengthen your hand in many directions. It would be entirely justified on account of the solid support which we are giving in munitions and organisers.

Before such recognition is accorded, however, I think it would be a very good thing if your suggestion of trying to secure a democratic programme about Russian land from Koltchak were carried through. In this connection it is worth noticing that Monsieur Tchaykovsky, the Head of the North Russian Government, the most democratic Government in the field against the Bolsheviks, is, it is believed, about to become a member of Koltchak's Government. The moment appears, therefore, very favourable for securing from the Koltchak Government a declaration of policy in regard to (a) the land and (b) a constitutional and non-autocratic regime, in return for their simultaneous recognition by the Allies, or at any rate by Great Britain.

I send you herewith a military paper which has been prepared by the General Staff, to the general policy of which I desire to obtain your approval and that of the Cabinet. If necessary Wilson and I can come over to see you on this subject, which seems to me to be of equal importance and urgency.

169. (*Memo. by Lloyd George, 30 August 1919, Lloyd George Papers, F/9/1/15*)

I earnestly trust the Cabinet will not consent to committing British resources to any fresh military enterprises in Russia. They have decided to withdraw from Siberia, from Archangel, from the Baltic, and after furnishing General Denikin with one more packet, to let the Russians fight out their own quarrels at their own expense. I hope nothing will induce the Ministry to deviate from this decision.

As to the 'great opportunities' for capturing Petrograd which we are told were 'dangling at our finger tips', and which we never grasped, we have heard this so often of other 'great opportunities' in Russia which have never materialised in spite of lavish expenditure on their prosecution. We have already this year spent over 100 millions in Russia. We have sent some excellent troops there. Early in the year there were 'great opportunities' of liberating Moscow, and we were assured it was within our grasp. We sent every assistance in our power to Admiral Kolchak to exploit those opportunities, not merely by helping him to equip his forces but by sanctioning a military expedition which was to penetrate far into Russia in order to join hands with him. The liberating army—or at least what is left of it—is now running as hard as it can back to Omsk, and is meditating a further retreat to Irkutsk. The failure was certainly not due to any default on our part. It is due to facts which are none the less stubborn because some of our advisers have habitually refused to take cognisance of them.

General Yudenitch never had a chance of taking Petrograd. The Esthonians, so far from co-operating with him, distrusted him as much as the Bolsheviks, and the result of his operations up till now has been to drive the Esthonian Republic to make a separate treaty with the Bolsheviks. He is a notorious reactionary, as much distrusted by the Esthonians as by the Russian people. He is not a man of any military distinction, and there is no proof that he is capable of leading such an enterprise as he meditated. If North Russia were groaning under Bolshevik tyranny and the Esthonians and Latvians were eager to join in a war of liberation, there would now have been an army numbering hundreds of thousands sweeping over North West Russia. The fact that out of a population of several millions the anti-Bolsheviks have only mustered 20 or 30,000 men is another indication of the complete misreading of the Russian situation, upon which the military policy has been based.

As to General Gough, I have read the instructions given him by the Chief of the Staff when he went to Helsingfors, and unless secret instructions were given him of which the Cabinet had no knowledge—and I cannot believe that—then General Gough ought to be reprimanded for taking upon himself a responsibility inconsistent with his orders. I have always thought that the choice of General Gough for this mission was an injudicious one. Whatever his qualities, he was utterly unsuited for a task requiring great judgment. If Russia were anxious to overthrow Bolshevik rule, the help we have given her would have provided her with a full opportunity. We have discharged faithfully our honourable obligations to Denikin and to Kolchak. We have never entered into any with Yudenitch and I hope we shall not do so. The British public will not tolerate the throwing away of more millions on foolish military enterprises.

I am anxious for another reason to have done with these military ventures in Russia as soon as possible. I cannot help thinking that they have taken away the mind of the War Office from important administrative tasks which urgently needed attention. If the amount of intense and concentrated attention which has been devoted to the running of these Russian wars had been given to reducing our expenditure, I feel certain that scores of millions would have been saved. 'Russia does not want to be liberated'. Whatever she may think of the Bolsheviks, she does not think it worth while sacrificing any more blood to substitute for the men of the Yudenitch type. Let us therefore attend to our own business and leave Russia to look after hers.

170. (*Churchill to Lloyd George, 20 September 1919, Lloyd George Papers, F/9/1/19*)

Here are a few late Russian papers which speak for themselves.

I am sorry you could not see Mr. Dukes. He would interest you greatly. Perhaps you will find time next week.

I am frankly puzzled to know why you are opposed to the independence of the small Baltic States. The *Westminster Gazette* says that it is because we are under the influence of the Russian reactionaries. But so long as we do not have to guarantee their independence I do not see why we did not recognise it, even if the Russian reactionaries are displeased.

As a matter of fact now is the time to win good terms for the small states with the Russians, in return for their aid against the Bolsheviks.

In a little while the power of Russia will be re-established and then it will be too late.

You are always ready to seek and face the truth, & I hope you will not fail to do so in regard to Russia. Nothing can preserve either the Bolshevik system or the B. regime. By mistakes on our part the agony of the Russian people may be prolonged.

But their relief is sure. The only question open is whether we shall desert them in the crisis of their fate; & so lose all that we have worked so hard to win. You will see in my memo how much I have tried to harmonise my views with yours as it is my duty to do while I serve you. I do hope and trust that you will not brush away lightly the convictions of one who wishes to remain your faithful lieutenant & looks forward to a fruitful & active co-operation.

The plans you discussed with me about party matters will all miscarry if it is believed in the Conservative party that we are not the enemies of Bolshevism in every form & in every land.

171. (*Lloyd George to Churchill, 22 September 1919, Lloyd George Papers, F/9/1/20*)

Your letter distressed me. You know that I have been doing my best for the last few weeks to comply with the legitimate demand which comes from all classes of the country to cut down the enormous expenditure which is devouring the resources of the country at a prodigious rate. I have repeatedly begged you to apply your mind to the problem. I made this appeal to all departments, but I urged it specially upon you for three reasons: The first is that the highest expenditure is still military; the second that the largest immediate reduction which could be effected without damage to the public welfare are foreseeable in the activities controlled by your Department. The third is that I have found your mind so obsessed by Russia that I felt I had good ground for the apprehension that your great abilities, energy, and courage were not devoted to the reduction of expenditure.

I regret that all my appeals have been in vain. At each interview you promised me to give your mind to this very important problem. Nevertheless the first communication I have always received from you after these interviews related to Russia. I invited you to Paris to help me to reduce our commitments in the East. You there produce a lengthy and carefully prepared memorandum on Russia. I entreated you on Friday to let Russia be for at least 48 hours and to devote your weekend to preparing for the Finance Committee this afternoon. You promised faithfully to do so. Your reply is to send me a four page letter on Russia, and a closely printed memorandum of several pages—all on Russia. I am frankly in despair. Yesterday and to-day I have gone carefully through such details as have been supplied about the military expenditure, and I am more convinced than ever that Russia has cost us not merely the sum spent directly upon that unfortunate country, but indirectly scores of millions in the failure to attend to the costly details of expenditure in other spheres.

You confidently predict in your memorandum that Deniken is on the eve of some great and striking success. I looked up some of your memoranda and your statements made earlier in the year about Kolchak, and I find that you use exactly the same language in reference to Kolchak's successes.

The Cabinet have given you every support in the policy which they have laid down, and which you have accepted. I am not sure that they have not once or twice strained that policy in the direction of your wishes. The expedition to Kotlass was hardly a covering one to protect the retirement of Ironside's troops. The sequel has shown that it was quite unnecessary from that point of view. It was in the nature of an attempt to cut through in order to join hands with Kolchak. Nevertheless you received all support in your effort. That failed, but it was not the fault of the Cabinet that it did not succeed.

You proposed that the Czecho-Slovaks should be encouraged to break through the Bolshevik armies and proceed to Archangel. Everything was done to support your proposal. Ships were promised for Archangel if they succeeded. Deniken has been supplied with all the munitions and equipment that he needed. Still you vaguely suggest that something more could have been done and ought to have been done.

I abide by the agreed policy. We have kept faith with all these men. But not a member of the Cabinet is prepared to go further. The various Russian enterprises have cost us this year between 100 and 150 millions, when Army, Navy and Shipping are taken into account. Neither this Government nor any other Government that this country is likely to see will do more. We cannot afford it. The French have talked a good deal about Anti-Bolshevism, but they have left it to us to carry out the Allied Policy. Clemenceau told me distinctly that he was not prepared to do any more. Foch is distinctly and definitely opposed to these ventures at the Allied expense. Their view is that our first duty is to clear up the German situation. I agree with them.

I wonder whether it is any use my making one last effort to induce you to throw off this obsession which, if you will forgive me for saying so, is upsetting your balance. I again ask you to let Russia be, at any rate for a few days, and to concentrate your mind on the quite unjustifiable expenditure in France, at home, and in the East, incurred by both the War Office and the Air Department. Some of the items could not possibly have been tolerated by you if you had given one-fifth of the thought to these matters which you devoted to Russia.

I would only add one word about the Baltic States. You want their independence recognised by the Allies in return for an undertaking by them to attack the Bolsheviks. It is quite clear from their communications that that would not satisfy them in the least, and that they would ask (1) that we should guarantee that independence; (2) that we should supply them with the necessary equipment and cash to enable them to maintain their armies. Are you prepared to comply with these two requests? There is no other member of the Cabinet who would. It would be the height of recklessness to do so. Whether the Bolsheviks or the anti-Bolsheviks get the upper hand, they would not recognise the independence of these States as it would involve the permanent exclusion of Russia from the Baltic. Would you be prepared to make war with an Anti-Bolshevik regime if they attempted to reconquer these States and to secure the old Russian ports of Riga and Reval? If not, it would be a disgraceful piece of deception on our part to give a guarantee. In the second place, do you wish this country to maintain armies in the field of Esthonians, Latvians and Lithuanians to invade Russia? Unless you do, it is idle to hurl vague reproaches at your colleagues. The reconquest of Russia would cost hundreds of millions. It would cost hundreds of millions more to maintain the new Government until it had established itself. You are prepared to spend all that money, and I know perfectly well that is what you really desire. But as you know that you won't find another responsible person in the whole land who will take your view, why waste you energy and your usefulness on this vain fretting which completely paralyses you for other work?

I have worked with you now for longer than I have probably co-operated with any other man in public life and I think I have given you tangible proof that I wish you well. It is for that reason that I write frankly to you.

THE LIMITS OF SUPPORT TO POLAND

172. (*Curzon to Rumbold (Warsaw), 27 January 1920, D.B.F.P. III, no. 664*)

Extract

Yesterday M. Patek had an interview with the Prime Minister on the subject of the Bolshevik offer of peace to Poland. The Prime

Minister stated formally to M. Patek that, while it was not for Great Britain to advise Poland, which must take the full responsibility for deciding as between peace and war, the British Government certainly did not advise war. He then explained to M. Patek the situation as he saw it. Six months ago there was a great converging movement against Bolshevism, including Koltchak, Denikin, Poland, the Baltic States, Finland and the British at Archangel. Poland at that time was only a unit in a great combined movement pressing the Bolsheviks on all sides. Now, on the other hand, Poland was alone. The Allies had withdrawn from Russia. Koltchak had disappeared. Denikin had been defeated. Esthonia had made an armistice, and, if his information was correct, Latvia intended to follow suit immediately. There was clearly, therefore, grave risk that Poland might be left to face a Bolshevik concentration by itself. The Prime Minister therefore wished to make it perfectly clear to the Polish Government that the British Government did not wish to give Poland the slightest encouragement to pursue the policy of war, because if it were to give that advice it would incur responsibilities which it could not discharge.

The Prime Minister then gave certain reasons for his opinion that Bolshevism did not constitute a serious military menace outside its own borders. The danger from its propaganda was perhaps as great as ever, but he did not believe that it would be possible for the Soviet authorities to organise a really formidable army for offensive purposes against the West, while there was reason for thinking that the revolutionaries were becoming afraid of the military instrument they had created. A military *coup d'état* in Russia might be a very formidable menace to Poland. He did not think that the Bolshevik armies, in view of the great desire of the population for peace, now constituted a military menace against any well-organised State. Their transportation and manufacturing resources were not sufficient to admit of great offensive operations. In addition, there was nothing in the shape of food or raw materials to attract an army to march into Poland, Hungary, or Germany.

The conversation then turned upon the character of a possible peace between Poland and Russia. The Prime Minister made it clear that, in his opinion, the principal difficulty would be the fact that the Polish armies had advanced far beyond the racial boundary into considerable territories which contained large Russian majorities. The Prime Minister said that if the Poles made a sincere attempt to make an equitable peace and the Bolsheviks either refused peace or, having made peace, proceeded to repudiate it, Great Britain would feel bound to assist Poland to the best of its power. He was sure that it would be possible both for the French and British Governments to rouse their people, exhausted as they were by five years' war, to make fresh efforts if Poland had made a sincere attempt to make peace on fair terms and the Bolsheviks rejected it and attacked Poland instead. If, on the other hand, Poland insisted on retaining within Poland areas which were indisputably Russian according to the principles generally applied by the Peace Conference, and if the Bolshevik Government refused the peace on this ground and attacked Poland in order to recover Russian districts for Russia, it would be very difficult, if not impossible, for the British Government to get public opinion to support military or financial outlay in these circumstances.

173. (*Resolution of the Hythe Conference*,[1] *9 August 1920, App. II, Cab/23/22/46*)

I. The Allies are agreed:
  (1) That the only ground upon which they can undertake hostile action against Russia is to assist the Polish people to maintain their independence within their ethnographic frontier:
  (2) That they will not interfere in the internal affairs of Russia provided Russia does not interfere in the affairs of other nations:
  (3) That they will not declare a final breach with Russia until the result of the Minsk negotiations is clear;
  (4) That if the Polish Government, after hearing the policy of the Allies as defined in these Resolutions, comes to terms with Russia, the ground for Allied action against Russia lapses, unless the Treaty of Versailles is thereby infringed.

II. On these conditions, and if the Soviet Government attempts to impose terms on Poland incompatible with its independence, the Allies are agreed to take common action to assist the Polish people to defend their independence, provided:

[1] This is a condensed version of three resolutions—see D.B.F.P. 1st series, VIII, pp. 747–55.

(a) That their action will not involve the despatch of further Allied troops to Poland:

(b) That the Polish Government accepts and acts upon the military advice tendered to it by the Allies.

III. The common action they will take in the event of Russia not respecting the independence of Poland, and until such time as that recognition is given, will be as stated in the accompanying Note.

IV. The British Government, after consulting the other Allies, *will inform* the Soviet Government and MM. Kameneff and Krassin that the Allies have initiated the action they propose to take to support Poland in its struggle for independence, and that unless an agreement of the above character has been reached between Poland and Russia by Sunday night next, relations of all kinds will be broken off and MM. Kameneff and Krassin will be required to leave England immediately, unless in the interval they have engaged or engage in propaganda, in which case their stay will be immediately terminated.

NOTE

The military and naval means available for exercising pressure on the Soviet Government with a view to obtaining a guarantee for the independence of Poland may be summed up as follows:

A declaration by the Allied Governments to the Polish Government, saying:

If the Polish Government does not accept the Russian armistice or peace terms, and if it is decided to struggle energetically for the independence of the country, it is asked to declare this publicly and to come to an understanding with the Allied Governments as to the measures to be taken with this object in view, and which would include:

(a) *On the part of the Polish Government:*

(i) The designation of a Commander-in-Chief of the Polish Armies without any other functions, assisted by Allied Officers:

(ii) The maintenance of the Polish Army at a strength of 22 Divisions completed as far as possible to their normal effectives:

(iii) The defence at all costs of the line of the Vistula in case the line held at this moment by the Polish armies cannot be maintained.

(b) *On the part of the Allied Governments:*

(i) The supply to the Polish Army maintained at 22 Divisions of the means of armament and various materials and, in addition, of officers for this Army:

(ii) Interruption of contact between Russia and the outside world, whether by naval action or by international action:

(iii) Support to General Wrangel's army:

(iv) The propaganda accompanied by proposals effected in Baltic States, in Roumania and in the Caucasus:

(v) Employment of the means necessary for the maintenance of the communications of the Allied Powers with Poland.

THE OBJECT OF THE GENOA CONFERENCE

174. (*Cabinet Minutes, 28 March 1922, Cab/23/29/21*)

(3) The Prime Minister said that perhaps it would assist his colleagues in their consideration of the Genoa Conference if he were to state the case in the form of two propositions:

(a) The economic proposition, namely, the economic conditions under which our traders can be induced to undertake trade in Russia.

(b) The larger question at the base of our economic troubles, namely, the position of unrest in the East, which disturbs the trader and makes him suspicious.

With regard to the second point, there was a state of something like menace along the Russian frontier. Russia was full of suspicion of the intentions of Roumania, Poland, Finland, and other neighbouring countries, who were equally suspicious of Russia. One half of Europe was living under a condition of menace of war, and it was absolutely necessary to restore the sense of peace in Europe. The first object of the Genoa Conference should therefore be to establish a pact among all the nations of Europe against aggression. Russia must undertake not to attack Roumania, Latvia, Lithuania, Poland and Finland, and *vice versa.* Until some such condition of peace was established there would not be an effective revival of trade. The President of the Board of Trade had prepared a valuable document, after consultation with leading business representatives, which indicated serious industrial and commercial prospects for at least two years to come (Papers C.P.-3890). Mr. Baldwin's Memorandum showed that very little diminution of unemployment was to be expected in the near future, owing in part to the international situation. The problem of unemployment would need to be considered also apart from the discussion which would take place in Genoa.

With regard to Russia, we had made efforts to restore trading relations with that country which had been only partially successful, because the Soviet Government had failed to carry out the conditions as strictly as we had a right to expect: but the fact remained that Russia was still outside the comity of nations, and until that fact was changed the full restoration of trade would be difficult. Our first object should be to establish peace, and our second object to establish complete commercial relations with Russia. This raised the question of the extent to which those objects involved the recognition of Russia. He did not believe it was possible to get trade going until there was some degree of recognition. Access to Courts of Law was essential to the carrying on of trade. Therefore some measure of recognition was absolutely essential. Three questions arose at that stage:

(a) Should the recognition be complete?
(b) If complete, should there be a time element introduced?
(c) To what extent is Great Britain prepared to act alone?

He thought it was generally agreed that Great Britain should not act absolutely alone. On the other hand, if we said that we would never recognise Russia until all were agreed, that would be to give notice to countries (e.g. France) which stand least in need of Russian trade, to exercise a vote on any possible agreement. No self-respecting Delegates could go to Genoa fettered in that way. He agreed that whatever action was taken should be taken by Europe as a whole.

Next, as to the question of a probationary period during which it would be possible to test the *bona fides* of the Soviet Government, the Home Secretary had circulated a Paper recording an interview with a Russian trader, who represented a very important Corporation. According to this trader, Lenin was personally largely responsible for the promulgation of the recent economic laws, which amount to an abandonment of Communism. If the Russian Delegation came to Genoa having practically surrendered their Communistic principles and willing to enter into negotiation with Capitalistic communities, we ought to give all necessary support to the anti-Communistic elements in Russia, and declare that if Communistic principles are abandoned we are ready to assist in the economic development of Russia. He was prepared, in the name of the Cabinet, to tell the Delegates that they would not be accorded full diplomatic and ceremonial representation until the Powers had had an opportunity of satisfying themselves that a genuine attempt had been made to carry out the decisions reached at Genoa. In the case of Germany there had been a considerable interval between the signing of the Pact and the granting of full diplomatic representation.

The Lord Privy Seal suggested that there should be the kind of recognition which enabled each Power to protect its citizens.

The Prime Minister agreed, and said there should be some inducement put on Russia to expedite the carrying out of her obligations.

The Secretary of State for the Colonies asked if Russia was to have Consuls?

The Prime Minister replied that that was already part of the Trade Agreement, but he thought they were called 'Agents'. The appointment of Consuls would be subject to the assent of the Government. The proposal was that Russia should have a Chargé d'Affaires in London, and we should have a similar representative in Moscow. He suggested that the Chargé d'Affaires should occupy a position like that occupied for a period by Dr Sthamer.

The Lord Privy Seal said that if the case of Dr Sthamer did not quite fit, a new precedent could be made. The preliminary to any form of recognition was the full acceptance in substance of the Cannes conditions: recognition was limited by excluding the Chargé d'Affaires from presentation at Court, and full recognition would only be granted after further decision by the Cabinet.

The Prime Minister, in reply to a question by the President of the Board of Education, said he thought the French would agree to co-operate on the lines now proposed. So also would Dr Benes.

The Secretary of State for Foreign Affairs said that he attached great importance to the phrase used by the Prime Minister as to the desirability of acting with Europe as a whole. It was impossible to be more precise at present, as no one knew the degree of Russia's acceptance of the Cannes conditions. Only in its later stages would the Genoa Conference be in a position to come to a decision as to recognition or no recognition, or the sort of recognition. In his view either the Russians at that stage would have established claims to confidence and recognition or they would not. It would be ridiculous for us to stand out for or against recognition if the great majority of the other Powers were opposed. He himself attached more importance to acting with Europe than to any other point. That had been the most valuable result of the recent Conference on the Near East.

The Lord Chancellor, in reply to questions by Lord Curzon and Mr Baldwin, stated that *de jure* recognition was used in contrast with *de facto*, and implied that as a matter of law in all Constitutional and ceremonial matters you admit a nation fully into the comity of nations. If the former position was one where the representative was an Ambassador, you restored that representation unless there had been a notable contraction of area, as, for example, in the case of Austria. In effect, anything that went beyond *de facto* recognition was *de jure*.

The Secretary of State for India remarked that what was now proposed was a limited *de jure* recognition.

The Secretary of State for the Colonies said that he saw considerable difficulty in giving a final authority to the British Delegates in this important matter without a reference back to the Cabinet here. This was the last the Cabinet would hear on the subject and the decision of the three Delegates would be filed in Genoa whether the conditions laid down were fulfilled or not. He recalled that the Russian Trade Agreement had been accepted by the Cabinet on the understanding that if its terms were violated it could be terminated. As a matter of fact its terms had since been repeatedly broken. Now we were asked to go still further to meet the Soviet Government.

He had not much confidence in any Russian trade revival in the next two or three years which would exercise any important influence on employment in this country. He thought it was right to meet the Russian representatives in Genoa. He then read a most gloomy account from our representative at Moscow which indicated that the sole purpose of the Soviet Delegation at Genoa would be to use the occasion to improve their prestige at home. This, he said, could be supported by innumerable quotations from the utterances of Soviet leaders. They would sign papers which they did not mean to honour and would go back reinforced by the fact of having contracted negotiations with the chief capitalist country of Western Europe. This would enable them to rivet their shackles even more closely on the ignorant peasants. Meanwhile there were 3 million intelligent Russians living in exile and when they heard that it was proposed to grant *de jure* recognition it would strike them with despair. He was bitterly sorry that at a time of strong Conservative majorities in a country deeply devoted to the monarchy it was proposed to accord this supreme favour and patronage to the Bolsheviks. If there were going to be some alleviation of unemployment it would be different, but on that head he was sceptical.

He was bound also to take note that the Cabinet were to a large extent already committed at Cannes, and as he did not protest at the time he was to that extent involved. He wished there had been an opportunity of considering these questions at the time. In the case of the Anglo-French Pact there had been a special Cabinet decision. He wished it had been possible for the Cabinet to meet in a similar way to discuss the conditions of the Economic Conference. He was grateful to the Prime Minister for the distinction he had drawn between partial *de jure* recognition for trade and full diplomatic recognition. He should like to know what line the Prime Minister proposed to take in his statement to the House of Commons. The Resolution committed the Government to recognition of the Soviet Republic. That would cause pain in many quarters and it would be helpful if the Prime Minister would state that the intention was to take only such practical steps as were necessary for the restoration of trade.

The Prime Minister said that he proposed to say substantially to the House of Commons what he had that morning told the Cabinet. He was going to say definitely that H.M. Government were disappointed with the actions of the Russian Government and must be assured at Genoa that there was a bona fide acceptance of the conditions laid down.

The Lord Privy Seal said that inasmuch as a number of Ministers would be at Genoa and others might be scattered for the

Easter vacation it would be desirable to give the Delegates a limited discretion, within which they could act, Ministers being meanwhile kept fully informed of the course of the proceedings. The limits which had emerged in the course of the discussion were broadly as follows:

(a) We are not to act in isolation nor without a general consensus of opinion.

(b) There can be no advance in our diplomatic relations with Russia unless they accept the substance of the Cannes conditions.

(c) In the event of their accepting these conditions and of our Delegates, in the course of the negotiations, concluding that the acceptance is bona fide, we will grant that diplomatic recognition which is required to make the agreement a success, but will not give full ceremonial recognition beyond that involved in the appointment of a Chargé d'Affaires.

The Prime Minister remarked that these were tremendous restrictions and while the Delegates could not be bound to details the governing consideration was that indicated by Mr Chamberlain when he said that *in substance* the conditions of Cannes must be accepted. Payment of debts incurred by predecessors, for example, was at the root of civilised government.

The Secretary of State for the Colonies asked if it were proposed to say to France that if she did not take our line no further progress would be made with the Anglo-French Pact. In his opinion that would be to use an unfair threat.

The Secretary of State for Foreign Affairs said the position had been made quite clear to the French at Cannes when it was laid down that the conclusion of the Pact would not be pursued until other questions outstanding between us had been cleared away.

The Prime Minister said that he had not intended to use any threat in the way suggested by Mr Churchill but he believed it would be useful to reserve the Pact to bring pressure on France in connection with Reparations and the treatment of Germany generally.

The Secretary of State for Foreign Affairs said that he had ascertained in reference to a point made earlier in the discussion by the Prime Minister that the Treaty with Germany had been ratified in January 1920. We had sent a Chargé d'Affaires to Berlin (Lord Kilmarnock) and the Germans had sent a Chargé d'Affaires (Dr Sthamer) to London, who six months later became their Ambassador, but during that six months although he did go to Court he was not received by the King. He thought it would probably be necessary to create a new diplomatic practice in the case of the Russian representative.

The Minister of Labour said that he feared the Resolution and the procedure to be followed on Monday by the Government would be regarded as an astute device to turn a difficult political corner.

The President of the Board of Trade said it would go a long way to minimise criticism of the Government if the Prime Minister in his speech would state that full *de jure* or diplomatic recognition would only be given to Russia after a probationary period and subject to ratification by Parliament.

The Prime Minister said that the decision of the Genoa Conference would certainly come before the House of Commons.

The Cabinet agreed that:

(a) The British Delegates to the Genoa Conference should be given discretion to conduct the negotiations subject to the following limitations in respect of the recognition of the Soviet Government:

    (i) The British Government should not act in isolation nor without a general consensus of opinion among the States represented at Genoa;

    (ii) There can be no advance in British diplomatic relations with Russia unless the Russian Government fully accepts the substance of the Cannes conditions;

    (iii) In the event of their accepting these conditions and of the British Delegates, in the course of the negotiations, concluding that the acceptance is bona fide, the British Government will, during a probationary period, receive a Chargé d'Affaires in London and will send a British Chargé d'Affaires to Russia to facilitate the execution of the agreement. But the British Government will not grant full and ceremonial diplomatic representation to the Russian Government until experience has shown that the agreement has been loyally observed on the part of the Russian Government. The Russian Chargé d'Affaires will not be received by the King nor invited to any Court function. Under the terms of this arrangement, Russian subjects will have access to British courts of justice, and British subjects to Russian courts of justice, which latter will be reconstituted for that purpose.

(b) The results of the Genoa Conference should be subject to approval by Parliament.

Chapter 6

The Peace Settlement and After
1919–22

THE OBJECT OF THE PEACE

175. (*War Cabinet 491B, 26 October 1918, Cab/23/14*)

Extract

The Prime Minister pointed out that if the League of Nations was effective there would be no wars, and the question would not arise. He himself agreed with Mr. Chamberlain that he could see no difference between sea warfare and land warfare. President Wilson's proposals really amounted to the taking of measures to render sea power ineffective in a way that he did not render land power ineffective. We ought to state quite definitely that we could not associate ourselves with this doctrine. Public opinion in this country would never stand any faltering on the question. He felt, however, that it was very difficult to say it in a telegram without giving offence to the President. By saying it in a speech you could use all sorts of diplomatic and friendly phrases, and so render it innocuous without losing the force of what you wished to say.

Lord Curzon said it depended a good deal what would be the attitude of the other Powers in the Conference.

Sir Eric Geddes said that he did not think President Wilson wished really to press the Freedom of the Seas very strongly. He wished to leave it somewhat vague. In his view the President was rather bitten with the effectiveness of sea power, and this view was supported by the fact that he had now gone to Congress for a greatly increased Navy. He probably wished, under the League of Nations, to take a large share in the policing of the seas.

The War Cabinet decided that:

> The Prime Minister and Mr. Balfour should make it perfectly clear to the Conference that we do not accept the doctrine of the Freedom of the Seas, and that a notification to this effect must be made in some form to Germany before we entered

717

into peace negotiations. The method by which this should be carried out was left to the discretion of the Prime Minister and Mr. Balfour after they had discovered the views of other Allies and the general atmosphere of the Conference on the subject.

[*Desirability of an Armistice*]

(3) With reference to War Cabinet 491A, Minute 9, the War Cabinet resumed the discussion commenced on the previous day on the question of whether the British representatives at the forthcoming Conference should base their attitude on the assumption that we desired immediate peace or to continue the War.

Mr. Chamberlain reminded his colleagues that, on the previous day, he had expressed the view that the answer was that we ought to accept a good peace if we could get it at the present time, that Mr. Bonar Law had agreed with him, and that Lord Curzon had agreed in principle, but had pointed out that it depended on the interpretation given to the term 'a good peace'. His own feeling, on reconsideration, was that much depended on the position of the States to the East of Austria and Germany; on whether Germany was able to get a grip of these States; and whether we could prevent it. His own feeling was that the longer the War lasts the weaker these minor States would become.

The Prime Minister pointed out that there was an important school of thought, which at times made considerable appeal to him, who said that we ought to go on until Germany was smashed; that we ought to force our way on to German soil, and put Germany at our mercy; that we should actually dictate terms on German soil, very possibly such terms as we would now accept; but that the enemy should be shown that War cannot be made with impugnity. He felt that this preliminary question ought to be cleared up in our own minds before the forthcoming Conference with our Allies.

Mr. Balfour said that he himself would not go on with the War if we could now get the terms which he thought ought to be got. Those terms would include the loss of territory in Schleswig Holstein—(a point which had hitherto escaped observation)—as well as territory to the West of Germany of the most valuable kind from an aggressive point of view, since it contained coalfields and ironfields, and on the East territory containing coalfields which had belonged to Germany since the time of Frederick the Great. By these terms the Eastern frontier of Germany would be within 70 miles of Berlin. By these terms Germany would lose her Colonies. If these conditions could be secured it would be ludicrous to say that Germany was not beaten. The fact that our Armies were across the Rhine and had perhaps sacked Frankfurt would not really mean greater defeat to Germany.

The Prime Minister said that industrial France had been devastated and Germany had escaped. At the first moment when we were in a position to put the lash on Germany's back she said, 'I give up.' The question arose whether we ought not to continue lashing her as she had lashed France.

Mr. Chamberlain said that vengeance was too expensive in these days.

The Prime Minister said it was not vengeance but justice.

Mr. Balfour read an extract from President Wilson's conversations with Sir William Wiseman, in which he had stated that he would be ashamed if any American troops destroyed a single German town.

Mr. Bonar Law said his view was the same as Mr. Balfour's.

Lord Curzon said that Mr. Balfour had said he was perfectly clear about the conditions that must be imposed upon Germany. He himself laid great stress on including in these conditions the repair of the damage wrought to Belgium and France. He attached vital importance to the imposition of conditions which would render Germany impotent to renew the War. On this point we must have secure guarantees. He noticed that it was from this point of view that the Navy asked for the German Fleet, although he expressed no view himself in regard to this. What he was afraid of was lest Germany should be left with power to resume her nefarious plans, and lest she might be able to build up her power to force her way eastwards. In the wreckage of all civilisation and order in the East, he was apprehensive lest Germany, with her population humiliated, but not cowed by her defeat, might once more assert supremacy.

The Prime Minister said that in his mind he had summed up Lord Curzon's views as favouring a good peace, if it could be secured now.

Sir Eric Geddes said he did not want to get on German soil, he did not see that we could justify it, but he would insist on the surrender of so much of Germany's naval and military power as to reduce her to a second-class Power.

The Prime Minister summed up this view as he had summed up Lord Curzon's.

General Smuts said he had placed his views on Paper (*G.T. 6091*). In this he had pointed out that peace made at the present time would be a British peace. We had now got into our hands everything of material importance that we required; our communications were secure, as was our supply of raw material. By fighting for twelve months more we should get nothing more. Were we, he asked, to continue the War for the advantage of a Central Europe? The longer we continued the greater he believed would Germany's chance be of once more getting on top. In this War the weaker nations had gone to the wall—Russia, Roumania, Austria. In a continuance of the War, Europe would break up into a number of small nominally free nations. The only powerful unit on the Continent would be Germany. All Germany's rivals would disappear. In the anarchy and revolution that would follow the War, the strong hand of Germany would prevail. Hence, he did not see what was to be gained by pushing matters too far. If we were to beat Germany to nothingness, then we must beat Europe to nothingness, too. As Europe went down, so America would rise. In time the United States of America would dictate to the world in naval, military, diplomatic and financial matters. In that he saw no good.

Lord Reading said he did not want to repeat what had already been said. He would desire a good peace, but with a special view to security for the future. On this point he felt that we should be no more secure because we had invaded Germany and inflicted damage. As regards America, he took exactly the same view as General Smuts. Every month the War continued increased the power of the United States, which was gradually mobilising an enormous strength. At present it was in the main America and the British Empire that were dominating the situation, and we were in a position to hold our own. There were, however, influences, and important influences, in the United States which were getting the idea that America should dictate the conditions. Hence, by continuing the War it might become more difficult for us to hold our own.

The War Cabinet agreed that:

The Prime Minister and Mr. Balfour should, in the forthcoming Conferences at Paris, base their attitude on the question of an armistice on the assumption that the British Government desires a good peace if that is now attainable.

REPARATIONS: THE BRITISH CASE

176. (*War Cabinet 536, 25 February 1919, Cab/23/9*)

Extract

1. With reference to War Cabinet No. 535, Minute 3, the Prime Minister explained that the question of indemnities had reached a stage in the discussion in Paris at which he thought the War Cabinet should consult together before deciding on their future attitude. He had therefore asked the British delegates to the Inter-Allied Indemnity Commission to come over and report the position.

Mr. Hughes said that the Commission had been engaged up to the present in discussing general principles, that is to say, what categories of loss and damage came under reparation and what did not come thereunder. After two or three weeks' discussion the Committee found themselves divided into two sections; on the one hand, the representatives of the United States held that we were precluded from including the cost of the war in our claim for reparation. We had taken the position that we were entitled to include the cost of the war, and neither side had receded from the attitude taken up. The Commission had therefore reached an *impasse*, and it had been agreed that the matter should be referred back to the Supreme War Council with a request to the Council to interpret the precise meaning of the terms accepted on the 5th November.

Lord Sumner said that the Americans had suggested that instead of the Commission interpreting the documents which were before it, they should ask the representatives who had signed the documents exactly what they had meant. The British attitude was that it was idle to do this as they were quite certain that Britain had never intended to give up her right to the inclusion of the cost of the war in reparation.

The Prime Minister asked what were the views of the French.

Mr. Hughes said that the French views had been set forth by M. Klotz and M. Loucheur. Their attitude could be summed up by saying that they recognised the principle that the right of the Allied and Associated Powers to reparation was absolute, an order of priority being reserved for certain claims.

Lord Sumner said that the French delegates had spoken specially in favour of our attitude. The attitude of the Belgians and the Italians was rather doubtful—Belgium, in particular, wished to know what they would get by way of reparation for destruction if the whole cost of the war were included in reparation. The Japanese also were in favour of including the cost of the war.

The Chancellor of the Exchequer said he understood that the French views were the same as ours on the question of integral reparation, but they went on to say that, having fixed a sum to be claimed, claims for reparation and damage actually done should have precedence over the cost of the war. As they meant, however, to put their claims for damage very high, the inclusion of the claim for the cost of the war would not adversely affect them, but the exclusion of the claims would be very damaging to us.

Mr. Hughes said there were two questions to consider:

(1) The attitude of the Americans, who denied that under the terms of peace made on the 5th November we had any right to claim costs of the war.
(2) The attitude which would be very strongly taken by the French and the Belgians in favour of priority.

The first question had been referred to the Supreme War Council, and the second could not be considered until the answer of the Council had been secured.

The Prime Minister pointed out that the urgent question was to reach a conclusion on the amount Germany could pay; even if we took a long time to decide the distribution of this amount, it would not stand in the way of peace, and it was very important that we should make peace soon in order that trade might be restarted.

Lord Cunliffe suggested that whatever we decided as to Germany's capacity to pay, she would say that she could not pay it. He hoped that the Sub-Committee, of which he was chairman, which was considering Germany's capacity, would report at the beginning of the following week. He doubted, however, if the report would be unanimous. They were unanimous that what

Germany could pay in the next twelve or eighteen months amounted to about a thousand millions. He thought also that the American members would agree that Germany would be able to pay a further eleven or twelve thousand millions during the next 37 years. He doubted whether the French would agree to the adoption of such a small figure. He desired the guidance of the War Cabinet as to whether the British delegates should agree to this figure. Personally, he was of the opinion that Germany could pay a great deal more, but it was a matter of guesswork; the payment of any big sum would have to be spread over about 50 years.

Mr. Bonar Law said that it had been suggested that Germany should pay by means of an annual tribute over a series of years, which would include the interest and sinking fund on the debt. The problem to decide was, what she could pay annually.

Lord Cunliffe said that this would be an increasing amount yearly as Germany's prosperity revived.

The First Lord said that it was difficult to arrive at a definite figure of what Germany could pay. There was evidence to show that she was spending money now in what we would consider an illegitimate way, for example, financing expeditions against Poland and Northern Russia. Where did this money come from? He thought we should place an embargo on the purposes on which Germany should be allowed to spend money.

The Secretary of State for War asked whether any conclusion had been come to as to the form in which payments should be made. How was the actual transference of objects of value to be carried out?

Lord Cunliffe said that this would have to be done in the ordinary way by means of goods or by credit. In reply to the Prime Minister, who asked if we should be compelled to take German goods as payment, Lord Cunliffe said that we would only take ships, and the French only coal.

The Secretary of State for War said that he understood that Germany would build up credit in South America and other markets, and that we should buy goods on this credit.

Lord Cunliffe concurred.

The Prime Minister said the second question was the order in which payments would be made. He had wired to Paris, although he had not had time to consult his colleagues before doing so, to the effect, that if we agreed to the French proposal that reparation for damage should have first claim, we were not likely to obtain anything from Germany. The French might make very extravagant claims upon which it was impossible for us to sit in judgment. No one knew what would happen in thirty or forty years' time. It was impossible to be sure that we should continue to obtain 700 millions per annum from Germany for the whole of that time. He would prefer that we made certain of securing something during the first ten years. If Germany later refused to pay, we could only compel her to do so by going to war with her. The United States would certainly not go to war, nor did he think would our people undertake another war in order to collect a debt. In all probability France would not go to war, and certainly if her claims for reparation had already been met, she would not do so in order to enable us to collect the rest of the debt.

Lord Sumner said that in his opinion the French did not know what their claim would be. They were at present engaged in legislating to set up local commissions which should go into the question of the value of the towns and houses which had been destroyed. They could not give a definite figure on any point. When it came to deciding claims, all they could do would be to put forward to the Allied Governments a claim *ad misericordiam*. Our claim for ships sunk was quite as valid as theirs for houses destroyed, and ultimately he thought they would be prepared to come to an amicable agreement.

The Prime Minister thought that there were two ways of dealing with the French request for priority:

1. To make no distinction between reparation and indemnity;
2. To give part priority only to reparation in some agreed proportion.

It was imperative that we should not admit the French claim that the whole figure for reparation should have absolute priority.

The Secretary of State for War was of the opinion that our external debts in countries like the United States should be included in the claims for reparation. Our debt to America was over 1,000 millions. We had depended upon the United States for food and raw materials, and we had managed to get these commodities on account of the credit which we had built up in that country. The damage to our finances and our trade that had thus been incurred was just as real as the material damage to France and Belgium. He thought our external debts should have priority next to claims for reparation for concrete instances of destruction. France, too, was in debt to the United States, and he thought that it would be a good thing if Germany could take over our debt and the French debt to the United States.

Lord Curzon asked what guarantees could be secured that Germany would pay. The threat of war might be effective for ten years, but thereafter what guarantee or sanction for payment would there be?

Mr. Bonar Law pointed out that if Germany acknowledged the debt at all she could only get rid of it later by repudiation, and that would not be easy.

Lord Cunliffe thought it was being assumed that Germany would be able to pay what we demanded, and at the same time keep up a great army and navy. The intention was, however, to impose such a burden that she would not be able to maintain large armed forces.

The Prime Minister said that he wished to make sure of getting something; he was far more certain of what we would get in the first ten years than in the second ten years, and still more certain of securing something in the second ten years than in the third ten years.

Lord Sumner said that the Commission were trying to obtain at once all they could without crippling Germany. Germany would then have to enter into commercial relations with various countries, and they would find it difficult to repudiate their debt later on.

The Chancellor of the Exchequer said that the German debt would be partly in the hands of individuals and partly in the hands of the Allied Governments. The debt to individuals she could not repudiate, but she might recover sufficiently to feel strong enough to repudiate the debt to the Governments.

Lord Cunliffe said that the Allied Governments must convert the German debt into negotiable securities and then transfer these into the hands of individuals.

Mr. Bonar Law said that the debt could only be paid in gold, goods, or credit. Had they considered whether Germany could find 700 millions yearly for this purpose?

Lord Cunliffe said that five years ago no one would have

thought we could have borrowed sufficient money to carry on the war. The German debt would have to be paid mostly in credit, and he thought that Germany would find any amount of credit—the United States, in any case, were quite prepared to grant them credit.

Mr. Hughes said that if we merely asked for reparation, perhaps 500 or 600 millions would cover it.

The Prime Minister pointed out that we owed the United States 1,000 millions; we had transferred 500 millions to them in securities and 400 millions in bullion. Our claim for material damage amounted to 800 millions, and this total of 2,700 millions would all have to be included in claims for reparation.

Sir John Bradbury pointed out that the figures given by the Prime Minister were our gross losses. We had transferred away a great deal of bullion, but we had also had a great deal transferred to us, and in this respect we were not much worse off than before, and if France and Russia paid their debts to us we should not on balance be losers.

Mr. Hughes said that unless the Supreme War Council declared that they had not intended to waive their right to claim the costs of the war in their note of the 5th November, and had not in fact done so, and the Reparation Commission supported their view, Britain could not even claim reparation for the 1,000 millions owed to America, for this was clearly a debt as was the remainder of the 6,000 or 7,000 millions we had raised by war loans. Therefore it followed that, unless we could claim costs of the war, Britain and the Empire would get little or nothing.

The Prime Minister said that the British Cabinet stood by the demand that reparation should include indemnities. He thought that the Allies, perhaps, with the exception of the United States, would stand by us in this interpretation of reparation.

Churchill urges a quick settlement with Germany

177. (*Churchill to Lloyd George, 20 June 1919, Lloyd George Papers, F/8/3/55*)

I have read the memoranda by General Smuts and Mr Barnes on the subject of the Peace negotiations with the Germans. In my opinion it is of profound importance to reach a settlement with the present German Government, and to reach it as speedily as possible. Although no doubt the Allied armies can advance rapidly into Germany, we shall only find ourselves involved in greater difficulties with every step of our forward movement. Large masses of the German population will come upon our hands and we shall have to feed them and make them work. We shall be involved in an infinite series of political and social questions of the most painful complexity, and the rigorous enforcement of the renewed blockade would aggravate these difficulties. (2) Our military strength is dwindling every day, not only through demobilisation but through the growing impatience of all ranks of the army to return home. The formidable pre-occupations which are arising in the East, where British interests are so pre-eminently engaged, must be taken into consideration before a policy which commits us to a long occupation of Germany in force is resorted to.

(3) The newspapers and public opinion at home, so far as it is vocal, claims the enforcement of the most extreme terms upon the vanquished enemy. At the same time, however, all classes demand the rapid demobilisation of the army, the release of innumerable categories of soldiers, and the removal of restrictions of all kinds and of all precautions inseparable from a state of war. The same crowd that is now so vociferous for ruthless terms of peace will spin round to-morrow against the Government if a military breakdown occurs through the dwindling forces which are at our disposal. It is one thing to keep a compact force for a long time in comfortable billets around Cologne in a well-administered and adequately rationed district. It is quite another to spread these young troops we have over large areas of Germany holding down starving populations, living in houses with famished women and children, and firing on miners and working people maddened by despair. Disaster of the most terrible kind lies on that road, and I solemnly warn the Government of the peril of proceeding along it. A situation might soon be reached from which the British moral sentiment would recoil. I consider that we shall commit a political error of the first order if we are drawn into the heart of Germany in these conditions. We may easily be caught, as Napoleon was in Spain, and gripped in a position from which there is no retreat and where our strength will steadily be consumed. Meanwhile, what is going to happen in India, in Egypt, in the Middle East, and in Turkey?

(4) I wish to place on record my opinion that the military forces at our disposal are not adequate in numbers, and still less in morale, for the prolonged execution of the kind of policy that is now coming into view. You cannot carve up and distribute at pleasure the populations of three or four once enormous Empires with a few hundred thousand war-weary conscripts and 150,000 slowly organising volunteers. Our strength is ebbing every day, and although the excitement of a swift advance on Berlin might pull all ranks together for the moment, all the difficulties which I now envisage will recur with greatly increased force the moment the forward movement ceases.

(5) On every ground, therefore, I strongly urge settling up with the Germans now. Now is the time, and it may be the only time, to reap the fruits of victory. 'Agree with thine adversary whilst thou art in the way with him'. Everything shows that the present German Government is sincerely desirous of making a beaten peace and preserving an orderly community which will carry out its agreement. It seems to me quite natural that they should put forward a series of counter propositions, and we ought to take these up seriatim with patience and goodwill and endeavour to split the outstanding difference. In this way we shall get a genuine German acceptance of a defeated peace and not be drawn into new dangers measureless in their character.

(6) The British Empire is in a very fine position at the present moment, and we now require a peace which will fix and recognise that position. Let us beware lest in following too far Latin ambitions and hatreds we do not create a new situation in which our advantages will largely have disappeared. Settle now while we have the power, or lose perhaps for ever the power of settlement on the basis of a military victory.

CHURCHILL'S FOREIGN POLICY

178. (*Churchill to Lloyd George, 24 March 1920, Lloyd George Papers, F/9/2/20*)

I write this as I am crossing the Channel to tell you what is in my mind.

Since the armistice my policy would have been 'Peace with the German people. War on the Bolshevik tyranny'. Wittingly or unavoidably you have followed something very near the reverse.

Knowing the difficulties and also your great skill and personal force—so much greater than mine—I do not judge your policy and actions as if I could have done better, or as if anyone could have done better. But we are now face to face with the results. They are terrible. We may well be within measurable distance of universal collapse and anarchy throughout Europe and Asia. Russia has gone into ruin. What is left of her is in the power of these deadly snakes. But Germany may perhaps still be saved. I have felt with a great sense of relief that we may be able to think and act together in harmony about Germany: that you are inclined to make an effort to rescue Germany from her frightful fate—which if it overtakes her may well overtake others. If so time is short and action must be simple. You ought to tell France that we will make a defensive alliance with her against Germany, *if and only if* she entirely alters her treatment of Germany and loyally accepts a British policy of help and friendship towards Germany. Next you should send a great man to Berlin to help consolidate the Anti-Spartacist–Anti-Ludendorff elements into a strong left centre block. For this task you have two levers (1) Food and credit which must be generously accorded in spite of our own difficulties (which otherwise will worsen) (2) Early revision of the Peace Treaty by a Conference to which New Germany shall be invited as an equal partner in the rebuilding of Europe. Having these levers it ought to be possible to rally all that is good and stable in the German nation to their own redemption and to the salvation of Europe. I pray that we may not be 'Too Late'.

Surely this is a matter far more worth while taking your political life in your hands for than our party combinations at home important though they be. Surely also it is a matter which once on the move would dominate the whole world situation at home and abroad. My suggestion involves open resolute action by Britain under your guidance, and if necessary independent action. In such a course I would gladly at your side face political misfortune. But I believe there would be no misfortune and that for a few months longer Britain still holds the title deeds of Europe. As part of such a policy I should be prepared to make peace with Soviet Russia on the best terms available to appease the general situation, while safeguarding us from being poisoned by them. I do not of course believe that any real harmony is possible between Bolshevism and present civilization. But in view of the existing facts a cessation of arms and a promotion of material prosperity are inevitable: and we must trust for better or for worse to peaceful influences to bring about the disappearance of this awful tyranny and peril.

Compared to Germany, Russia is minor: compared to Russia, Turkey is petty. But I am also very anxious about your policy towards Turkey. With military resources which the Cabinet have cut to the most weak and slender proportions, we are leading the allies in an attempt to enforce a peace on Turkey which would require great and powerful armies and long costly operations and occupations. On this world so torn with strife I dread to see you let loose the Greek armies—for all sakes and certainly for their sakes. Yet the Greek armies are your only effective fighting force. How are you going to feed Constantinople if the Railways in Asia Minor are cut and supplies do not arrive? Who is going to pay? From what denuded market is the food to come? I fear you will have this great city lolling helplessly on your hands, while all around will be guerrilla and blockade. Here again I counsel prudence and appeasement. Try to secure a really representative Turkish Governing authority, and come to terms with it. As at present couched the Turkish Treaty means indefinite anarchy.

I have felt bound to write you these convictions of mine derived from a study of all the information at our disposal. Do not take them in ill part. I am most sincerely desirous of continuing to work with you. I am all with you in our home affairs. My interests as well as my inclinations march with yours, and in addition there is our long friendship which I so greatly value.

ANGLO-FRENCH RELATIONS

179. (*Hardinge to Curzon, 13 June 1921, Hardinge MSS., 1921*)

Extract

There has been an interesting and rather curious development during the last few days that I think I should report to you, although there is nothing sufficiently tangible at present to give substance for a despatch. It was only a fortnight ago that the question of an Alliance with England was being seriously discussed in the Press, which I think was largely due to Northcliffe's advocacy in the 'Times'. At first it received a certain amount of favourable consideration and there is little doubt that the idea was well received in Government circles although it was given a good deal of criticism elsewhere. At the present moment, opposition to the idea is fairly general, and public opinion is being educated to think that England wants the Alliance, not for the protection of France against Germany but to help her out of her present difficulties. I am convinced in my own mind, and I have a certain amount of evidence to show it, that the chorus of the Press is due to a 'mot d'ordre' from the Quai d'Orsay, the attitude there being that the Government would have liked it but that it came at the wrong moment, and realising that the majority of the Chamber would be opposed to it, they had to stop it. The fact is, this Chamber in no sense represents the Government and the Government have consequently to be very wary in their proceedings. There is no doubt that there is a feeling of deep disappointment that they did not go into the Ruhr, and this they attribute entirely to the action of the Prime Minister. There is also very strong feeling about Upper Silesia and that we are supporting Germany in opposition to Poland and to the detriment of France. There is also the supposition that we are playing our own game in the Near East without regard to the interests of France, and consequently there is a certain bitterness of feeling growing up against us here. I do not attach great importance to it and think it will not last as soon as questions like that of Upper Silesia have been definitely settled and the time will come when they will once more feel that they cannot stand alone.

180. (*Lloyd George–Briand conversation, 21 December 1921, D.B.F.P. 1st series, XV, no. 110*)

Extract

M. BRIAND asked the Prime Minister whether he might give him a sketch of a proposed Alliance between France and Great Britain.

MR. LLOYD GEORGE said that he would be very glad to consider such a sketch. He had already had his attention called to the conversations which had taken place between Lord Curzon and the French Ambassador in London. Might he ask M. Briand a few questions on that subject? Was it the idea that the guarantee of the Alliance should go beyond that concluded in Paris in 1919?

M. BRIAND said he had in mind a very broad Alliance in which the two Powers would guarantee each other's interests in all parts of the world, act closely together in all things and go to each other's assistance whenever these things were threatened.

MR. LLOYD GEORGE said that opinion in Great Britain was hardly prepared for so broad an undertaking as that. So far as the Western frontier of Germany was concerned, it would be possible to give France complete guarantee against invasion. The British people were not very much interested in what happened on the Eastern frontier of Germany; they would not be ready to be involved in quarrels which might arise regarding Poland or Danzig or Upper Silesia. On the contrary there was a general reluctance to get mixed up in those questions in any way. The British people felt that the populations in that quarter of Europe were unstable and excitable; they might start fighting at any time and the rights and wrongs of the disputes might be very hard to disentangle. He did not think, therefore, that this country would be disposed to give any guarantees which might involve them in military operations in any eventuality in that part of the world. On the other hand, he repeated, public opinion would readily give a guarantee against a German attack upon the soil of France.

M. BRIAND said that he conceived of an Alliance on a larger scale than Mr. Lloyd George had outlined. He quite understood that there was no passion in the hearts of the British public for giving unqualified support to countries in Eastern Europe. But from the French point of view the first result of a firm understanding would be to reduce the military burden [?s] on France and make them more proportionate to her power to carry them. This was the earnest wish of at least three-fourths of the population of France and their belief was that it could only be done by means of a close compact between France and Great Britain. It was not impossible to imagine other nations coming into the compact including Germany herself. He thought that there was much to be said for some arrangement similar to the Quadruple Pacific Treaty just concluded in Washington. That would not bind the Powers to very strict military obligations but would provide for their taking counsel together in a crisis in the event of threats to their interests and the 'status quo'. Such an arrangement might include three or four Powers but the nucleus of it should be a complete Alliance between Great Britain and France, around which other Nations would gather. He repeated with emphasis that Germany should be a party to the Pact.

MR. LLOYD GEORGE said that English public opinion was hardly prepared at the present moment to contemplate such an extensive alliance, but there would be a majority in Parliament and in the country for a plain guarantee to France against invasion, although in point of fact the guarantee would be opposed by a stronger minority to-day than two years ago. But Monsieur Briand contemplated something which went beyond the two countries. If we could draw in Germany, so much the better. He would like to consult his colleagues on M. Briand's suggestion and resume the conversation when they met at Cannes.

REPARATIONS AND WAR DEBTS: THE CANNES CONFERENCE

181. *(Cabinet Minutes, 22 December 1921, Cab/23/27/93)*

[Forthcoming visit of M. Briand]

The Cabinet were informed by the Chancellor of the Exchequer that when arrangements had been made for the forthcoming Conference with M. Briand, it had been contemplated as possible that the representatives of the United States of America, France and Great Britain, would have entered upon a general discussion of the various large outstanding economic questions, including the question of inter-allied debts. At such a discussion it would have been possible for Great Britain in the event of the United States of America agreeing to a cancellation of her European indebtedness, to have similarly cancelled the debts owed to her by the Allies, and also possibly to have foregone any claim to further reparation from Germany, except claims in respect of actual damage sustained. A policy of this character would have left France in a position to obtain from Germany reparation for her devastated regions. M. Loucheur had been willing to entertain proposals of this character, and it was not out of the question that he might have been willing, as part of a general settlement, to forego the French pension claim against Germany.

As a result of tentative enquiries made in responsible quarters, it was, however, certain that any suggestion to the United States Government to enter upon discussions of this character would meet with a very hostile reception. While certain of the mercantile and trading classes in the Eastern States might be favourable to some general arrangement, the view of the great majority of Americans was that the debts should be paid, and that the failure to pay them was the primary cause of the present distress in the United States. The attitude of the Finance Committee of the Senate was of a similar character, and in a recent discussion on the subject of the funding of Allied Debts, that Committee had laid down that such funding should be subject to the condition that there should be no cancellation, either of interest or principal, and that there should be no acceptance by the United States Treasury of the Bonds of one country in satisfaction of the American debt of another. In these circumstances, American participation in any general discussion must be ruled out and the Allies must turn to the smaller problem of German reparation.

The position as regards German reparation was that on the 15th January and 15th February next, Germany would have to find two instalments amounting to a sum of 30 to 35 millions sterling, and it was pretty clear that the utmost that in the present circumstances the German Government could produce would be £10 to £12 millions. In the main the money would have to go to Belgium by reason of her priority. It must be borne in mind that France was at present receiving reparation Coal on very lucrative terms, and in fact she was only being debited in the accounts of the Reparation Commission for coal at a price of 8/4 per ton. Notwithstanding the great size and extravagant cost of her Army of Occupation, the amount received by her in respect of German coal was more than sufficient to pay for the cost of the Army of Occupation.

If Germany defaulted on the instalments, the question arose whether she should be granted a moratorium. Undoubtedly her inability to pay was due to a very large extent to her own action. As a result of the generous subsidies given by the German Government, the State Budget showed a deficit, while the German manufacturers were in receipt of enhanced profits, some of which they were converting into foreign credits. Herr Rathenau was of opinion that these credits were not more than enough to finance German industry, but while doubts might be felt on this point, it was quite clear that it would be most difficult for the German Government to lay their hands upon the actual money. The real fact was that the German Government was a very weak Government, in fear of Bolshevism on the one hand, and a revival of Prussianism on the other. Any moratorium granted to Germany should be upon conditions, such as the cessation of all subsidies, the balancing of the State Budget, the stoppage of note printing, the calculation in gold of customs duties, the re-constitution on more independent lines of the Reichsbank, and the raising of the internal price of coal in Germany.

The experts were unanimously of opinion that if the Allies were to insist on Germany making considerably heavier payments than she could at present afford to make, she would before the winter collapse into a hopeless state of chaos. M. Loucheur had admitted that France did not desire the collapse of Germany. When asked whether in the event of default the French Government would occupy the Ruhr he had, speaking for himself, deprecated such occupation, but this might not, of course, be the view of the French Government, which might be forced by French public opinion into violent action.

It was quite clear that M. Briand would suggest that Great Britain should lend Germany the money to enable her to satisfy the coming instalments. This, in effect, would be equivalent to Great Britain paying Germany's reparation, which she was not in a position to do, but even if she could find the money on this occasion, she would undoubtedly be pressed to take the same course in the case of future instalments. M. Briand would also no doubt press Great Britain to give up some part of the 38 million pounds which she had received under the August Agreement. This money represented a contribution towards the cost of the British Army of Occupation, and it would be most objectionable to hand any part of it over to France, as by so doing undoubtedly a deficit would be created in next year's Budget. It would be possible to say to France that if she would agree to the moratorium, Great Britain would be prepared to waive her claim to any part of the excess values under the Rathenau-Loucheur Agreement.

Some discussion then took place as to the possibility of marketing a portion of the 'A' Bonds, it being represented that even if these Bonds were sold at a very substantial discount, they would still fetch cash which would be very acceptable to the French Government. On the other hand it was pointed out that these Bonds might be of great value in the future, and that it would be mistaken policy to part with them for a more or less nominal figure at the present moment.

The suggestion was then made that the difficulties of the

French Government were largely attributable to the fact that France had not adopted a proper financial policy. She was still maintaining a very expensive army, fleet, and air service, and was engaging in costly adventures in the Near East. So long as she refused to economise, it would be mistaken policy for Great Britain to deal tenderly with her on the reparation question.

Attention was also drawn to the instability of M. Briand's position, and it was pointed out that if he returned from England empty handed, he would probably fall; particularly in view of the strong opposition which had been raised to his Angora policy. The view was expressed that if M. Poincaré were to return to power, it might be possible to come to some more satisfactory settlement with him than with M. Briand.

A discussion next took place on the question of Anglo-American indebtedness and the view was expressed that the moment was not yet ripe for making any definite proposals on the subject to the American Government. It was pointed out that if Great Britain once started paying interest on the debt she would have to continue to pay, and that the effect of such payment would be to enable the American Government to reduce taxation and so place the American manufacturer in a favourable position as regards his British competitor. It was pointed out that Great Britain was at present materially assisting the American Government at the Washington Conference and by the Irish settlement and that it would be a mistaken policy to initiate any payment of interest except under the greatest pressure.

A suggestion was made that France might be willing to disarm if she could be given a defensive alliance with Great Britain, but it was pointed out that the French Government were opposed to such an alliance, and it was suggested that if M. Briand threatened to occupy the Ruhr if Germany defaulted, that it might be sufficient to threaten her with isolation and the termination of the Entente.

M. Briand might ask that the difficulty should be considered at a Meeting of the Supreme Council, but it was pointed out that France would be in a minority on the Council in wishing to occupy the Ruhr.

The suggestion was then made that in order to help France, an effort should be made to persuade Belgium to postpone her priority in favour of France, provided Great Britain made some similar contribution; but it was pointed out that the present attitude of the Belgian Government on the subject was very uncompromising. It was then urged that a National Economic Conference should be summoned forthwith to consider the whole European situation, and that this suggestion would give M. Briand the time which he much needed to make his arrangements.

In connection with this last suggestion, reference was made to the enormous importance to Great Britain of the economic reconstruction of Europe and especially of Eastern Europe. It was clear that the rehabilitation of Russia could only be properly effected by Germany, and proposals had been made that the Allies should facilitate the task of Germany in this respect and that a substantial proportion of the German profits derived from a revived Russia should be earmarked for reparation purposes. Herr Stinnes and Herr Rathenau were strongly in favour of a scheme on these lines, and it was proposed that the British Ministers should discuss the whole situation with M. Briand and M. Loucheur. It was, however, pointed out that before any scheme of this character could be brought into operation, the consent and co-operation of the Soviet Government would be necessary, and it would clearly involve some foreign control of the Russian Railways and Customs and the making of definite guarantees in respect of the Russian debt.

The Cabinet agreed:

(i) That in the conversations with M. Briand and M. Loucheur the Prime Minister should be perfectly free to examine all aspects of proposals for dealing with the problem of German reparations and inter alia a scheme for the formation of a syndicate of the Western Powers (and possibly the United States) for the economic reconstruction of Russia, subject to possible conditions, e.g. recognition of Russian debts, the control of Russian Railways and Customs and diplomatic recognition of the Soviet Government.

(ii) That before diplomatic recognition of the Soviet Government was agreed to, the Cabinet should be consulted and that in the meantime Ministers were in no way committed.

The Secretary of State for the Colonies wished his view recorded, that while he regarded a tripartite trade agreement as premature at present, he had no objection to it in principle. He dissented, however, from any decision being taken at this stage, and, in the absence of several colleagues, to accord diplomatic recognition to the Soviet Government.

The Secretary of State for India also wished it to be recorded that in his view any scheme concerning Russia must depend on the cessation of the organised activities conducted under the auspices of the Russian Government against the British Empire—activities against which he had already protested.

Note.—The Secretary of State for Foreign Affairs, who had left the Room before the latter part of the above discussion had taken place and who had received no intimation that the question would be raised, asks to have his view recorded that the Foreign Office should be consulted before a decision on any of the above subjects is taken and more especially to reserve his opinion as to diplomatic recognition of the Soviet Government—a matter vitally affecting the foreign policy of the Empire and our relations with our Allies.

HARDINGE ON THE MAIN PROBLEMS IN ANGLO-FRENCH RELATIONS

182. (*Hardinge to Curzon, 3 February 1922, Hardinge MSS., 1922*)

I am most grateful to you for sending me your memorandum on the question of an Anglo-French Alliance. It is a most comprehensive document dealing with the question from every point of view and I may say that it does not contain a single word anywhere with which I am in disagreement, but the last four paragraphs are those which interest me most for they contain, in my opinion, the outlines of a policy which might be possible, provided the French would readily make an attempt to act with us more loyally and more upon lines of a common policy, in the future. I am all for accepting as a test of their attitude, their conduct in the approaching negotiations with you and the Italians on questions connected with the Near East. It will depend upon the French attitude whether a successful issue will result, but the two points upon which I lay the greatest stress as showing French animus at the present time, are the question of submarines and that of Tangier. I told you either in a letter or a private telegram about three weeks ago, that the 'mot d'ordre' had been given to write up the question of submarines. At that moment public opinion in France was absolutely callous on the subject, but never has there been a more successful press campaign, for the question is now regarded as vital and as one of 'amour propre' and at the same time the fact is not concealed that the aim and object of these submarines is to deal a blow at England, should the necessity arise. People tell me that at present there is no question of building the submarines, because they do not want to spend the money on them and that they merely demand the right to build them should they desire to do so. To that argument I think we could very safely reply that so long as the French claim the right or make budget provision for the construction of submarines, we shall demand repayment in full of the five hundred and fifty million sterling which they owe to us and on which they have paid us nothing so far. Again, I am told that if we make a military and naval Convention with them, by which we guarantee them against invasion by Germany, they will readily renounce their right to build submarines if we guarantee the safety of their coasts. So after all, it looks as though this submarine question may be one of blackmail to compel us to give the French a guarantee against invasion by Germany.

But I would not be satisfied with a promise of the French not to construct submarines without a clear renunciation by them of their claim on Tangier. In my opinion, the whole aim and intention of the French to obtain control or possession of Tangier is as a weapon to be used against us in case of need. Not only would it be a perfect submarine base, but also a base for aeroplanes, by which Gibraltar would be rendered practically valueless and our lines of communication with Egypt and India would be cut. Now will be the opportunity to deal with Tangier and not to go into niggling details as to what rights the French or we are to have there, but simply to tell them 'Hands off Tangier. No preponderating French influence in Tangier.'

What I have said in this letter may possibly appear to you unrealisable. I do not think so, if we do our utmost to meet the French squarely on the subject of reparations and especially cash payments from Germany. That to them is the crux of everything and if we, at the same time support them as much as we can in the to them vital question of German disarmament, much might be obtained, but there should be no concession on our part of any kind without an entire change of attitude on the part of the

French. If Briand felt that he could come back from Cannes with satisfactory assurances about reparations, disarmament and an English guarantee against invasion, I am quite confident that he would be ready to make you considerable concessions as regards the Near East, submarines, and even Tangier.

I hear that the French experts on the Near East have not gone down to Cannes and I suspect that they are very anxious that the Conference should be held here since it would give them a decided advantage in many ways, especially to influence public opinion by their many underhand ways and intrigues. This should be prevented at all costs. I am quite convinced that Paris is the very worst place in Europe to hold a Conference for the discussion of the Near East, since it is full of Levantines, Orientals and cosmopolitan financiers. On the other hand a pro-Greek P.M. with barging in tendencies is a danger.

183. (*Hardinge to Curzon, 23 February 1922, Hardinge MSS., 1922*)

Extract

I saw somewhere, I cannot remember where, that it was proposed to deal with the question of submarines before the conclusion of the Pact. My personal opinion is that at the present moment it is not worth our while to introduce another subject of controversy with the French especially about submarines, since I believe that they have no intention of building more than those for which they budgeted, and secondly it seems to me absolutely foolish to bother about the French having submarines as a menace to us since the real arm of menace to us which the French possess is their air force. I am told that we have four squadrons in England at the present time. The French have 140 squadrons at present and by this time next year they will have 240 squadrons. Consequently they could destroy England with their aeroplanes long before any submarines could come out of a French harbour to do any damage to our trade. I really think that the French air force is real militarism on the part of France . . .

The problem of Syria

184. (*Memo. by Balfour, 11 August 1919, D.B.F.P. 1st series, IV, no. 242*)

Extract

The effect which the Syrian question is producing on Anglo-

French relations is causing me considerable anxiety—an anxiety not diminished by the fact that very little is openly said about it, though much is hinted. The silence which the French press maintains about the Prime Minister's declaration that under no circumstances will Britain accept a Syrian mandate, is itself ominous. All know it, none refer to it; and it has done little or nothing to modify the settled conviction of the French Government and the French Colonial Party that British officers throughout Syria and Palestine are intriguing to make a French mandate in these regions impossible.

These misunderstandings are no doubt in part due to the same cause as most misunderstandings—namely, a very clear comprehension by each party of the strength of his own case, combined with a very imperfect knowledge of, or sympathy with, the case of his opponent. In this particular instance, for example, I have never been able to understand on what historic basis the French claim to Syria really rests. Frenchmen's share in the Crusades of the Middle Ages, Mazarin's arrangements with the Turk in the seventeenth century, and the blustering expedition of 1861, lend in my opinion very little support to their far-reaching ambitions. I could make as good a case for Great Britain by recalling the repulse inflicted by Sir Sydney Smith on Napoleon at Acre, and a much better case by asking where French claims to Syria or any other part of the Turkish Empire would be, but for the recent defeat of the Turks by British forces, at an enormous cost of British lives and British treasure.

If, however, we start from the French assumption, that they have ancient claims in Syria and the Middle East, admitted as it has been in all the recent negotiations, then we must in fairness concede that they have something to say for themselves; and it is well to understand exactly what that something is.

Suppose, then, we were to ask M. Clemenceau to speak his full mind in defence of the attitude of resentful suspicion adopted almost universally by his countrymen, I think he would reply somewhat in this fashion:

'In Downing Street last December I tried to arrive at an understanding with England about Syria. I was deeply conscious of the need of friendly relations between the two countries, and was most anxious to prevent any collision of interests in the Middle East. I therefore asked the Prime Minister what modification in

the Sykes–Picot Agreement England desired. He replied "Mosul."
I said, "You shall have it. Anything else?" He replied, "Palestine." Again, I said, "You shall have it." I left London somewhat
doubtful as to the reception this arrangement would have in
France, but well assured that to Great Britain at least it would
prove satisfactory.

'What, then, was my surprise when I found that what I had
given with so generous a hand was made the occasion for demanding more. Mosul, it seems, was useless unless Palmyra was
given also. Palestine was no sufficient home for the Jews unless
its frontiers were pushed northward into Syria. And, as if this
was not enough, it was discovered that Mesopotamia required
a direct all-British outlet on the Mediterranean; that this involved,
or was supposed to involve, the possession by England of Palmyra; so that Palmyra must follow Mosul and be transferred from
the French sphere to the British.

'All this was bad; but worse remains to be told. In the early
days of the Peace Conference it was agreed that, speaking generally, conquered territory outside Europe should be held by the
conquerors under mandate from the League of Nations. Who
under this plan was to be the mandatory for Syria? This, perhaps,
could only be finally settled when other Turkish problems were
dealt with. But who was not to be mandatory could be settled, so
far as England was concerned, at once. Accordingly, the Prime
Minister took occasion formally to announce that under no circumstances would England either demand the mandate or take it;
she valued too highly the friendship of France. Nothing could be
more explicit. Yet at the very moment when the declaration was
made, and ever since, officers of the British army were occupied in
carrying on an active propaganda in favour of England. Rumours
were spread broadcast regarding France's unpopularity with the
Arabs, and though the rumours were false everything was done
to make them true. There could be but one object in these
manoeuvres, namely, to make the British mandate, which had
been so solemnly, and doubtless so sincerely, repudiated in Paris,
a practical necessity in the East. England's pledged word would
be broken, because England had so contrived matters that it
could not in fact be fulfilled. Syria would thus go the way of
Egypt, and an incurable injury would be inflicted on Anglo-
French relations.'

This, or something very like it, represents, I am convinced, the present frame of mind of M. Clemenceau. The French Foreign Office, the French Colonial Party, the shipping interests of Marseilles, the silk interests of Lyons, the Jesuits and the French Clericals, combine to embitter the controversy by playing on French historical aspirations with the aid of mendacious reports from French officials in Syria. Relations between the two countries on this subject are getting more and more strained, so that it does most seriously behove us to consider the method by which this cloud of suspicion can best be dissipated, and an arrangement reached which shall be fair to both countries and of benefit to the Eastern World.

PEACE WITH TURKEY

185. (*Memo. by Montagu, 18 December 1919, C.P. 326, Cab/24/95*)

In a short time now, in accordance with what the Prime Minister told us last Friday night, it will be the duty of the Cabinet to make up its mind finally about the conditions of peace with Turkey. I therefore wish to address to my colleagues once more a few arguments on a question of such vital importance to the peace of the British Empire.

I would urge at the outset that we should keep this aspect of the question in view above all others. We are now practically alone in the peace negotiations with our French Allies. I have never noticed in the whole course of the peace negotiations that they have had any other motive than the well-being of France, and it will not be for France to taunt us if we emulate at least their patriotism and consider our own interests and the interests of our Empire.

I approach this question firstly as the representative of the Indian Empire at the Peace Conference, and from a consideration of the interests and views of India.

Let me say that I know of no other question on which Indian opinion, of whatever race, colour or creed, is so unanimous. The members of my Council here, the Viceroy's Government, Hindus and Mohammedans, whose opinion is expressed in speech and in writing, in letter and in telegram, Governors and Lieutenant-Governors, Chief Commissioners and Political Agents, have all only one view, that it is to the interest of India to adopt the policy which I advocate, and that any other policy will be fraught with grave danger to the peace of the East and will be resented throughout our Indian Empire. This is not a question of opinion, but of fact. I am responsible for conveying to my colleagues such facts as these. They can disregard them if they wish, but if I do not succeed in bringing home to them the facts of the case I shall have failed in my duty to those whom I represent. India is unanimous and nothing has so much made for the unity of Hindus and Mohammedans in India; nothing will give so great an opportunity for the extremist to foment discontent as a peace which is not in accord with India's views.

The Cabinet is entitled to disregard the warnings and the facts, but I would once more respectfully say that India has the same claim to be considered in these matters as Australia has in the destinies of the Pacific. It was largely by Indian troops that Turkey was conquered, and Turkey's fate affects the internal and external security of our Indian Empire.

What then is the peace that I advocate? I cannot describe it better than in the Prime Minister's own words:

'Nor are we fighting to destroy Austria-Hungary or to deprive Turkey of its capital, or of the rich and renowned lands of Asia Minor and Thrace, which are predominantly Turkish in race.'

. . . . .

'Outside Europe we believe that the same principles should be applied. While we do not challenge the maintenance of the Turkish Empire in the homelands of the Turkish race with its capital at Constantinople—the passage between the Mediterranean and the Black Sea being internationalised and neutralised—Arabia, Armenia, Mesopotamia, Syria and Palestine are in our judgment entitled to a recognition of their separate national conditions.'

The Prime Minister has assured the Cabinet that this is not a pledge, that it was an offer to Turkey to make peace. All I can say is that there were no words in the speech (which set out the war aims of the British Empire) which support this construction. But I do not want to argue whether it was a pledge or not; I merely wish to state that it was understood in India (I was there when it was telegraphed out) to represent the war aim of the British Empire then, and that it represents the policy which I would urge upon the Cabinet now.

I would further observe that even if it was an offer to Turkey of which she did not avail herself, if it would have satisfied the British Empire then I cannot see why it should not satisfy the British Empire now. All arguments that to leave the Turk in Constantinople would be dangerous to British interests and to the peace of Europe go by the board if we were ready to endanger the British Empire and the peace of Europe at the beginning of 1918.

It is further said that if Turkey is not turned out of Constantinople, it will be regarded throughout the East as an admission that the Turk is not beaten. I cannot conceive that this argument can be put forward seriously. When you force the Turk to surrender his sovereignty over Palestine, Arabia, Mesopotamia and, I hope, Kurdistan; when you force him to submit to the neutralisation and to the international control of the Straits, and to the demolition of the forts which guard them, that he can possibly claim, or that anybody could possibly believe, that he was not beaten, is to my mind as ludicrous as to suggest that Carpentier did not beat Beckett because he did not cut off his head. And in the East, vendettas, revenge, the sullen nursing of a wrong after punishment has been enforced is a policy which finds no favour.

But it is not only a consideration of the Indian aspect which I regard as so serious. It is from the point of view of the Middle East that I also urge my case. Turn the Turk out of Constantinople by means of your troops there if you like, and then, with a sense of grievous wrong not righted, what will the Turk do? Surely his course is clear. He will join the forces of disorder in the world, link up with the Bolsheviks, and through his many agents make trouble for us in Mesopotamia, Syria, Palestine, Egypt, Northern Asia, right to the confines of China, in Afghanistan and in India, where 'Turkey irredenta' will be a sore for many years to come. During all the long delays he has gathered strength, and you will be making a peace which will endanger for many months or years to come the peace of the world. You will require hundreds of thousands of troops, and you will not be able to use Indian troops either. All the time that the Turk is fighting, unrest and riot and danger will be present in India. If I thought that this peace would be accepted, and that after its signature peace would reign in the world, unjust and unfair as it is, I would be inclined to

745

accept it; but it is because I am convinced that, even if the Turkish Government accepts it, it will mean fighting, and because I am convinced that all the time fighting is going on British interests in countries for which we are responsible will suffer, that my anxieties and objections are doubled.

I would observe, further, that it has been reported to the Cabinet that M. Clemenceau expressed his willingness to leave the Turk in Constantinople, but that he would adhere to our wishes. The French have always been jealous of our position *vis-à-vis* Muslim opinion in the world. They have viewed with envious eyes our success in the East as contrasted with their failure in Algeria, and my anxieties are increased by the certainty that it will be upon us of all the Allies that the responsibility for turning the Turk out will fall in the opinion of the world.

And on the other hand, what do we gain? The possibility, or as I think the certainty, of using armed force and losing control of the rulers of Turkey; whereas if the Turkish Government was kept in the homelands of Thrace, we should be able to see that it did everything we required in maintaining peace in Asia Minor and withdrawing its forces from Kurdistan and Armenia. The Government is continually seeking means of economy. I know of nothing which will make for greater expenditure than to make a peace which will involve us in large military commitments.

So far as I am aware, whenever this matter has been discussed in the Cabinet the majority, at any rate, shared my view. I would urge them to adhere to that opinion, an opinion which is also shared, so far as I am aware, by all our military and naval advisers.

Yesterday I received from Lord Milner a letter, from which I quote the following: 'I should like to have had a word with you about Turkey. I tried very hard once more before I left, but I fear with little success, to urge the view that the Turk, however much controlled, should not be cut up, but that the "homeland of the Turkish race", including Constantinople and Adrianople, and of course Anatolia, should be left as *one State* under the sovereignty of the Sultan, with an international commission to look after his finances and exercise such general supervision as might prevent any excessive oppression of non-Turkish minorities. I know this would be best for us in Egypt, and, I believe, in India. I think it would be best for us in the whole of the Muslim East.'

I quote this from an absent colleague, who, I think my colleagues will agree, knows more of the Middle East than any other member of the Government.

Finally, I would urge that much depends upon the form of the peace. Let us avoid any language which would appear to presume to interfere with the Khalifate or with the religious observances of Mohammedans and with the guardianship of their Holy Places from Adrianople to Basra.

Let us, above all, do nothing which would appear to put us in opposition to what I conceive to be a Mohammedan ambition, the ultimate voluntary federation of these great Muslim countries as members of the League of Nations—a view which I understood in Paris was not viewed unfavourably by Mr. Balfour. Any expression of favour of this course would do something to soften the blow which the disappearance of the last great Mohammedan Power must inevitably produce.

186. *(Memo. by Curzon, 7 January 1920, C.P. 407, Cab/24/96)*

I ask to place on record my earnest and emphatic dissent from the decision arrived at by the majority of the Cabinet yesterday—in opposition to the advice of the Prime Minister and two successive Foreign Secretaries—to retain the Turk in Constantinople. I believe this to be a short-sighted and, in the long run, a most unfortunate decision.

In order to avoid trouble in India—largely manufactured and in any case ephemeral—and to render our task in Egypt less difficult—its difficulty being in reality almost entirely independent of what we may do or not do at Constantinople—we are losing an opportunity for which Europe has waited for nearly five centuries, and which may not recur. The idea of a respectable and docile Turkish Government at Constantinople, preserved from its hereditary vices by a military cordon of the Powers—including be it remembered, a permanent British garrison of 10,000–15,000 men—is in my judgment a chimera.

Nor will it be found that the decision, if carried into effect in Paris, will either solve the Turkish problem or calm the Eastern world.

The Turk at Constantinople must have very different measure meted out to him from the Turk at Konia. He will retain a sovereignty which will have to be a mere simulacrum, and those who have saved him will, unless I am mistaken, presently discover that his rescue has neither satisfied him nor pacified Islam.

But beyond all I regret that the main object for which the war in the East was fought and the sacrifice of Gallipoli endured— namely, the liberation of Europe from the Ottoman Turk—has after an almost incredible expenditure of life and treasure been thrown away in the very hour when it had been obtained, and that we shall have left to our descendants—who knows after how much further sacrifice and suffering?—a task from which we have flinched.

I may add that the refusal of the Cabinet to endorse the scheme prepared by M. Berthelot and myself was resolved upon without any consideration by them of what the rival scheme will be, *i.e.*, a Turkish State still centred at Constantinople but under international supervision. When produced it may cause some surprise.

The limitations of the League of Nations

187. (*Memo. by Balfour, 15 March 1920, C.P. 898, Cab/24/100*)

1. The two telegraphic messages from the Supreme Council about the Turkish Peace only reached the meeting of the League of Nations at the end of its sittings, and it was impossible to discuss them with any completeness, still less to pass a final judgment upon them.

2. It was however agreed informally by M. Bourgeois and the rest of my colleagues, that I should attempt to give a general impression of the difficulties, which at least a majority of them feel, with regard to the policy sketched out in the two telegrams.

3. The first of these deals with Armenia, and the proposal it contains amounts to this: That the League of Nations should accept a position equivalent to that of a Mandatory Power. That an (as yet undefined) Armenia should be placed under its 'protection', and that it should thus provide an 'effective guarantee for the future security of the proposed State'.

4. The second proposal deals with minorities in Turkey, and suggests that the League of Nations should be saddled with the same responsibilities as regards the Clauses for protecting minorities in Turkey as it has accepted with regard to the corresponding Clauses in some of the European Treaties.

5. As regards the suggestion that the League of Nations should become in fact the mandatory for Armenia it is evident that as yet, and probably for a long time to come, the League of Nations is not and cannot be adequately equipped to carry out duties which may well prove to be of the most onerous kind. It is understood that France is to be mandatory in Syria; Great Britain in Mesopotamia. But these two Nations possess the resources of Great Powers, and are well aware that these resources may be seriously called upon if they are adequately to fulfil their mandatory functions. The League of Nations have *no* resources, nor have they at present the machinery for creating them. And there is a serious danger that if they were to undertake a responsibility, which powerful and well organised nations apparently shrink from accepting, they will break down under the strain.

6. The League is of course perfectly ready to act as the supervising authority under the mandatory system. It is to it presumably that the mandatories now being called into being in various parts of the world, will be called upon to report, and we have every hope and expectation that it will exercise, where necessary, a salutary influence in the development of the mandated territories. It is more than doubtful however whether it should itself directly undertake large responsibilities of a mandatory character; especially in remote and half civilised regions where civilised opinion, the chief weapon of the League, carries but little weight. There is no useful analogy to be drawn between the case of Armenia and the case (say) of Dantzig.

7. Somewhat similar considerations must be borne in mind when dealing with the protection of minorities in Asia Minor. We may well hope that the League may perform most valuable functions in securing the observance of the minority clauses in European Treaties. It will strengthen the hands of the Governments, for example at Bucharest or Warsaw, in the suppression of local abuses. It will give the minorities themselves the consciousness that there is an organised public opinion outside their own State prepared to support them. And if unhappily abuses should arise, the machinery of the League may be quite adequate to secure their suppression.

8. The position is very different in Asia Minor. Civilised public opinion has no influence whatever in that country; indeed since

civilised public opinion is for the most part Christian opinion, it is a danger rather than a strength to Christian minorities. Outrages against these minorities are usually inflicted by irregular bands whom the Turkish Government would immediately disavow and over whom, as they would protest, (it may be with truth), they had no power of control.

9. The League of Nations with no force at its immediate disposal, would have no weapon except remonstrance; and remonstrance has been tried in Turkey for 100 years with singularly little effect.

10. Of course if Turkey is placed under a Mandatory Power the League of Nations would gladly undertake the same duties with regard to that Power that it is ready to accept with regard to other Mandatory Powers. This is a point, however, on which the League have so far no information.

11. Speaking generally it must be remembered that the chief instruments at the disposal of the League are Public Discussion; Judicial Investigation; Arbitration; and in the last resort, but only in the last resort, some form of Compulsion. These are powerful weapons, but the places where they seem least applicable are those remote and half barbarous regions, where nothing but force is understood, and where force is useless to preserve order unless it can be rapidly applied. It would seem that in those parts of the world to which this description applies the League of Nations can only play an effective part if there be a mandatory through whom it can act. If no such mandatory can be found, it cannot, as at present constituted, play the effectual part of a substitute.

12. I must repeat that I alone am responsible for these opinions; but that I believe them to be largely shared by my colleagues.

TURKISH POLICY MISMANAGED

188. (*Hardinge to Harcourt-Butler, 9 April 1920, Hardinge MSS., 1920*)

Extract

You are right in saying that the Government have not been happy in their treatment of the Turkish question. Nothing could have been more mismanaged, and we are only at the beginning of our trouble with Turkey over the conditions of peace. All those with experience and knowledge of Turkey and of Near Eastern politics have been ignored and the views of cranks and enthusiasts adopted. The merest tyro who has lived in Turkey would know that the Turks would never agree to give up Smyrna and Adrianople to the Greeks whom they both hate and despise, and if they refuse to accept the Treaty, which is more than probable, or if they accept the Treaty and do not carry out its provisions, who is going to force them, and where are the men and the money to come from with which to do it? Nobody seems to have thought of this. The Turks will stand the loss of Arabia, Syria, Armenia and the Islands, but not Adrianople or Smyrna, which they regard, and not without some excuse, as Turkish towns.

REVISION OF THE TREATY OF SÈVRES

189. *(Conference of Ministers, 18 February 1921, Cab/23/24/14)*

Extract

In reply to a question why the substitution of the Enos–Media line for Chatalja damaged British interests, Lord Curzon stated that British interests were not directly affected except through the fact that this would mean that there would be no chance of a real peace. The Greeks would have to be turned out, and the Bulgarians would immediately come in.

The Secretary of State for India asked whether it was advisable for the Government definitely to decide beforehand what they would alter in the Treaty of Sèvres and what they would not; would it not be better to wait and see the various claims put forward by the Delegations at the Conference, and then decide what course of action to adopt?

The Prime Minister was inclined to agree. He went on to say that he was of opinion that Mustapha Kemal was really looking towards the East rather than to the West. He thought that Mustapha Kemal was basing his strength in Azerbaijan and would like to know if he could be encouraged in that direction. Azerbaijan could not possibly remain independent, and would have to be either Turkish or Bolshevist.

Lord Curzon, continuing, said that it must be remembered that a large portion of the population of Azerbaijan was Turkish and Mohammedan, and their presence would create less harm to us than that of the Bolsheviks. Then also there was the existence of Georgia, which State the Government had only the other day recognised *de jure*, a course to which he himself had been opposed. The existence of Georgia was one of the main difficulties in the problem of the Caucasus. He did not say this because he felt any animosity against the Georgians; on the contrary, one must admire the way in which they had resisted the blandishments of the Soviet Government. It was, however, of the utmost importance to prevent the Turks from getting back to Batum.

The Secretary of State for the Colonies said he would be prepared to hand Azerbaijan to the Turks.

The Secretary of State for India suggested that the Foreign Office should consider two points:

(a) Whether a Constitution, on lines somewhat similar to that of Roumelia, could not be applied to Thrace;
(b) Whether it would not assist in a settlement of the Near Eastern question to invite the Arabs to be represented at the Conference in the following week.

The Secretary of State for Foreign Affairs hoped that the occasion of the forthcoming Conference would be used to bring about an agreement between the French and the Arabs, but he doubted if the best way to do this was by the latter being invited to take part in the general negotiations. They had no *locus standi* in the matter. King Hussein having declined to sign the Treaty of Sèvres. He thought the best way was for the British representatives at the Conference to deal direct with M. Berthelot.

A suggestion was made that, as we might be prepared to make concessions to the French regarding Mustapha Kemal, the French, as a *quid pro quo*, should make concessions which would facilitate agreement with the Arabs at Baghdad and Damascus and in Transjordania.

The Secretary of State for India said that he felt certain that either the Angora or the Constantinople Turks would raise the question of the guardianship of the Holy Places, and if King Hussein was confronted with the possibility of his subsidy being cut off he would be more inclined to come to some arrangement with the Sultan on this question.

The Secretary of State for the Colonies expressed regret at the suggestion that we should cast aside the Arab conception of guarding the Holy Places, and pointed out that whilst there was much to be said in favour of Mustapha Kemal keeping the Turkish flag flying in places in which he was interested, yet he had little to do with the tombs of Mecca and Medina.

The Secretary of State for India explained that he did not mean to suggest that the Turk should ever go back to Arabia, only that some arrangement might be come to by which his spiritual authority over the Holy Places was maintained.

The Lord President of the Council said he had not been in a position to follow closely the financial and military considerations of this question, but in his opinion they had perverted the policy of the Allies in regard to Turkey. Putting aside, however, this aspect of the question, he thought the position a deplorable one. Of all the nations who entered the War, the Bulgarians and the Turks had the worst record, and Turkey, which owed its continued existence to France and England, had behaved in an abominable manner and caused untold misfortunes. He considered that the Turks had proved themselves quite hopeless. They had had more opportunities and had shown themselves more incompetent than any race in the world. Whilst the Arabs had contributed their quota to the intellectual attainments of the world, and had produced the Mohammedan religion, the Turks could make no such claim; nor had they shown any administrative ability. There was plenty of evidence to show that the Turk was not capable of ruling. He had no great opinion of the Border States who had cast off the Turkish yoke, but it was significant that once they were freed from the blighting influence of the Turks they had become increasingly civilised. Mr Balfour, continuing, said that if there had been no War and the evolution of the Middle East had continued, there was much to be said for the Foreign Secretary's proposals regarding Smyrna; but in present circumstances he thought the arrangement worse than that set out in the Treaty of Sèvres. It was bound to offend the Greeks, and, after all, they were our Allies during the War. When M. Venizelos was recently in England he (Mr Balfour) had asked him about the defensive powers of Smyrna, and M. Venizelos had said that Smyrna could hold its own and that Mustapha Kemal as a fighting force had been greatly exaggerated. M. Venizelos had asserted that Smyrna volunteers would be prepared to defend the Smyrna district. It had been stated that unless peace was made with Mustapha Kemal there would be no peace in the East. If this peace was arranged, Kemal would say that he was the only person who had been able to stand against the Great Powers, and it would add immensely to his prestige. He (Mr Balfour) did not believe that the policy suggested would bring peace, and he viewed the revision of the Treaty with the utmost reluctance. He would strive to confine the Turks within strictly Turkish limits. Our Allies who wished the Treaty revised were hoping for some selfish advantage thereby.

Doubt was expressed as to whether Greece would be able to bear the financial burdens involved in meeting a potential Kemalist threat that might continue for an indefinite period.

The Prime Minister reminded the Conference of the undertaking given by M. Venizelos at Lympne, that he could, if given permission by the Allies, inflict a defeat on Mustapha Kemal within a fortnight; and he had carried out his promise within ten days. Why should it be assumed that the Greeks could not defend Smyrna, and that Mustapha Kemal, with no support at all, could keep an army in being indefinitely? Smyrna was a rich port and could, he was informed, raise a numerous body of volunteers. It was stated that Mustapha Kemal was being financed by the Bolsheviks, but he doubted this, and in any case they did not possess unlimited resources. He did not think the British Delegates should go into this Conference with the feeling that Mustapha Kemal was a force before which we must bow down. To surrender to Mustapha Kemal would not bring peace, but fresh trouble in the East.

The Secretary of State for India asked if sufficient consideration had been given to Mustapha Kemal, not as a military danger but as a figure representing all those interests who were united against the Treaty of Sèvres? With reference to the remarks regarding the Turkish proportion of the population of certain places, he would like it to be recorded that he did not accept the figures which were based on Greek returns. Further, he would like to add that he attached more importance to the future of Adrianople than to Smyrna.

The Secretary of State for the Colonies regretted the turn the discussion had taken. We could either make peace with the Turks or we could fight the Turks. He could only bring himself to support Lord Curzon's policy with difficulty, but he did not believe that any solution of the problem would be found on the lines indicated by the Prime Minister or Mr. Balfour, the result of which would be indefinite disorder over all the regions under review. If the outcome of the forthcoming Conference were a continuance of the present state of degeneration and the absence of an effective peace with the Turks, his task of pacifying the Middle East would be rendered impossible. He could only regard such a proposal with dismay.

The Secretary of State for India stated that he had accepted the Treaty of Sèvres, but he was bound to press for its revision, because it was demonstrable that it had not brought peace, and because he was being constantly appealed to by those he represented, to press for a revision. He agreed with Mr. Churchill.

The Prime Minister stated that they were all agreed that the main object to work for was a permanent peace, but he could not accept the sharp alternatives, put by Mr. Churchill, of surrender or war as the only possible alternatives.

MILITARY SITUATION IN THE MIDDLE EAST,

190. (*War Office Memo., 19 February 1921, C.P. 2608, Cab/24/120*)

Extract

20. As regards Mesopotamia and Persia, it is outside the scope of this paper to discuss in detail this situation, but there is ample evidence to show that the Bolsheviks are pursuing relentlessly their aim of striking at British power in both these countries. This they will continue to do by turning to account the instrument for propaganda placed in their hands by the terms of the present Turkish Treaty. Thus they may increase the likelihood of a recrudescence of the Mesopotamian troubles of this summer, which would force us to despatch large reinforcements if our position is to be maintained.

VI. CONCLUSION

21. An endeavour has been made to show that in Europe the situation is not such as will necessarily involve British military commitments, but the disappearance of Wrangel, the capitulation of Armenia, the imminent threat to Georgia and the downfall of Venizelos confront us with a situation in the Middle East with which it may be beyond our power to cope without a change of policy.

22. In the opinion of the General Staff recent events have shown clearly that whatever may be the outcome of the present crisis in Greece, it is unsafe to rely upon the Greek Army to cover the Allied position in Turkey. The temporary success of the recent operation by the Greek Army in Asia Minor, which consisted of a reconnaissance in force by one Army Corps of two divisions to the line of the Anatolian railway between Eskishehr and Bilejik, followed by a withdrawal to its former line, must not be allowed to influence our distrust in its ability to cover this position. It would appear that Mustapha Kemal had granted a suspension of hostilities in this area, and it may be that the Greek thrust caught his army at a time when, owing to its want of discipline, it was somewhat disintegrated. On the other hand, should the suspicions of General Headquarters, Constantinople, be correct, that Mustapha Kemal and the Greeks are in collusion, the value of the Greek successes is even less.

The General Staff are, therefore, of opinion that His Majesty's Government must be prepared either to

(*a*) Send reinforcements to Constantinople.
(*b*) Withdraw the existing British troops, or
(*c*) Re-adjust the Allied policy.

The first alternative, owing to the present state of the British military resources is out of the question as a permanent measure. As regards the second, however desirable from a military point of view, a question of high policy is involved, and in any case a temporary reinforcement to effect withdrawal might be necessary. The General Staff, however, believe that a drastic revision of the territorial terms of the Turkish Treaty in respect of Smyrna, the province of Kars, and possibly of Thrace, would induce the Turkish Nationalists to break with the Russian Soviet Government. In short, the change in the Government of Greece, though it alters the situation of the British and Allied troops temporarily for the worse at Constantinople, gives the opportunity to make gracious concessions to the Turks, and so wean them from their alliance with the Russian Bolsheviks, by this means recreating Turkey as a buffer State between the Entente Powers and Russia, and removing some of the principal underlying causes of unrest throughout the British dominions in Egypt, Mesopotamia and India.

The Peace Settlement and After, 1919–22

THE CABINET PREPARED TO FIGHT FOR GALLIPOLI AND
CONSTANTINOPLE

191. (*Cabinet Minutes, 7 September 1922, Cab/23/31/48*)

Extract

1. LORD CURZON explained that we had been working up to the
present situation since last March, when he had negotiated in
Paris an agreement signed by all the Allied Powers. The failure
to give effect to that agreement was due to the consistent treachery
of France. The French Government had been in constant communication with Kemal and had urged him to pay no attention to
what had been agreed to at Paris. Delays were first caused owing
to the difficulties made by France in arranging for a meeting to
discuss the terms for an Armistice. Later on further delay was
caused by the proposal to establish a commission to enquire into
the atrocities committed by the Kemalists against the Greek
population. Again the French threw obstacles in the way of the
enquiry. It had been finally agreed that the enquiry should be
conducted by the Red Cross Society, but the French had refused
to contribute their quota to the cost of the enquiry.

SIR ALFRED MOND suggested that the Turks would not agree
to an armistice except on outrageous terms, and, if these terms
were not accepted, they would proceed to destroy the whole
Greek Army. He enquired what course we should take then.

MR. CHURCHILL was of opinion that we ought not to bind
ourselves to any bargain with the Turks to ensure the safety of
the Greek Army which would in any way compromise our European policy. The Asiatic arrangements should be kept separate.
The line of deep water separating Asia from Europe was a line
of great significance, and we must make that line secure by every
means within our power. If the Turks take the Gallipoli Peninsula and Constantinople, we shall have lost the whole fruits of our
victory, and another Balkan war would be inevitable. He suggested the possibility of making Bulgaria play a part in the
arrangement should be considered. Although Bulgaria had been
hostile to us in the war, she had been brought in against her will
by the treacherous intrigues of the King, the Prime Minister and
the Commander-in-Chief. The Bulgarians were the best fighting
people in the Balkans, and we should endeavour to bring them in
as a factor in the situation.

THE PRIME MINISTER stated that he felt some considerable doubt about the whole Turkish attack. He suspected that defeat had been engineered by Constantine, who had found himself in a position in which he was unable either to advance or to retreat. He had therefore moved two divisions from Asia Minor to Thrace and had replaced the Commander-in-Chief by a courtier who was reputed to be mentally defective. He was doubtful if the Greek Army had suffered a complete *débâcle*. The Turks had claimed to have captured only 10,000 prisoners. He entirely agreed that we should stand by the European part of the Paris agreement. In no circumstances could we allow the Gallipoli Peninsula to be held by the Turks. It was the most important strategic position in the world and the closing of the Straits had prolonged the war by two years. It was inconceivable that we should allow the Turks to gain possession of the Gallipoli Peninsula and we should fight to prevent their doing so. The Peninsula was easily defended against a great Sea Power like ourselves and if it were in the occupation of a great Sea Power it would be impregnable. He considered that the suggestion of the Secretary of State for the Colonies as regards Bulgaria to be a valuable one, but an insuperable difficulty in the way was that the Roumanians and Yugo-Slavians are bitterly hostile to the Bulgarians. He considered that it was possible the Greeks under the new Commander-in-Chief may fight and improve the situation.

LORD LEE stated that, during his recent visit to Constantinople, he had formed the opinion that our prestige there was far higher than that of the French or the Italians. The Turks say that, while the French constantly give them information as regards the action of their Allies, they never received from us information as to our Allies. We had only 1,000 men in the Ismid Peninsula and it is probable that they would be withdrawn to help in maintaining order in Constantinople. He believed that our fleet at Constantinople would be sufficient to deter Kemal from attempting to take Constantinople. The Gallipoli Peninsula was occupied by French and Italian troops. There were no British troops there, although we had a small detachment of troops at Chanak on the southern shore. He considered it desirable that there should be some British troops in the Gallipoli Peninsula, as it was possible that the French might surrender the Peninsula to the Turks.

CHURCHILL suggested that the Chief of the Imperial General

Staff should be asked to furnish a report as to the military consequence of the evacuation of the Ismid Peninsula.

THE PRIME MINISTER stated that, if the Kemalists made an attempt on Constantinople, the British Fleet should certainly fire on them, just as we had informed the Greeks that the British Troops would oppose them if they attempted to advance on Constantinople. We should be strictly impartial in this matter. He considered that the danger that the French might surrender the Gallipoli Peninsula to the Turks should be met by strengthening our naval forces by a patrolling flotilla.

The Cabinet agreed:

(1) That while using every effort to bring hostilities between Turks and Greeks to a speedy end the Secretary of State for Foreign Affairs should continue to base his Near East Policy on the Agreement concluded by the Allies in Paris in March last.

(2) That the maintenance of the control of the deep sea water separating Asia and Europe was a cardinal British interest, and any attempt by the Kemalists to occupy the Gallipoli Peninsula should be resisted by force.